ASP.NET 2.0

A Developer's Notebook™

Other Microsoft .NET resources from O'Reilly

Related titles Visual Basic 2005:
    A Developer's Notebook
Visual C# 2005:
    A Developer's Notebook
Visual Studio Hacks

ASP.NET Cookbook
Programming ASP.NET
Programming C#
C# Cookbook

**.NET Books
Resource Center** *dotnet.oreilly.com* is a complete catalog of O'Reilly's books on .NET and related technologies, including sample chapters and code examples.

ONDotnet.com provides independent coverage of fundamental, interoperable, and emerging Microsoft .NET programming and web services technologies.

Conferences O'Reilly brings diverse innovators together to nurture the ideas that spark revolutionary industries. We specialize in documenting the latest tools and systems, translating the innovator's knowledge into useful skills for those in the trenches. Visit *conferences.oreilly.com* for our upcoming events.

Safari Bookshelf (*safari.oreilly.com*) is the premier online reference library for programmers and IT professionals. Conduct searches across more than 1,000 books. Subscribers can zero in on answers to time-critical questions in a matter of seconds. Read the books on your Bookshelf from cover to cover or simply flip to the page you need. Try it today with a free trial.

ASP.NET 2.0

A Developer's Notebook™

Wei-Meng Lee

O'REILLY®

Beijing · Cambridge · Farnham · Köln · Paris · Sebastopol · Taipei · Tokyo

ASP.NET 2.0: A Developer's Notebook™
by Wei-Meng Lee

Published by O'Reilly Media, Inc., 1005 Gravenstein Highway North, Sebastopol, CA 95472.

O'Reilly books may be purchased for educational, business, or sales promotional use. Online editions are also available for most titles (*safari.oreilly.com*). For more information, contact our corporate/institutional sales department: (800) 998-9938 or *corporate@oreilly.com*.

Editor:	John Osborn
Production Editor:	Genevieve d'Entremont
Cover Designer:	Edie Freedman
Interior Designer:	David Futato

Printing History:

June 2005:   First Edition.

 This book uses RepKover™, a durable and flexible lay-flat binding.

ISBN: 0-596-00812-0

[M]

Contents

The Developer's Notebook Series

So, you've managed to pick this book up. Cool. Really, I'm excited about that! Of course, you may be wondering why these books have the odd-looking, college notebook sort of cover. I mean, this is O'Reilly, right? Where are the animals? And, really, do you *need* another series? Couldn't this just be a cookbook? How about a nutshell, or one of those cool hacks books that seem to be everywhere? The short answer is that a developer's notebook is none of those things—in fact, it's such an important idea that we came up with an entirely new look and feel, complete with cover, fonts, and even some notes in the margin. This is all a result of trying to get something into your hands you can actually use.

It's my strong belief that while the nineties were characterized by everyone wanting to learn everything (Why not? We all had six-figure incomes from dot-com companies), the new millennium is about information pain. People don't have time (or the income) to read through 600-page books, often learning 200 things, of which only about 4 apply to their current job. It would be much nicer to just sit near one of the uber-coders and look over his shoulder, wouldn't it? To ask the guys that are neck-deep in this stuff why they chose a particular method, how they performed this one tricky task, or how they avoided that threading issue when working with piped streams. The thinking has always been that books can't serve that particular need—they can inform, and let you decide, but ultimately a coder's mind was something that couldn't really be captured on a piece of paper.

This series says that assumption is patently wrong—and we aim to prove it.

A Developer's Notebook is just what it claims to be: the often-frantic scribbling and notes that a true-blue alpha geek mentally makes when working with a new language, API, or project. It's the no-nonsense code that solves problems, stripped of page-filling commentary that often serves more as a paperweight than an epiphany. It's hackery, focused not on what is nifty or might be fun to do when you've got some free time (when's the last time that happened?), but on what you need to simply "make it work." This isn't a lecture, folks—it's a lab. If you want a lot of concept, architecture, and UML diagrams, I'll happily and proudly point you to our animal and nutshell books. If you want every answer to every problem under the sun, our omnibus cookbooks are killer. And if you are into arcane and often quirky uses of technology, hacks books simply rock. But if you're a coder, down to your core, and you just want to get on with it, then you want a Developer's Notebook. Coffee stains and all, this is from the mind of a developer to yours, barely even cleaned up enough for print. I hope you enjoy it...we sure had a good time writing them.

Notebooks Are...

Example-driven guides

As you'll see in the "Organization" section, developer's notebooks are built entirely around example code. You'll see code on nearly every page, and it's code that *does something*—not trivial "Hello World!" programs that aren't worth more than the paper they're printed on.

Aimed at developers

Ever read a book that seems to be aimed at pointy-haired bosses, filled with buzzwords, and feels more like a marketing manifesto than a programming text? We have too—and these books are the antithesis of that. In fact, a good notebook is incomprehensible to someone who can't program (don't say we didn't warn you!), and that's just the way it's supposed to be. But for developers...it's as good as it gets.

Actually enjoyable to work through

Do you really have time to sit around reading something that isn't any fun? If you do, then maybe you're into thousand-page language references—but if you're like the rest of us, notebooks are a much better fit. Practical code samples, terse dialogue centered around practical examples, and even some humor here and there—these are the ingredients of a good developer's notebook.

About doing, not talking about doing

    If you want to read a book late at night without a computer nearby, these books might not be that useful. The intent is that you're coding as you go along, knee deep in bytecode. For that reason, notebooks talk code, code, code. Fire up your editor before digging in.

Notebooks Aren't...

Lectures

    We don't let just anyone write a developer's notebook—you've got to be a bona fide programmer, and preferably one who stays up a little too late coding. While full-time writers, academics, and theorists are great in some areas, these books are about programming in the trenches, and are filled with instruction, not lecture.

Filled with conceptual drawings and class hierarchies

    This isn't a nutshell (there, we said it). You won't find 100-page indices with every method listed, and you won't see full-page UML diagrams with methods, inheritance trees, and flow charts. What you will find is page after page of source code. Are you starting to sense a recurring theme?

Long on explanation, light on application

    It seems that many programming books these days have three, four, or more chapters before you even see any working code. I'm not sure who has authors convinced that it's good to keep a reader waiting this long, but it's not anybody working on *this* series. We believe that if you're not coding within 10 pages, something's wrong. These books are also chock-full of practical application, taking you from an example in a book to putting things to work on your job, as quickly as possible.

Organization

Developer's Notebooks try to communicate different information than most books, and as a result, are organized differently. They do indeed have chapters, but that's about as far as the similarity between a notebook and a traditional programming book goes. First, you'll find that all the headings in each chapter are organized around a specific task. You'll note that we said *task*, not *concept*. That's one of the important things to get about these books—they are first and foremost about doing something. Each of these headings represents a single *lab*. A lab is just what it sounds like—steps to accomplish a specific goal. In fact, that's the first heading you'll see under each lab: "How do I do that?" This is the central question of each lab, and you'll find lots of down-and-dirty code and detail in these sections.

Some labs have some things not to do (ever played around with potassium in high school chemistry?), helping you avoid common pitfalls. Some labs give you a good reason for caring about the topic in the first place; we call this the "Why do I care?" section, for obvious reasons. For those times when code samples don't clearly communicate what's going on, you'll find a "What just happened" section. It's in these sections that you'll find concepts and theory—but even then, they are tightly focused on the task at hand, not explanation for the sake of page count. Finally, many labs offer alternatives, and address common questions about different approaches to similar problems. These are the "What about..." sections, which will help give each task some context within the programming big picture.

And one last thing—on many pages, you'll find notes scrawled in the margins of the page. These aren't for decoration; they contain tips, tricks, insights from the developers of a product, and sometimes even a little humor, just to keep you going. These notes represent part of the overall communication flow—getting you as close to reading the mind of the developer-author as we can. Hopefully they'll get you that much closer to feeling like you are indeed learning from a master.

And most of all, remember—these books are...

All Lab, No Lecture

—Brett McLaughlin, Series Creator

Preface

Who This Book Is For

ASP.NET 2.0: A Developer's Notebook is written for programmers who are already familiar with ASP.NET 1.x (1.0 or 1.1) and who have used a previous version of Visual Studio .NET (either 2002 or 2003) to build ASP.NET web applications. Our aim is to introduce you, through a series of hands-on labs, to the new features of ASP.NET 2.0 using the Visual Studio 2005 development environment.

In order to get the most out of this book you'll need a copy of Visual Studio 2005 that supports Visual Basic. You are encouraged to work your way through the labs, as they are purposefully small and to the point; however, the complete source code (along with an Errata) is available on O'Reilly's web page for this book, *http://www.oreilly.com/catalog/aspnetadn/*.

ASP.NET 2.0: A Developer's Notebook covers very little of the material that an experienced ASP.NET 1.x programmer already knows: our goal is to help you to build on your current knowledge, not to waste your time with old material.

TIP

If you are not yet familiar with ASP.NET, you may prefer to read *Programming ASP.NET* by Jesse Liberty and Dan Hurwitz, which teaches ASP.NET from the ground up.

As the examples in this book are all written in Visual Basic 2005, C# programmers will have to do some conversion. However, the syntactical differences between the two languages are minor and make the conversion process trivial. For more information, see the *C# and VB.NET Conversion Pocket Reference* by Jose Mojica (O'Reilly).

Similarly, this book does not try to be exhaustive in its treatment of how you go about building web applications with ASP.NET 2.0 and the Visual Studio 2005 development environment. Instead, I introduce you to what is new in ASP.NET 2.0, the development environment and the class libraries, and to equip you for further exploration of those areas that are likely to be of particular interest to you.

How This Book Is Organized

ASP.NET 2.0: A Developer's Notebook is organized in eight chapters, with each chapter focusing on a particular set of new features in ASP.NET. In some chapters, the labs can be read independently of each other; in others, it is more logical to read through the labs in sequence, when the material in each lab builds on the previous one. In any case, the examples are structured so that you can learn the concepts very quickly by following the steps outlined.

In Chapter 1, I walk you through the new steps you follow with Visual Studio 2005 to set up ASP.NET 2.0 web applications, and then highlight some of the changes in the new development tool. I also discuss some of the most interesting controls that are new to ASP.NET 2.0. In addition, ASP.NET 2.0 comes with some neat improvements to the old ways of doing things, such as cross-page posting, inserting client script into the page, and more. These new improvements are also covered in this chapter.

In Chapter 2, you will learn about Master Pages, a new feature supported by ASP.NET for visual page inheritance, which is similar to Windows Forms inheritance. With ASP.NET 2.0, you can now create a single Master page that contains the common elements used by the pages of your site. You can then create web pages that inherit from the Master page, to enforce a common look-and-feel across your entire site. In addition to Master Pages, you will also learn how to use the new navigational controls in ASP.NET 2.0. These controls, known as SiteMapPath and Menu, allow you to add navigational links to your site without much coding.

In Chapter 3, you will learn how to create portal web sites using the Web Parts Framework. Web sites today contain a wealth of information, so much so that a poorly designed site can easily overwhelm users. To better help users cope, portal web sites (such as MSN) often organize their data into discrete units that support a degree of personalization. Information is organized into standalone parts and users are allowed to rearrange those parts to suit their individual working styles.

Such personalization also lets users hide parts that contain information in which they have no interest. What's more, users can save their settings so that the site will remember their preferences when they return. In ASP.NET 2.0, you can use the new Web Parts Framework to build web portals that offer this kind of modularization of information and personalization.

In Chapter 4, you will learn to use new controls that reduce the coding necessary to do data access. Data access is one of the most common tasks that you're likely to perform when you write web applications. This is evident in the number of new data controls that ship with Visual Studio 2005. One of the most important is the new GridView control, which is a much improved version of the venerable DataGrid control of previous versions (the older DataGrid control is still supported in ASP.NET 2.0, though). In addition, ASP.NET 2.0 ships several new data source controls that make it easier to consume a variety of data sources. In this chapter, you will learn how to use the various new data controls—GridView, DetailsView, and DataList—together with the new data source controls, such as SqlDataSource, ObjectDataSource, and XmlDataSource. With all these controls, data access is now much easier than before, and you can spend more time working on your business logic.

In Chapter 5, you will discover the new security controls in ASP.NET 2.0 that aim to simplify the life of a developer. Using these new security controls, you can now perform user login, registration, changing of password, and more, with no more effort than dragging-and-dropping controls onto your web form. Powering these new controls are the Membership APIs, which perform the mundane tasks of user management without you having to write your own code. In this chapter, you will learn how the use the new security controls to secure your site. You will also learn about the Membership APIs and how they can be used to perform user administration.

In Chapter 6, you will learn about some of the productivity improvements in ASP.NET 2.0. For example, in ASP.NET 1.x, because pages are dynamically compiled and cached the first time a user loads a page, an ASP.NET 1.x web application is typically slower the first time it is loaded. In ASP. NET 2.0, you can now precompile a site so that it's already compiled when the first user links to it. ASP.NET 2.0 also supports fragment caching, which means that you can cache parts of your page rather then the entire page. Consuming web services is also made easier with the automatic generation of a web proxy class based on a WSDL document. Simply drop a WSDL document into the *App_Code* folder, and the web proxy class will be automatically generated. Finally, ASP.NET 2.0 includes the Client Callback Manager, which allows you to update your page with information from the server without performing a postback.

In Chapter 7, you will learn how to create personalizable web sites using the Profile service. Personalizing your web site enhances the experiences of your users, by preserving information about visitors so that it can be reused when they come to your site again. In ASP.NET 2.0, the new Profile service gives you a way to store information about your users.

Finally, in Chapter 8, you will learn about how you can maintain a consistent look-and-feel for your web site using themes and skins. In this chapter, you will learn about the new Themes and Skins feature in ASP.NET 2.0 and how you can use it to maintain a consistent user interface for your application. In addition, localization in ASP.NET 2.0 has gotten easier with the new auto-culture handling mechanism. You will learn how to create applications that support multiple cultures.

Where Can I Learn More?

While I try to show you as many of the new features in ASP.NET 2.0 as I can, it is not possible to cover them all in the scope of this book. Microsoft has made many enhancements to Visual Studio 2005 and ASP.NET 2.0, and often there is more than one way of doing the same thing.

Thus, the end of each lab includes a section entitled "Where Can I Learn More?" Here I will point you to books, magazine articles, online resources, MSDN articles, and Visual Studio 2005 Help topics where you can find more detail or obtain another perspective. When I refer to the *MSDN Help Topics*, I am generally referring to the MSDN Library that is available to you through the installed Visual Studio 2005 Help, or online at *http://msdn.microsoft.com/library*. The MSDN Library contains a wealth of resources and should be the first place you visit if you have a question about a particular feature of ASP.NET. Online articles are also a very useful way to learn more about a particular feature of ASP.NET. I would also encourage you to check out some of the following good magazines where you can read more about ASP.NET:

- *MSDN Magazine*
- *CoDe Magazine*
- *Visual Studio Magazine*
- *.NET Developer Journal*

What You Need to Use This Book

I am assuming that you are somewhat familiar with how ASP.NET works in principle, and so in this book I have concentrated on the new features in ASP.NET 2.0. Also, the code examples in this book are all written in Visual Basic 2005, so you should be well versed in Visual Basic to take advantage of this book. If you are a C# programmer, converting the examples from VB to C# should not take too much effort. For this task, I suggest you take a look at *C# and VB.NET Conversion Pocket Reference* by Jose Mojica, published by O'Reilly Media, Inc.

You'll want a computer with a version of Visual Studio 2005 installed that supports Visual Basic, along with some form of SQL Server (SQL Server Express is fine).

You can also do the labs in this book using the new Visual Studio Express Editions. Specifically, you'll need Visual Web Developer 2005 Express Edition.

Conventions Used in This Book

The following typographical conventions are used in this book:

Plain text
> Indicates menu titles, menu options, menu buttons, and keyboard accelerators (such as Alt and Ctrl). Plain text is also used for the names of controls, files, classes, interfaces, methods, properties and other elements when these names are used in conjunction with their type (e.g., Page class).

Italic
> Indicates new terms, URLs, email addresses, filenames, file extensions, pathnames, directories, and Unix utilities.

`Constant width`
> Indicates commands, options, switches, variables, attributes, keys, functions, types, classes, namespaces, methods, modules, properties, parameters, values, objects, events, event handlers, XML tags, HTML tags, macros, the contents of files, or the output from commands.

Constant width bold

Shows commands or other text that should be typed literally by the user.

Constant width italic

Shows text that should be replaced with user-supplied values.

TIP

This icon signifies a tip, suggestion, or general note.

WARNING

This icon indicates a warning or caution.

Using Code Examples

This book is here to help you get your job done. In general, you may use the code in this book in your programs and documentation. You do not need to contact us for permission unless you're reproducing a significant portion of the code. For example, writing a program that uses several chunks of code from this book does not require permission. Selling or distributing a CD-ROM of examples from O'Reilly books *does* require permission. Answering a question by citing this book and quoting example code does not require permission. Incorporating a significant amount of example code from this book into your product's documentation *does* require permission.

We appreciate, but do not require, attribution. An attribution usually includes the title, author, publisher, and ISBN. For example: "*ASP.NET 2.0: A Developers Notebook* by Wei-Meng Lee. Copyright 2005 O'Reilly Media, Inc., 0-596-00812-0."

If you feel your use of code examples falls outside fair use or the permission given above, feel free to contact us at *permissions@oreilly.com*.

Safari® Enabled

 When you see a Safari® enabled icon on the cover of your favorite technology book that means the book is available online through the O'Reilly Network Safari Bookshelf.

Safari offers a solution that's better than e-books. It's a virtual library that lets you easily search thousands of top tech books, cut and paste code samples, download chapters, and find quick answers when you need the most accurate, current information. Try it for free at *http://safari.oreilly.com*.

I'd Like to Hear from You

Please send comments, suggestions, and errata to *wei_meng_lee@hotmail.com*. You can also visit my web site at *http://www.developerlearningsolutions.com* for a list of articles that I have written on ASP.NET 2.0. Check out the Code Library section to download sample code for topics on .NET, ASP.NET 2.0, and the .NET Compact Framework.

Comments and Questions

Please address comments and questions concerning this book to the publisher:

O'Reilly Media, Inc.
1005 Gravenstein Highway North
Sebastopol, CA 95472
(800) 998-9938 (in the United States or Canada)
(707) 829-0515 (international or local)
(707) 829-0104 (fax)

We have a web page for this book, where we list errata, examples, and any additional information. You can access this page at:

http://www.oreilly.com/catalog/aspnetadn/

To comment or ask technical questions about this book, send email to:

bookquestions@oreilly.com

For more information about our books, conferences, Resource Centers, and the O'Reilly Network, see our web site at:

http://www.oreilly.com

Acknowledgments

I am very grateful to my editor, John Osborn, for giving me this opportunity to write a book on ASP.NET 2.0. His patience and attention to details have definitely made this book a better read. John has been more than an editor to me; he is more like a mentor. He has been very encouraging and edges me on when I am at a loss for words at times (literally!). A big thank you, John!

I am indebted to the following technical reviewers and editors who have taken time off their busy schedules and provided lots of valuable feedback to the drafts of this book (as well as answering my strings of questions). They are: Thomas Lewis, Jonathan Hawkins, Jesse Liberty, David Mercer, G. Andrew Duthie, Jason Alexander, Tommy Lee, and Ron Buckton. Thomas Lewis (ASP.NET 2.0 evangelist at Microsoft) deserves a special mention, as he has been very patient in answering my questions on the changes in the early days of the beta of ASP.NET 2.0. Thank you, Thomas!

Thanks are also due to Rod Paddock (Editor In Chief) and Markus Egger (Publisher) from CoDe Magazine (*http://www.code-magazine.com*) for graciously granting me the permission to reproduce my ASP.NET article "Localizing ASP.NET 2.0 Applications," available in the March/April 2005 issue of *CoDe Magazine*. I also want to take this opportunity to thank Lori Piquet at DevX (a division of Jupitermedia Corp.), who has always been very supportive of my articles on ASP.NET 2.0.

As always, it has been a pleasure working with the O'Reilly team. Did people ever tell you that you guys rock?

About the Author

Wei-Meng Lee is a technologist and founder of Developer Learning Solutions (*http://www.developerlearningsolutions.com*), a technology company specializing in hands-on training on the latest Microsoft technologies.

Wei-Meng speaks regularly at international conferences and has authored and coauthored numerous books on .NET, XML, and wireless technologies, including *Windows XP Unwired* and the *.NET Compact Framework Pocket Guide* (both from O'Reilly). He writes extensively for the O'Reilly Network on topics ranging from .NET to Mac OS X.

Wei-Meng is currently a Microsoft Regional Director for Singapore.

What's New?

Within a few short years, ASP.NET has become one of the favorite tools of web applications developers, and now it's about to undergo its second major upgrade. Microsoft is making major improvements to the product based on feedback from its millions of customers and the company's own experience in developing and deploying web applications. Moreover, the market for web development tools has become increasingly competitive with the rise of open source PHP and Macromedia Flash, both of which have steadily gained market share.

Among its many improvements, ASP.NET 2.0 ships with more ready-to-use controls than ever, making your life as a web application developer easier, and reducing considerably the amount of code you need to write to achieve professional results. In fact, a stated aim of the Microsoft web development tools team is to reduce the amount of code you write to perform common web site tasks by up to 70%. In addition, ASP.NET 2.0 comes with some neat improvements, such as cross-page posting and the ability to insert client script into a page. You will learn about some of these improvements in this chapter.

The new features in ASP.NET 2.0 can be grouped into three broad categories: new Controls and control functionality, improvements to the Page Framework, and new Services and APIs.

Controls

ASP.NET 2.0 ships with several new controls to make the life of a web application developer easier. In ASP.NET 2.0, there are now new controls that help you to perform data access, site navigation, login, and personalization using Web Parts.

Page Framework

ASP.NET 2.0 supports some useful additions to its Page framework such as visual inheritance, technically known as Master Pages. Besides Master Pages, ASP.NET 2.0 also supports "theming" through Themes and Skins, allowing you to maintain a consistent look-and-feel for your web sites. Another noteworthy feature in ASP.NET is the improved support for localization, which reduces the amount of work you need to do to internationalize your web applications.

Services and APIs

Behind the various new controls in ASP.NET 2.0 lie the foundation services and APIs that do the heavy lifting needed to support the controls. For example, behind the new Login controls you'll find the new collection of Membership APIs, which perform such tasks such as user authentication, registration of new users, etc. Besides using the new controls, you can directly make use of these APIs in code.

Table 1-1 summarizes some of most important new features of ASP.NET 2.0.

Table 1-1. Summary of new features in ASP.NET 2.0

Controls	Page Framework	Services and APIs
Data Controls	**Master Pages**	**Membership**
Includes controls that simplify the connection to data sources, as well as the new GridView and DetailsView controls.	Visual page inheritance for Web Forms.	The core service for user management, such as user creation, deletion, authentication, retrieval of passwords, etc.
We will discuss this topic in Chapter 4.	We will discuss this topic in Chapter 2.	We will discuss this topic in Chapter 5.
Login Controls	**Themes and Skins**	**Role Management**
Contains controls that make web site user management and user authentication easy and efficient.	Maintain consistent look-and-feel for the entire site by using Skins definitions grouped by themes.	Manages the assignment of roles to users, such as add user to role, delete user from role, enquire if user is in role, etc.
We will discuss this topic in Chapter 5.	We will discuss this topic in Chapter 8.	We will discuss this topic in Chapter 5.
Web Parts	**Localization**	**Site Maps**
Provides the infrastructure for creating Web Parts.	Simplify the steps needed to globalize and localize your web applications.	Supports the retrieval of site information, as well as display of site maps.
We will discuss this topic in Chapter 3.	We will discuss this topic in Chapter 8.	We will discuss this topic in Chapter 2.

Table 1-1. Summary of new features in ASP.NET 2.0 (continued)

Controls	Page Framework	Services and APIs
Navigation Controls Contains controls that display site information and menus. We will discuss this topic in Chapter 2.	**Compilation** Supports dynamic compilation of business logic without the need for explicit recompilation when the code is changed. Also supports automatic generation of Web Services proxy class using WSDL. We will discuss this topic in Chapter 6.	**Profile** Supports the personalization of Web sites through the Profile object. We will discuss this topic in Chapter 7.
Additional Standard Controls Contains controls such as ImageMap, FileUpload, MultiView, and TreeView. We will discuss these controls in Chapters 1 and 2.		

This chapter starts with a walkthrough of the steps you now follow to create a web application with Visual Studio 2005, and then dives into a few of the coolest new controls and control functionality.

TIP

If the professional editions of Visual Studio 2005 are too expensive for you, try the Visual Web Developer 2005 Express Edition, a lightweight, easy-to-use, and easy-to-learn development tool focused exclusively on web development. It is primarily targeted at hobbyist developers and students who may find the cost of Visual Studio 2005 prohibitive. At the time of this writing, Microsoft has not yet announced pricing for the Visual Web Developer 2005 Express Edition but is widely expected to sell this version for a nominal amount.

Create a New Web Project

The way you create a new web application project has changed in Visual Studio 2005. In Visual Studio .NET 2003, you select File → New Project on the Visual Studio menu and then select the kind of project you want to create (Web, Windows, Windows Services, and so on) in the New Project Dialog. In Visual Studio 2005, you open a new web project with the New Web Site... command in the File menu.

With Visual Studio 2005, it's now easier than ever to start building an ASP.NET web application. You've got to try it to believe it!

Visual Studio 2005 Editor Settings

When you launch Visual Studio 2005 for the first time, you will be asked to choose a default setting for the IDE. Among the list of settings available are:

- Web Development Settings
- Visual Basic Development Settings
- Visual C# Development Settings

Depending on which setting you choose, you will get a slightly different menu setup.

How do I do that?

To get a feel for how you create a new web application in Visual Studio 2005, try walking through the following steps. First we'll open the application, pick a location to host it for development, and then add a second web form. Finally, we will see how we can debug the application.

1. You can change the IDE settings (listed in the sidebar "Visual Studio 2005 Editor Settings") via Tools → Import and Export Settings.... Since this book is all about web development, we naturally suggest you select Web Development Settings. Launch Visual Studio 2005. If you selected the Web Development Settings option in Visual Studio 2005, go to the File menu and select New Web Site..., as shown at the top of Figure 1-1. If you have chosen any other setting, go to the File menu and choose New → Web Site... (see the bottom part of Figure 1-1).

2. When the New Web Site dialog box appears, select a project template from the Templates pane. Since we're creating a blank ASP.NET web site in this lab, select the ASP.NET Web Site template.

3. In the New Web Site dialog, you need to choose a development language and a place to locate the project. We'll be using Visual Basic as our language of choice throughout this book, so from the Language drop-down listbox, select Visual Basic.

   Visual Studio 2005 provides four ways to develop a web site. For this lab, you'll use the File System option. Choose File System from the Location drop-down list. This new ASP.NET 2.0 option frees you from having to use IIS (Microsoft Internet Information Server) for development. Instead, Visual Studio 2005 provides its own built-in web server, which it launches when you run the web application.

Figure 1-1. Creating a new web site in Visual Studio 2005

Use *C:\ASPNET20* as the location of your application and *chap01-WebSite1* as its name. Type the complete pathname, *C:\ASPNET20\chap01-WebSite1*, into the drop-down combo box to the right of the Location box.

Figure 1-2 shows the completed New Web Site dialog.

No more worries about creating virtual directories on your web server! Visual Studio 2005 comes with a file-based web server for developing ASP.NET 2.0 applications. Now you can also develop ASP.NET 2.0 web applications on a Windows XP Home Edition PC, which traditionally does not include IIS.

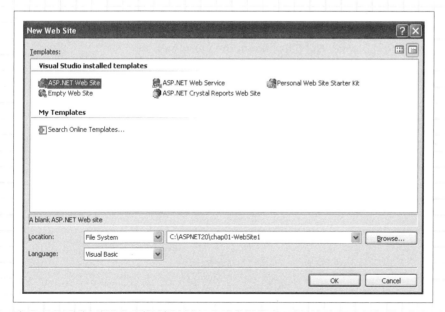

Figure 1-2. Selecting a project language, template, and location

If you do wish to use IIS for development purposes, select HTTP from the Location drop-down list and enter a URL for the application instead, such as *http://localhost/chap01-WebSite1*.

Order of Installation

If you wish to use IIS to develop your ASP.NET web applications, you must install IIS before installing Visual Studio 2005. By default, Windows XP does not install IIS, and so you need to retrieve your Windows XP Installation CD and then use Control Panel → Add or Remove Programs → Add/Remove Windows Components → Components: Internet Information Services (IIS) to add IIS yourself.

In the event that you have installed Visual Studio 2005 before installing IIS, you need to associate IIS with ASP.NET. You can do so by using the *aspnet_ regiis* utility (located in *C:\WINDOWS\Microsoft.NET\Framework\<version>*) with the –i option, like this:

```
aspnet_regiis -i
```

4. Once you have selected your template, language, and location, click OK. Visual Studio creates your project, and the Solution Explorer should display the files shown in Figure 1-3.

Figure 1-3. The Solution Explorer

5. By default, ASP.NET creates a folder named *App_Data* and an initial application page, a Web Form named *Default.aspx* with a code-behind page named *Default.aspx.vb* (to see the contents of this file, click the + symbol to the left of Default.aspx icon in the Solution Explorer).

Switching Between Design View, Source View, and Code-Behind View

In Visual Studio 2005, a Web Form is displayed in Source View by default. In Source View, you can modify the various attributes of the form and the controls contained within it. To switch to Design View, click on the Design button at the bottom of the screen. In Design View, you can visually inspect the page and drag and drop controls onto the form. To view the code-behind of the form, you can simply double-click on the form and the code-behind will appear. In Code View, you write your business logic for your application as well as service the events raised by the various controls on the page. Figure 1-4 shows the three views.

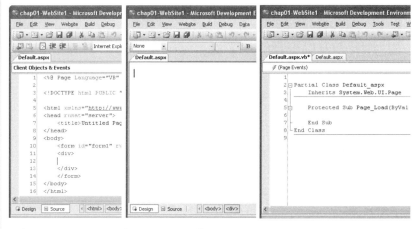

Figure 1-4. Switching between the different views

6. To add a new item (such as an additional Web Form) to your project, you can right-click the project name and select a template from the Add New Item... dialog box shown in Figure 1-5.

   Notice that you have the option to "Place code in separate file." If this option is unchecked, your code will reside in the same file as your Web Form. For all the examples in this book, you will place the code in a separate file. Hence, check the "Place code in separate file" option. Click Add.

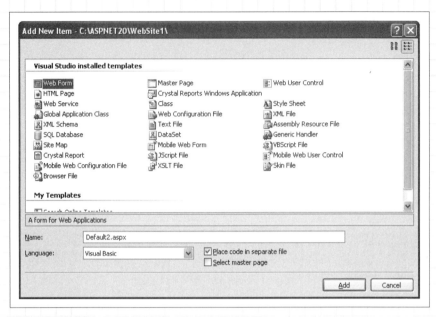

Figure 1-5. Adding a new item to your web project

TIP

If you wish to debug your application (by using F5), you need to have a *Web.config* file in your project. By default, if there is no *Web.config* file when you try to debug your application, Visual Studio will prompt you to add one.

In Visual Studio 2005 (unlike Visual Studio .NET 2003), *Web.config* is not automatically added to your project. To add a *Web.config* file yourself, simply go to the Add New Item... dialog box, and select Web Configuration File from the "Visual Studio installed templates" window.

What about...

...modifying the code generated by the Visual Designer?

If you look at the code-behind of a Web Form, you will realize that the bulk of the user interface code generated by Visual Studio is no longer visible, as it has been in ASP.NET 1.x. Instead, you see a partial class:

```
Partial Class Default_aspx

End Class
```

You add your business logic to this partial class. Unlike ASP.NET 1.x, where the code-behind contains code generated by the Visual Designer,

ASP.NET 2.0 does not display this section. Instead, at compile time, the Visual Designer automatically generates the partial class needed to implement the user interface and merges it with your code-behind.

The New Partial Keyword

One of the language enhancements in .NET 2.0—available to both VB2005 and C# 2.0 programmers—is support for partial classes. In a nutshell, partial classes mean that your class definition can be split into multiple physical files. Logically, partial classes do not make any difference to the compiler. During compile time, it simply groups all the various partial classes and treats them as a single entity.

One of the greatest benefits of partial classes is that they allow a clean separation of business logic and the user interface (in particular, the code that is generated by the Visual Studio Designer). Using partial classes, the UI code can be hidden from the developer, who usually has no need to access it anyway. Partial classes also make debugging easier, as the code is partitioned into separate files. This feature also helps members of large development teams work on their pieces of a project in separate physical files.

…choosing another location for your web application?

Visual Studio 2005 provides four possible locations for a web application. If you are developing a simple web application (or are just trying out some of the new features in ASP.NET), the quick and easy way to build the application is to use the File System method. This method is also useful for developers who do not have a web server (such as IIS) installed on their machine, or for developers who are using Windows XP Home Edition as their development workstation.

If you already have a web server installed on your machine and you want to use it to host your web application, you can choose the Local IIS method. Doing so allows your web application to be accessed from other machines during development time.

If your web server is located remotely, such as in a hosting environment, then you could use the FTP method. Use FTP Sites if your hosting vendor supports FTP access. Alternatively, you can host your application on another remote server through HTTP using the Remote Web Site option. To use this option, the remote server must be configured with the FrontPage Server Extensions.

Improved Debugging Support in ASP.NET 2.0

In ASP.NET 1.x, you need to explicitly set a start page in your project so that a specific page is loaded when you press F5 to debug the application. In ASP.NET 2.0, you can still set a specific page as the start page if you want. However, you can also set the start page as the currently selected page (currently selected either because you're editing it or because you selected the page in Solution Explorer). This feature saves you the trouble of setting a start page when you just want to debug a page you're working on at the moment.

This option is configurable via the Start Options item in the project Property Pages dialog (right-click a project name in Solution Explorer and then select Property Pages), as shown in see Figure 1-6.

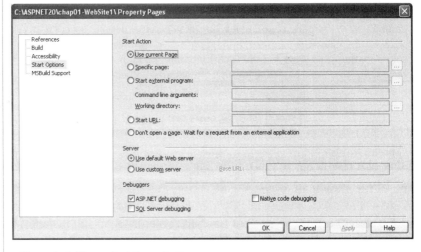

Figure 1-6. The project Property Pages

Where can I learn more?

Visit the Visual Studio 2005 home page at *http://lab.msdn.microsoft.com/vs2005/* for information on the latest changes to Visual Studio 2005.

If you prefer to use the Visual Web Developer 2005 Express Edition, head over to *http://lab.msdn.microsoft.com/express/vwd/default.aspx* for information on how to download a trial copy.

Use Multiple Languages

You're no longer restricted to using a single language for your web applications.

Unlike ASP.NET 1.x, which requires that you use the same language throughout a web application, ASP.NET 2.0 lets you vary your languages from page to page within a project.

TIP

While support for multiple languages is a useful feature, developers should use it in moderation (and only if necessary). Going with multiple languages in a single project is likely to increase the effort required in maintaining the project, particularly if the application ends up being maintained by someone who's not familiar with all the languages used.

Figure 1-7 shows a project with three pages, each of which is programmed with a different language: VB.NET (*Default.aspx*), C# (*Default2.aspx*), or VJ# (*Default3.aspx*).

TIP

VJ# does not support code-behind pages, so none appear for *Page3.aspx* in the Solution Explorer window.

Figure 1-7. A project with pages using different languages

How do I do that?

To verify that you can really mix languages in an ASP.NET 2.0 web application, in this lab you will create an application that uses two languages: VB.NET and C#.

1. Using the project created in the last lab, add a new Web Form by right-clicking the project name in Solution Explorer and then selecting Add New Item…. Select Web Form from the list of installed templates.

---

2. In the Add New Item dialog, you can choose the language you want to use, as shown in Figure 1-8. ASP.NET 2.0 supports three languages: VB2005, C#, and VJ#. Use the default name of *Default2.aspx* and choose the C# language. Click Add.

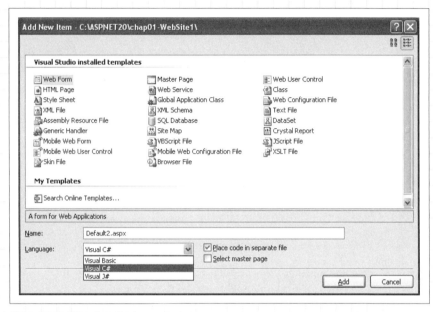

Figure 1-8. Choosing the language to use

3. In the Code View of *Default.aspx*, code the following:

```
Protected Sub Page_Load(ByVal sender As Object, _
                        ByVal e As System.EventArgs) _
                        Handles Me.Load
    Page.Title = "Page written in Visual Basic"
End Sub
```

4. In the Code View of *Default2.aspx*, code the following:

```
void Page_Load(object sender, EventArgs e)
{
    Page.Title = "Page written in C#";
}
```

5. To test the application, select *Default.aspx* in Solution Explorer and press F5. In IE, note the title of the window. Now, change the URL to load *Default2.aspx*. Figure 1-9 shows the effect of loading the two forms.

Figure 1-9. Loading two forms in an application written in two different languages

What about...

...using other .NET-supported languages such as C++, Python, or Perl?

Visual Studio 2005 will support only VB2005, C#, and VJ# for web development. The other languages are, however, available for other types of non-web projects.

Where can I learn more?

There is a good discussion on mixing languages in a .NET project at *http://weblogs.asp.net/dreilly/archive/2003/05/17/7164.aspx*. So before you go ahead and write your next ASP.NET web application using both VB.NET and C# (or J#), check out what other developers have to say.

Set the Focus of Controls

In earlier versions of ASP.NET, assigning focus to a control involves writing client-side script (such as JavaScript). In ASP.NET 2.0, this process has been much simplified, and you can now set the focus of a control via its Focus() method. Consider the example shown in Figure 1-10. If the user clicks on the Single radio button, you would expect the focus to now be assigned to the Age text box. If the Married option is selected, the Spouse Name text box should get the focus.

Look, no JavaScript! Now you set the focus of controls using the new Focus property.

How do I do that?

To try out the new Focus() method, work through the following steps to implement the form shown in Figure 1-10.

1. In Visual Studio 2005, create a new ASP.NET 2.0 web application and name it *C:\ASPNET20\chap01-ControlFocus*.

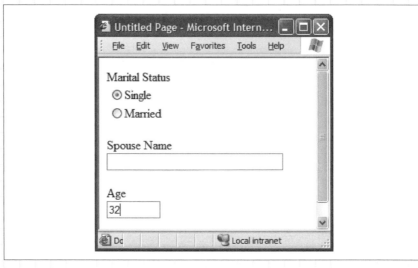

Figure 1-10. Setting the focus of controls

2. Add a radio button list and two text box controls to the default Web Form and give them the names shown in Figure 1-11.

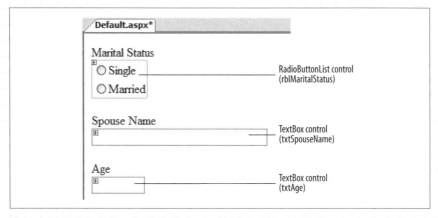

Figure 1-11. Populating the default form with the various controls

3. Populate the RadioButtonList with two items: Single and Married. To do so, switch to Source View and add the following bold lines:

```
<asp:RadioButtonList ID="rblMaritalStatus"
    runat="server" AutoPostBack="True">
    <asp:ListItem>Single</asp:ListItem>
    <asp:ListItem>Married</asp:ListItem>
</asp:RadioButtonList><br />
```

4. To ensure that the Spouse Name text box gets the focus when the user selects the Married radio button, and the Age text box gets

the focus when the user selects the Single radio button, you need to set the AutoPostBack property of the RadioButtonList control (rblMaritalStatus) to true. This can be done either in the Tasks Menu of the RadioButtonList control (check the Enable AutoPost-Back option) or via the Properties window.

5. To implement the desired focus rules described in the previous step, double-click the RadioButtonList control to reveal the code-behind, and add the following code to the page:

```
Protected Sub rblMaritalStatus_SelectedIndexChanged( _
        ByVal sender As Object, _
        ByVal e As System.EventArgs) _
        Handles rblMaritialStatus.SelectedIndexChanged
    If rblMaritialStatus.SelectedValue = "Single" Then
        txtAge.Focus( )
    Else
        txtSpouseName.Focus( )
    End If
End Sub
```

TIP

You can also set the focus of a control through the SetFocus( ) method of the Page class. The syntax is:

```
Page.SetFocus(controlName)
```

What about...

...setting a default button on a Web Form?

In ASP.NET 2.0, you can set a default button on a form. For example, Figure 1-12 shows a page with two TextBox controls and two Button controls. You can configure the Submit button to be the default button so it is automatically clicked when a user presses the Enter key.

In ASP.NET 2.0, you can now set a default button on a page so that when the user presses the Enter key the button is automatically invoked.

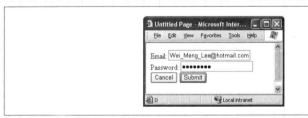

Figure 1-12. Setting the Submit button as the default button of the form

To try this out on your own, follow these steps:

1. Create a form like the one shown in Figure 1-13.

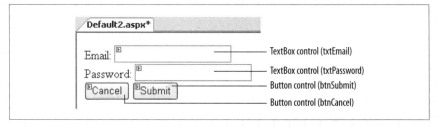

Figure 1-13. A Web Form with two TextBox controls and two Button controls

2. Switch the Web Form to Source View and then add the lines of code shown in bold. The defaultfocus attribute sets the control that will be assigned the focus when the form is loaded. The defaultbutton attribute sets the button to be activated when the Enter key is pressed:

```
<form id="form1" runat="server"
    defaultbutton="btnSubmit"
    defaultfocus="txtEmail"
    >
<div>
    Email:
    <asp:TextBox ID="txtEmail" runat="server" Width="174px"></asp:
TextBox>
    <br />
    Password:
    <asp:TextBox ID="txtPassword" runat="server" Width="153px"
        TextMode="Password"></asp:TextBox>
    <br />
    <asp:Button ID="btnCancel" runat="server" Text="Cancel" />
    <asp:Button ID="btnSubmit" runat="server" Text="Submit" /><br />
    <br />

</div>
</form>
```

3. Press F5 to load the form; note that the focus is on the Email text box (see Figure 1-14), and the Submit key is set as the default button.

Figure 1-14. The Email text box has the focus, and the Submit button is the default button

Where can I learn more?

The Focus() method in ASP.NET 2.0 works on the server side; hence, every time you need to set the focus of a control, you need to initiate a postback. If you want to set the focus of controls on the client side without a postback, check out the following two links:

- *http://www.ondotnet.com/pub/a/dotnet/2003/09/15/aspnet.html*
- *http://ryanfarley.com/blog/archive/2004/12/21/1325.aspx*

Define Multiple Validation Groups on a Page

By grouping controls into validation groups, you can now independently validate collections of controls.

In ASP.NET 1.x, all controls in a single page are validated together. For example, suppose you have a Search button and a Get Title button, as shown in Figure 1-15. If you use a RequiredFieldValidator validation control on the ISBN text box, then clicking the Search button will not result in a postback if the ISBN text box is empty. This is because the entire page is invalidated as long as one control fails the validation.

Figure 1-15. Multiple forms on a page

In ASP.NET 2.0, group validation allows controls in a page to be grouped logically so that a postback in one group is not dependent on another.

How do I do that?

The best way to explore this new feature is to create a form with multiple postback controls, add a validator to one of them, and then assign each control to a separate group. In this lab, you'll implement the form shown in Figure 1-15.

1. Launch Visual Studio 2005 and create a new web site project. Name the project *C:\ASPNET20\chap01-Validation*.

2. Populate the default Web Form with the Panel, TextBox, and Button controls shown in Figure 1-16.

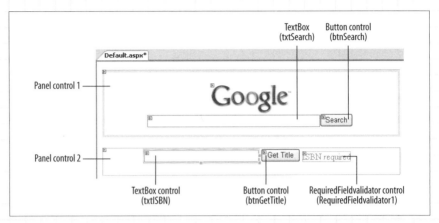

Figure 1-16. A page with multiple controls

3. In the top panel (Panel control 1), you'll configure the Search button to post the search string to the server, which in turn will redirect to Google's site. To do so, double-click the Search button (btnSearch) and enter the following code on the code-behind to redirect the search string to Google's site:

```
Sub btnSearch_Click(ByVal sender As Object, _
                    ByVal e As System.EventArgs) _
                    Handles btnSearch.Click
    Dim queryStr As String = HttpUtility.UrlEncode(txtSearch.Text)
    Response.Redirect("http://www.google.com/search?q=" & queryStr)
End Sub
```

4. The TextBox control contained in the bottom panel (Panel control 2) will take in an ISBN number and perhaps perform some processing (like retrieve details of a book from Amazon.com). Associate the RequiredFieldValidator control with the ISBN text box (you can configure it in Source View):

```
<asp:RequiredFieldValidator
    ID="RequiredFieldValidator1" Runat="server"
    ErrorMessage="RequiredFieldValidator"
    ControlToValidate="txtISBN"
    SetFocusOnError="True">
    ISBN required</asp:RequiredFieldValidator>
```

5. To divide the controls into two separate validation groups, switch to Source View and use the ValidationGroup attribute, as shown in the following code sample (highlighted in bold):

```
...

<asp:TextBox ID="txtSearch" Runat="server"
    Width="320px" Height="22px">
</asp:TextBox>
```

```
<asp:Button ID="btnSearch" Runat="server"
    Text="Search" ValidationGroup="SearchGroup" />

...

<asp:TextBox ID="txtISBN" Runat="server"
    Width="212px" Height="22px">
</asp:TextBox>

<asp:Button ID="btnGetTitle" Runat="server"
    Text="Get Title"
    ValidationGroup="BooksGroup" />

<asp:RequiredFieldValidator ID="RequiredFieldValidator1"
    Runat="server" ErrorMessage="RequiredFieldValidator"
    ControlToValidate="txtISBN"
    ValidationGroup="BooksGroup">ISBN required
</asp:RequiredFieldValidator>

...
```

6. Here, the Search button is assigned the SearchGroup validation group, while the Get Title button and the `RequiredFieldValidator` are both assigned to the BooksGroup validation group.

7. Press F5 to test the application. Now you can click the Search and Get Title buttons independently of each other.

T I P

Controls that do not set the ValidationGroup attribute belong to the default group, thus maintaining backward compatibility with ASP.NET 1.x.

What about...

...setting the focus on the field on error?

All validation controls in ASP.NET 2.0 now support the SetFocusOnError property. Simply set a validator control's SetFocusOnError attribute to True so that the browser will set the focus on the control on error.

In the previous example, if the RequiredFieldValidator control has the SetFocusOnError attribute:

```
<asp:RequiredFieldValidator
    ID="RequiredFieldValidator1" Runat="server"
    ErrorMessage="RequiredFieldValidator"
    ControlToValidate="txtISBN"
    ValidationGroup="BooksGroup"
    SetFocusOnError="True">
```

Then the ISBN text box will get the focus if you click the Get Title button when the ISBN text box is empty.

Where can I learn more?

If you are interested in simulating the validation group behavior of ASP.NET 2.0 in ASP.NET 1.x, check out *http://weblogs.asp.net/skoganti/archive/2004/12/05/275457.aspx*.

Insert Client Script into a Page

You can now insert client script into your web page as naturally as writing your server-side code.

There are times when you need to insert client-side JavaScript into your page to implement client-side functionalities. Take the example of an eBanking web application. If the user has not been active for a certain period of time after logging in, the application will prompt the user with a pop-up window asking if the user would like to continue. Employing a pop-up window is more likely to draw the user's attention than simply displaying the message on the web page, and this is best implemented with client-side script.

In ASP.NET 2.0, you can insert client-side script by using the ClientScript property of the Page class.

How do I do that?

To see how you can insert a client script into an ASP.NET 2.0 web application, you will create an application that displays the current time in a JavaScript window when the application is loaded.

1. In Visual Studio 2005, create a new web site project and name it *C:\ASPNET20\chap01-ClientScript*.

2. Double-click the default Web Form to switch to the code-behind.

3. In the Form_Load event, insert a client script onto the page using the RegisterClientScriptBlock() method. The following example inserts a JavaScript code that displays the current time on the server. The time will be displayed in a window, as shown in Figure 1-17.

```
Protected Sub Page_Load(ByVal sender As Object, _
                        ByVal e As System.EventArgs) _
                        Handles Me.Load
    '---inserting client-side script
    Dim script As String = _
        "alert('Time on the server is " & Now & "');"
    Page.ClientScript.RegisterClientScriptBlock( _
        Me.GetType, "MyKey", script, True)
End Sub
```

Figure 1-17. Executing a client script

The parameters of the RegisterClientScriptBlock( ) method are:

Type

The type of the calling page

Key

The key to identify the script

Script

Content of the script to be sent to the client side

AddScript

Indicates whether the script should be enclosed within a
<script> block. The script generated on the client-side would
look like this:

```
<script type="text/javascript">
<!--
alert('Time on the server is 7/18/2004 12:07:23 PM');//
-->
</script>
```

If the AddScript parameter is set to False, the script will not be
executed on the client side; instead, it simply will be shown on
the web page.

What about...

...including a script file?

Instead of inserting strings of client-side script into your application, you might have a much more sophisticated client-side application that is saved in a separate file. In this case, it is more effective for you to include the file directly rather than insert the scripts line by line.

Suppose you have a script file saved as *hello.js* and its content contains JavaScript code (without the <script> tag):

```
alert("Hello world, from JavaScript");
```

You can include this script in your page through the RegisterScriptInclude() method:

```
'--including script files
Dim scriptURL As String = "./hello.js"
Page.ClientScript.RegisterClientScriptInclude( _
    Me.GetType, "MyKey", scriptURL)
```

The generated output looks like this:

```
<script src="./hello.js" type="text/javascript"></script>
```

Where can I learn more?

MSDN has a comprehensive article on injecting client-side script from an ASP.NET server control: *http://msdn.microsoft.com/library/default.asp?url=/library/en-us/dnaspp/html/aspnet-injectclientsidesc.asp*.

Post to Another Page

ASP.NET 2.0 now allows you to post values from one page to another easily.

Most ASP.NET developers are familiar with the postback feature of ASP.NET server controls. However, in some cases, posting back to the same page is not the desired action—you might need to post to another. For example, you might need to build an application to perform some surveys. Instead of displaying 50 questions on one page, you would like to break it down to 10 questions per page so that the user need not wade through 50 questions in one go. Moreover, answers to certain questions might trigger a related set of questions in another page. In this case, using a conventional postback mechanism for your web pages is clearly not the solution. You might want to post the values (i.e., the answers to the questions) of one page to another. In this situation, you need to be able to cross-post to another page and, at the same time, be able to retrieve the values from the previous page.

In ASP.NET 1.0 and 1.1, there is no easy way to transfer to another page, and most developers resort to using Server.Transfer. Even so, passing values from one page to another this way is a challenge.

In ASP.NET 2.0, cross-page posting is much easier. Controls now inherently support posting to another page via the PostBackUrl attribute.

How do I do that?

To see cross-page posting in action, you will create an application that contains two pages. One page lets you choose items from a CheckBoxList control and then lets you cross-post to another page. You will learn how the values that were cross-posted can be retrieved in the destination page. In addition, you will see the difference between cross-page posting and the old Server.Transfer() method.

1. In Visual Studio 2005, create a new web site project and name it *C:\ASPNET20\chap01-CrossPagePosting*.

2. Populate the default Web Form with the controls shown in Figure 1-18. The CheckBoxList1 control contains CheckBox controls that let users choose from a list of values. When the "Post to Default2.aspx" button is clicked, you will post the values to *Default2.aspx* using the new cross-page posting feature in ASP.NET 2.0. The "Transfer to Default2.aspx" button uses Server.Transfer to load *Default2.aspx*.

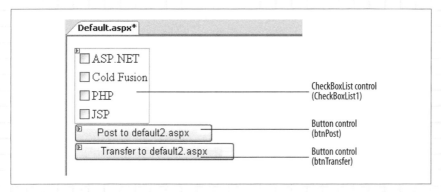

Figure 1-18. Populating the default Web Form

3. Add a new Web Form to your project and populate it with a Button control (see Figure 1-19).

Figure 1-19. Populating the Default2 Web Form

4. In *Default.aspx,* switch to Source View and add the PostBackUrl attribute to btnPost so that it can perform a cross-page post to *Default2.aspx:*

```
<asp:Button ID="btnPost"
    PostBackUrl="~/Default2.aspx"
    runat="server"
    Text="Post to Default2.aspx" />
```

5. For btnTransfer, add the following code-behind:

```
Protected Sub btnTransfer_Click(ByVal sender As Object, _
                                ByVal e As System.EventArgs) _
                                Handles btnTransfer.Click
    Server.Transfer("Default2.aspx")
End Sub
```

6. In order for *Default2.aspx* to access the value of the CheckBoxList1 control in *Default.aspx,* expose a public property in *Default.aspx.* To do so, switch to the code-behind of *Default.aspx* and type in the following code shown in bold:

```
Partial Class Default_aspx
    Inherits System.Web.UI.Page

    Public ReadOnly Property ServerSide() As CheckBoxList
        Get
            Return CheckBoxList1
        End Get
    End Property

    Protected Sub btnTransfer_Click(ByVal sender As Object, _
                                    ByVal e As System.EventArgs) _
                                    Handles btnTransfer.Click
        Server.Transfer("Default2.aspx")
    End Sub
End Class
```

You need to expose public properties in the first page in order for the other page to access it. This has the advantage of early binding and facilitates strong typing.

7. In *Default2.aspx,* you need to specify that *Default.aspx* is going to post to it by using the PreviousPageType directive. In *Default2.aspx,* switch to Source View and add the PreviousPageType directive:

```
<%@ Page Language="VB" AutoEventWireup="false"
       CodeFile="Default2.aspx.vb" Inherits="Default2_aspx" %>
<%@ PreviousPageType VirtualPath="~/Default.aspx" %>
```

8. When *Default.aspx* posts to *Default2.aspx,* all the information about *Default.aspx* is encapsulated in a special property known as PreviousPage. When *Default2.aspx* loads, you must first determine whether it was posted by *Default.aspx* or it gets loaded by itself. So check if PreviousPage contains a reference:

```
Sub Page_Load(ByVal sender As Object, ByVal e As System.EventArgs)
Handles Me.Load
    If PreviousPage IsNot Nothing Then
        ...
```

9. Then check if this is a cross-page post or a Server.Transfer by using the new IsCrossPagePostBack property. This property will be true if *Default.aspx* cross-posts to *Default2.aspx,* false if *Default.aspx* performs a Server.Transfer to *Default2.aspx:*

Check the IsCrossPagePost Back property to see if there is a cross posting.

```
If PreviousPage IsNot Nothing Then
    '--checks the type of posting
    If PreviousPage.IsCrossPagePostBack Then
        Response.Write("This is a cross-post")
    Else
        Response.Write("This is a Server.Transfer")
    End If
```

10. Finally, display the selections made in the CheckBoxList control in *Default.aspx*:

```
Response.Write("<br/>You have selected :")
Dim i As Integer
For i = 0 To PreviousPage.ServerSide.Items.Count - 1
    If PreviousPage.ServerSide.Items(i).Selected Then
        Response.Write( _
        PreviousPage.ServerSide.Items(i).ToString & " ")
    End If
Next
```

TIP

The ServerSide property refers to the property exposed in *Default.aspx.* The advantage to exposing properties in the page is that the data is strongly typed.

---

11. The entire block of code is as shown:

```
Protected Sub Page_Load(ByVal sender As Object, _
                        ByVal e As System.EventArgs) _
                        Handles Me.Load
    If PreviousPage IsNot Nothing Then
```

```
                    '--checks the type of posting
                    If PreviousPage.IsCrossPagePostBack Then
                        Response.Write("This is a cross-post")
                    Else
                        Response.Write("This is a Server.Transfer")
                    End If

                    Response.Write("<br/>You have selected :")
                    Dim i As Integer
                    For i = 0 To PreviousPage.ServerSide.Items.Count - 1
                        If PreviousPage.ServerSide.Items(i).Selected Then
                            Response.Write( _
                            PreviousPage.ServerSide.Items(i).ToString & " ")
                        End If
                    Next
                End If
            End Sub
```

To see the example in action, Figure 1-20 shows a cross-page post.

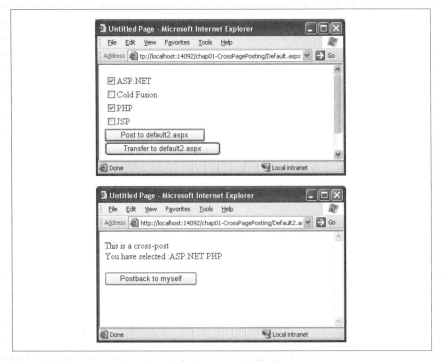

Figure 1-20. Cross-posting from Default.aspx to Default2.aspx

Figure 1-21 shows posting to *Default2.aspx* via the Server.Transfer method. Note the URL of both pages (they are the same for Server. Transfer).

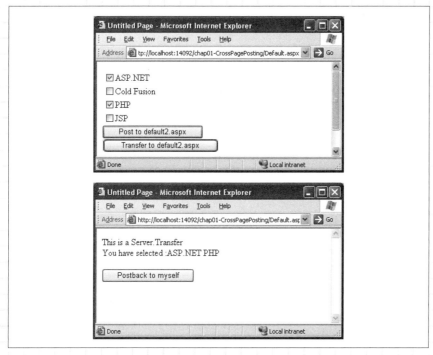

Figure 1-21. Using Server.Transfer to post from Default.aspx to Default2.aspx

If you click the button "Postback to myself" in *Default2.aspx*, you will notice that the information from *Default.aspx* is no longer displayed; a postback will clear the object reference in the PreviousPage property.

TIP

The main difference between a cross-page post and the use of Server.Transfer is that, in the case of the Server.Transfer, the URL does not change to the new page.

What about...

...having multiple pages post to the same page?

In this case, you would not be able to use the early binding mechanism accorded by the PreviousPage property, because the PreviousPageType directive predefines the type of a previous page:

```
<%@ PreviousPageType VirtualPath="~/default.aspx" %>
```

So if there are different pages posting to a common page, having this directive is not useful, because those pages may have different controls and types. Hence, a better way would be to use late-binding via the FindControl( ) method.

Example 1-1 shows how you can use the AppRelativeVirtualPath property of the PreviousPage property to get the address of the last page posted to it. The application then uses the FindControl( ) method to locate the controls within the source page.

Use the FindControl( ) method to locate values in the previous page if multiple pages post to one page.

Example 1-1. Locating the controls of the last page to post

```
If PreviousPage.AppRelativeVirtualPath = "~/Default.aspx" Then
    Dim serverSide As CheckBoxList
    serverSide = CType(PreviousPage.FindControl("checkboxlist1"), _
                    System.Web.UI.WebControls.CheckBoxList)
    If serverSide IsNot Nothing Then
        Dim i As Integer
        For i = 0 To serverSide.Items.Count - 1
            If serverSide.Items(i).Selected Then
                Response.Write(serverSide.Items(i).ToString & " ")
            End If
        Next
    End If
ElseIf PreviousPage.AppRelativeVirtualPath = "~/Default3.aspx" Then
    Dim userName As TextBox
    userName = CType(PreviousPage.FindControl("txtName"), _
                System.Web.UI.WebControls.TextBox)
    If userName IsNot Nothing Then
        Response.Write(userName.Text)
    End If
End If
```

TIP

If you attempt to cross-post between two different applications, the PreviousPage property will be set to Nothing (or null in C#).

Where can I learn more?

To learn more about the various ways to redirect users to another page, check out the Microsoft Visual Studio 2005 Documentation Help topic "Redirecting Users to Another Page."

Selectively Display Groups of Controls

Use the new MultiView and Wizard controls to selectively hide and display controls.

One task that is common in web applications is data collection. For example, you may need to create a page for user registration. On that page, you may want to collect a fair bit of information, such as username, birth date, and perhaps answers to survey questions (often used to collect subscriber information for controlled circulation magazines). A good practice is to split your questions across multiple pages so that the user need not scroll down a page that contains all the questions. Alternatively, ASP.NET 1.x developers often like to use the Panel controls to contain all the questions and then selectively display the relevant panels (and hide the other panels).

In ASP.NET 2.0, the MultiView control takes the drudgery out of creating multiple pages for this task. It allows controls to be contained within multiple View controls (a new control in ASP.NET 2.0), which you can then programmatically display.

How do I do that?

To see how the MultiView control works, you will create an application that contains a MultiView control with three View controls embedded in this control. You can then treat each View control like an ordinary Web Form and populate controls in it. You then connect these View controls together so that users can step through them in a specific order.

1. Launch Visual Studio 2005 and create a new web site project. Name the project *C:\ASPNET20\chap01-MultiView*.

2. Double-click the MultiView control (located in the Toolbox under the Standard tab) to add it to the default Web Form.

3. Double-click the View control (also located in the Toolbox under the Standard tab) and drag and drop it onto the MultiView control. Drag two more View controls onto the MultiView control.

4. Populate the View controls with the additional controls shown in Figure 1-22.

5. Double-click the Web Form to switch to its code-behind page. Add the code shown in Example 1-2 to service the Click events of all Button controls on *Default.aspx*.

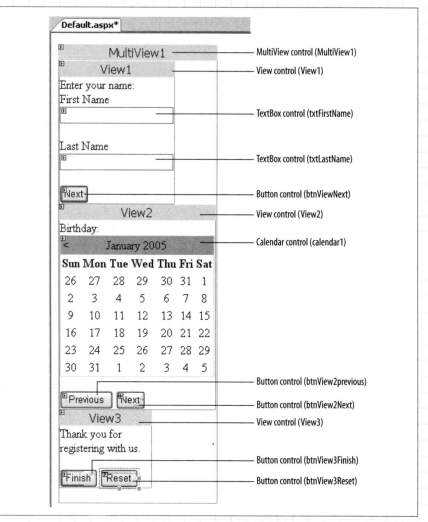

Figure 1-22. Populating the default Web Form with the various controls

Example 1-2. Event handler for all Click events on Default.aspx

```
Protected Sub btnAllButtons_Click(ByVal sender As Object, _
                         ByVal e As System.EventArgs) _
                         Handles btnView1Next.Click, _
                         btnView2Next.Click, btnView2Previous.Click, _
                         btnView3Finish.Click, btnView3Reset.Click
    Select Case CType(sender, Button).Text
        Case "Next"
            MultiView1.ActiveViewIndex += 1
        Case "Previous"
            MultiView1.ActiveViewIndex -= 1
        Case "Finish"
            Response.Write("You have registered as " & _
```

Example 1-2. Event handler for all Click events on Default.aspx (continued)

```
                    txtFirstName.Text & _
                    txtLastName.Text & "<br/>")
        Response.Write("Birthday " & _
                    Calendar1.SelectedDate)
        btnView3Finish.Enabled = False
        btnView3Reset.Enabled = False
      Case "Reset"
        MultiView1.ActiveViewIndex = 0
    End Select
End Sub
```

6. The ActiveViewIndex property of the MultiView control sets the View control to display. Set the ActiveViewIndex property of the MultiView control to 0 so that the first View control will be displayed when the page is loaded.

7. Press F5 to test the application. Figure 1-23 shows the results of stepping through the application.

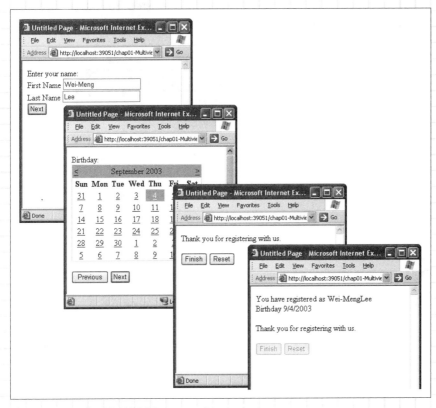

Figure 1-23. Using the MultiView control

Notice that for every change of view, a postback to the server occurs.

What about...

...a more efficient method for dividing screens that does not require a postback?

While this lab uses the MultiView control to split a long page into multiple views, the inherent disadvantage with this control is that every change of view requires a postback. Unless you need to access data on the server side, it is much more efficient to use the Wizard control, which performs similar tasks without a postback.

The Wizard control can be found in the Toolbox under the Standard tab. To try out the functionality of the Wizard control:

1. Launch Visual Studio 2005 and create a new web site project. Name the project *C:\ASPNET20\chap01-Wizard*.

2. Add the Wizard control to the default Web Form.

3. In the Wizard Tasks menu, click the Add/Remove WizardSteps... link (see Figure 1-24) to add one additional step to the control (by default, there are two steps created for you).

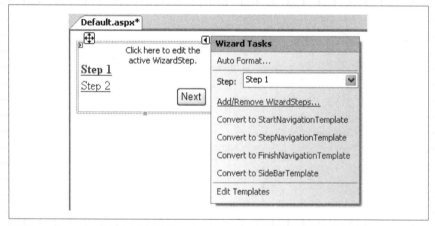

Figure 1-24. Using the Wizard control

The Wizard control is highly customizable. Make sure you check out the properties window for all its capabilities.

4. In the WizardStep Collection Editor window, click the Add button and then type "Step 3" in the Title text box (see Figure 1-25). Click OK.

5. Populate the Step 1 of the Wizard control with two TextBox controls, as shown in Figure 1-26. To go to the next step, select Step 2 in the Wizard Tasks menu.

6. Populate Step 2 with the Calendar control (use the default name of Calendar1), as shown in Figure 1-27.

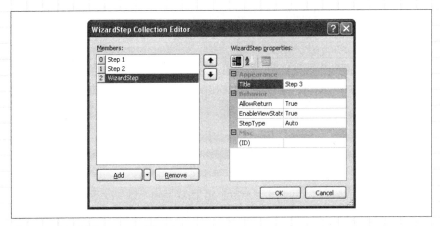

Figure 1-25. Adding a new Wizard step

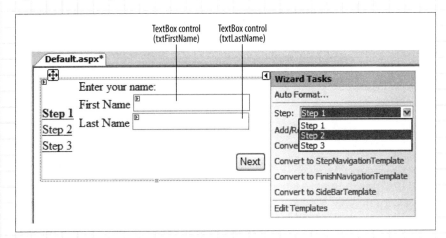

Figure 1-26. Populating Step 1

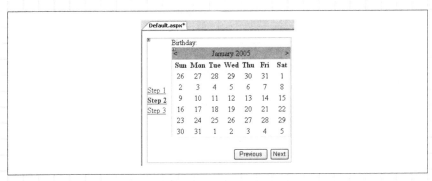

Figure 1-27. Populating Step 2

7. In Step 3, type the string as shown in Figure 1-28.

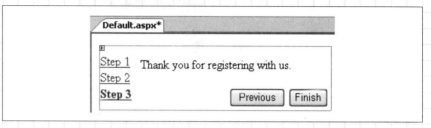

Figure 1-28. Populating Step 3

8. Double-click the Wizard control so that you can service the Finish-ButtonClick event when the user clicks on the Finish button in the final step (Step 3):

```
Protected Sub Wizard1_FinishButtonClick(ByVal sender As Object, _
    ByVal e As System.Web.UI.WebControls.WizardNavigationEventArgs) _
    Handles Wizard1.FinishButtonClick

    Response.Write("You have registered as " & _
            txtFirstName.Text & _
            txtLastName.Text & "<br/>")
    Response.Write("Birthday " & _
                    Calendar1.SelectedDate)
    Wizard1.Visible = False
End Sub
```

9. To test the application, press F5. Figure 1-29 shows the Wizard control in action.

TIP

In this example, the Wizard control does not perform a postback to the server when the user clicks on the Next or Previous button. However, if the user clicks on the Calendar control in Step 2, a postback does occur.

Where can I learn more?

Check out the Visual Studio 2005 Help entries for the MultiView and Wizard controls to learn more about their full capabilities. In particular, the Wizard control contains many properties for you to customize.

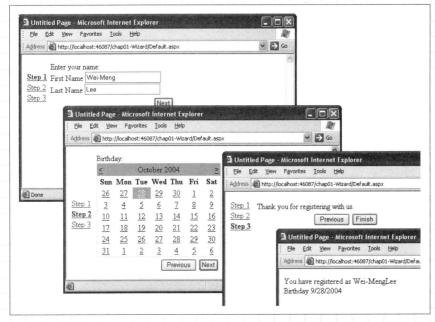

Figure 1-29. The Wizard control in action

Upload Files to Your Web Site

ASP.NET 2.0 now includes the FileUpload control, allowing web site users to upload files onto the web server for archival or file-submission purposes. For example, students typically need to upload their files to their school's server when they submit their assignment or project work. You'll find the FileUpload control in the Toolbox under the Standard tab.

Uploading files to your web site is made easy with the new FileUpload control.

How do I do that?

The Visual Studio designer represents the FileUpload control by adding an empty text box and a Button control to a Web page. To upload the selected file, you need to explicitly trigger an event, such as clicking a button (see the Submit button in Figure 1-30). In the following example, you will build an application that allows users to upload files to a particular directory on the server. You will also check the size of the file uploaded to ensure that users do not upload files that exceed an imposed limit.

1. Launch Visual Studio 2005 and create a new web site project. Name the project *C:\ASPNET20\chap01-FileUpload*.

2. In the Toolbox, double-click the FileUpload control located under the Standard tab to add the control to the default Web Form, *Default.aspx*.

Remember to add a Submit button so that you can invoke the FileUpload control.

3. Add a Button control to the default form, change its Text to "Submit", and name the button "btnSubmit".

4. Your form should now look like the one shown in Figure 1-30.

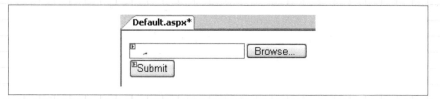

Figure 1-30. The FileUpload control on a Web Form

5. Right-click the project name in Solution Explorer and then select Add Folder → Regular Folder (see Figure 1-31). Name the new folder "uploads". This folder will be used to store the files uploaded by the user.

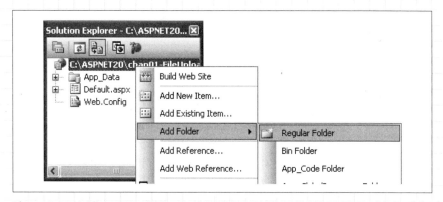

Figure 1-31. Adding a new folder to the project

6. Double-click the Submit button to reveal the code-behind. Enter the following code for the Submit button:

```
Sub btnSubmit_Click(ByVal sender As Object, _
                    ByVal e As System.EventArgs) _
                    Handles btnSubmit.Click
    ' get the application path
    Dim savePath As String = Request.PhysicalApplicationPath
    ' uploads to a special upload folder
    savePath += "uploads\"
    If FileUpload1.HasFile Then ' verify if there is file to upload
        savePath += FileUpload1.FileName
        ' existing file will be overwritten
        FileUpload1.SaveAs(savePath)
        Response.Write("File uploaded successfully!")
    Else
```

```
        Response.Write("No file to upload")
    End If
End Sub
```

TIP

You use the FileUpload1.SaveAs( ) method to save the file onto the specified directory. If there is a file of the same name, this method will simply overwrite it with the new file. Hence it is important that you do some error checking before writing the file to the server.

Wiring Up Event Handlers in ASP.NET 2.0

ASP.NET 2.0 provides a new way for you to wire up your event handlers, one that was unavailable in ASP.NET 1.x. To use this technique, add an attribute to the Web Form that identifies the event you wish to trap and the code to handle it. Then, add code for the handler to the code-behind page. For example, to handle the Click event of btnSubmit, add the OnClick attribute to the Source View of your form and then set it to point to an event handler in your code-behind. For example:

```
<asp:Button ID="btnSubmit"
 runat="server" Text="Submit"
 OnClick="Submit_Click" />
```

This technique eliminates the need for the Handles keyword in the handler code:

```
Protected Sub Submit_Click(ByVal sender As Object, _
                           ByVal e As System.EventArgs)
    ' code to handle the Submit button click
End Sub
```

You find out the path that the current application resides in by using the PhysicalApplicationPath property from the Request object. The HasFile property of the FileUpload control specifies if the user has selected a file to upload. The file selected is saved in the FileName property of the File-Upload control.

What about...

...limiting the size of uploaded files?

For security reasons, it is important to restrict the size of files that users may upload to your web site. (Allowing users to upload a file that is too large could potentially expose an app to a denial-of-service attack.) You

---

can check the size of the file uploaded by using the ContentLength property, as the following example shows:

```
' ensure size if below 3MB
If FileUpload1.PostedFile.ContentLength <= 3145728 Then
    savePath += FileUpload1.FileName
    ' existing file will be overwritten
    FileUpload1.SaveAs(savePath)
    Response.Write("File uploaded successfully!")
Else
    Response.Write("File size exceeds 3MB.")
End If
```

Where can I learn more?

If you want to learn more about how file uploading is done in ASP.NET 1.x, check out this article: *http://www.ondotnet.com/pub/a/dotnet/2002/04/01/asp.html*.

Create an Image Map

Modern web sites use image maps to allow users to navigate to another part of the site, or to initiate an action by clicking on one or more *hotspots* of an image. For example, you want to display a world map on a page so that users can click on specific parts of the map to see information about a particular country. ASP.NET 2.0 includes a new ImageMap control that allows you to create image maps easily and painlessly.

The ImageMap control can be found in the Visual Studio Toolbox under the Standard tab.

How do I do that?

To see how the ImageMap control works, you will use an ImageMap control to display the image of a Pocket PC. You will define three different hotspots of different shapes on the Pocket PC so that users are able to click on the different parts of the image to see more information.

1. In Visual Studio 2005, create a new web site project and name it *C:\ASPNET20\chap01-ImageMap*.

2. Double-click the ImageMap control in the Toolbox to add a control to the default Web Form.

3. In Solution Explorer, right-click the project name and add a new folder named *Images*, where you'll store the image used in this

project. Save an image named *dellaxim.jpg* (see Figure 1-32) into the new folder: *C:\ASPNET20\chap01-ImageMap\Images*.

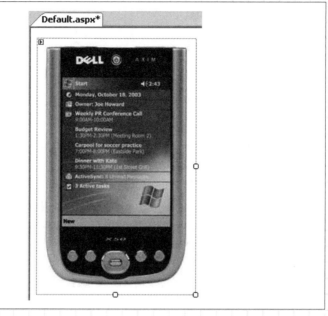

Figure 1-32. Displaying a Pocket PC using the ImageMap control

4. To display the image in the ImageMap control, set its ImageURL property to point to the file you just saved (*Images/dellaxim.jpg*). The ImageMap control will now display the image of a Pocket PC, as shown in Figure 1-32.

5. An image map works by providing one or more hotspots for users to click on, each initiating a particular action—for example, jumping to another page or altering the image itself. To define one or more hotspots, go to the Properties window for the ImageMap control, scroll down to the Hotspots property, and click on the Collections button (...) to invoke the HotSpot Collection Editor (shown in Figure 1-33).

   The ImageMap control supports three kinds of hotspot: circles (CircleHotSpot), rectangles (RectangleHotSpot), and polygons (PolygonHotSpot). The drop-down menu to the right of the dialog's Add button dialog lets you choose the type of hotspot to add. Once you add a hotspot, a Properties window appears that allows you to specify the location and dimensions of the hotspot, as well as its key properties. Figure 1-33 displays the properties of a CircleHotSpot that has a radius of 5 and *x* and *y* coordinates of 103 and 26, respectively.

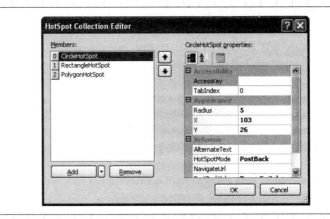

Figure 1-33. Adding hotspots to the ImageMap control

6. You can also specify your hotspots by hand. You can switch to Source View and add in the hotspots elements manually, like this:

```
<asp:ImageMap ID="ImageMap1" runat="server"
    ImageUrl="Images/dellaxim.jpg">
    <asp:CircleHotSpot HotSpotMode="PostBack"
        X="103" Y="26" PostBackValue="PowerSwitch"
        Radius="5" />
    <asp:RectangleHotSpot Top="48" Bottom="242"
        Left="30" NavigateUrl="./screen.aspx"
        Right="177" />
    <asp:PolygonHotSpot
        Coordinates="92,273,112,273,123,287,112,303,92,303,83,287"
        PostBackValue="Navigation" HotSpotMode="PostBack" />
</asp:ImageMap>
```

TIP

You can use Microsoft Paint to display the image and then position your cursor at the various hotspots you want to define. You can find the coordinates of the cursor at the bottom of the window.

The ImageMap control supports three types of hotspot: circles, rectangles, and polygons.

7. If you add the code shown in Step 6 or use the same attribute values to create hotspots with the HotSpot Collection Editor, you will end up with the hotspots shown in Figure 1-34.

Figure 1-34 shows an ImageMap with the three hotspots: a CircleHotSpot, a RectangleHotSpot, and a PolygonHotSpot. The CircleHotSpot defines the region containing the power switch of the Pocket PC as a circle hotspot, whereas the RectangleHotSpot defines the screen region as a rectangle hotspot. The PolygonHotSpot defines the navigational buttons on the Pocket PC as a polygon hotspot.

Chapter 1: What's New?

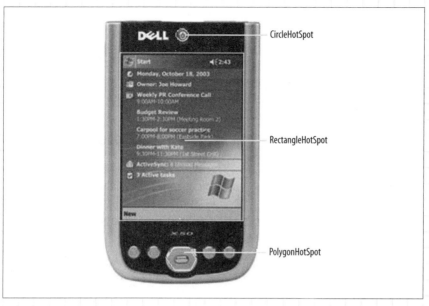

CircleHotSpot

RectangleHotSpot

PolygonHotSpot

Figure 1-34. Defining the hotspots in the ImageMap control

A HotSpot control supports one of four modes of behavior, defined by its HotSpotMode property:

Not Set

If a hotspot's HotSpotMode is set to "Not Set", its behavior will assume that of the HotSpotMode as defined in the ImageMap control.

Navigate

Another page can be loaded when a hotspot is clicked.

PostBack

A postback is sent to the server. This is useful in cases where you need to perform some action (such as increment a variable) when the user clicks on a hotspot.

Inactive

Disables the hotspot.

TIP

The HotSpotMode property of the ImageMap control defines the default behavior of all the hotspots in that control's HotSpot collection. A particular hotspot can override this behavior by setting its own HotSpotMode property.

---

8. To illustrate how a hotspot can be used to postback to a server, set the HotSpotMode property of the CircleHotSpot to PostBack and the PostBackValue property value to PowerSwitch. To receive the postback value on the server side, add an event handler to service the click event of the ImageMap control:

```
Protected Sub ImageMap1_Click(ByVal sender As Object, _
            ByVal e As System.Web.UI.WebControls.ImageMapEventArgs) _
            Handles ImageMap1.Click
    Dim str As String = "You have clicked " & e.PostBackValue
    Response.Write(str)
End Sub
```

9. Add a new Web Form to your project (right-click the project name in Solution Explorer, select Add New Item..., and then select Web Form) and name it *screen.aspx*. This page will be displayed when the user clicks on the RectangleHotSpot.

10. Use the RectangleHotSpot to navigate to another page by setting its HotSpotMode property to Navigate and setting the NavigateURL property value to screen.aspx.

11. Press F5 to test the application. Note how your mouse pointer changes when it hovers over the various hotspots.

What about...

...adding Tool Tip text to the hotspots?

You can add Tool Tip text to the various controls in the ImageControl control using the AlternateText property. Adding Tool Tip text to hotspots greatly improves the usability of your application, as users can view more information about a hotspot. You can add Tool Tip text in Source View:

```
<asp:CircleHotSpot
    HotSpotMode="PostBack"
    X="103" Y="26" Radius="5"
    PostBackValue="PowerSwitch"
    AlternateText="Power Switch" />
```

You can also add it programmatically:

```
Protected Sub Page_Load(ByVal sender As Object, _
                ByVal e As System.EventArgs) _
                Handles Me.Load
    ImageMap1.HotSpots(0).AlternateText = "Power Switch"
    ImageMap1.HotSpots(1).AlternateText = "Screen"
    ImageMap1.HotSpots(2).AlternateText = "Navigation"
End Sub
```

The next time the user's mouse hovers over the hotspots, he will see the Tool Tip text as shown in Figure 1-35.

Figure 1-35. Displaying the Tool Tip text

Where can I learn more?

Besides using the ImageMap control to implement an image map, you can use the ImageButton as an image map. To see how, check out this link: *http://samples.gotdotnet.com/quickstart/aspplus/samples/webforms/ctrlref/ webctrl/imagebutton/doc_imagebut.aspx.*

CHAPTER 2

Master Pages and Site Navigation

With Visual Studio 2005, ASP.NET now supports visual page inheritance, which is similar to Windows Forms inheritance, for those who have used that popular framework. With ASP.NET 2.0, you can now create a single Master page that contains the common elements used by the pages of your site. You can then create web pages that inherit from the Master page to enforce a common look and feel across your entire site.

In addition to Master Pages, ASP.NET 2.0 comes with new controls for easier page navigation. These controls, known as SiteMapPath and Menu, allow you to add navigational links to your site without much coding.

In this chapter:
- *Create a Master Page for Your Site*
- *Use a Master Page as a Content Page Template*
- *Modify a Master Page at Runtime*
- *Create a Site Map for Your Web Site*
- *Display Hierarchical Data Using the TreeView Control*
- *Populate a TreeView Control Programmatically*
- *Display Drop-Down Menus Using the Menu Control*

Create a Master Page for Your Site

Most web sites you see today have a consistent look and feel, with a company logo and perhaps a navigational menu repeated on every page. A good example is O'Reilly's web site, where every page displays the familiar O'Reilly tarsier logo across its top and a navigational menu on its left, as shown in Figure 2-1.

As an ASP.NET 1.x web developer, you've no doubt learned how to use Web User controls to encapsulate all the headers and navigational menus you use for your site and how to embed them onto every web page. The drawback, of course, is that if you wish to make modifications to any of these controls, you typically need to edit every single page by hand to modify its layout.

TIP

Using Master Pages to provide page headers is preferred over the use of Web User controls; only the Master page needs to be changed and the rest will follow!

Figure 2-1. Most web sites employ a common header and navigational menu

In ASP.NET 2.0, a new feature known as Master Pages addresses the limitations of using Web User controls for headers and navigational menu information. In ASP.NET 2.0, you can simply construct a Master page that includes your page header information. You then build each page of your site by first inheriting from the site Master page.

How do I do that?

To really understand how Master Pages work, you will build a web application using Master Pages in the next couple of labs. In this lab, you will create a Master page and populate it with some controls.

1. In Visual Studio 2005, create a new ASP.NET 2.0 web application and name it *C:\ASPNET20\chap02-MasterPages*.

2. Add a folder named *Images* to the project (right-click the project name in Solution Explorer and select Add Folder → Regular Folder). Copy the images shown in Figure 2-2 into the new *C:\ASPNET20\ chap02-MasterPages\Images* folder. You'll use these images to build your Master page.

TIP

The images can be downloaded from this book's support site: *http:// www.oreilly.com/catalog/aspnetadn/*.

Figure 2-2. The images in the Images folder

3. Now you'll create the Master page. Right-click the project name in Solution Explorer and then select Add New Item....

4. In the Add New Item dialog, select the Master Page template and use the default name, *MasterPage.master*, as shown in Figure 2-3. Click Add to create the page.

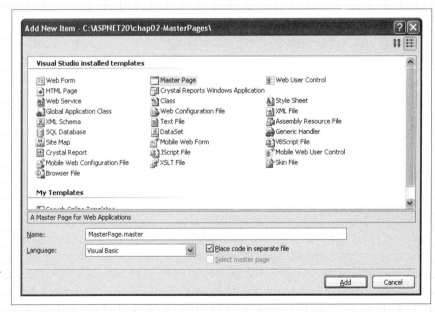

Figure 2-3. Adding a Master page to the project

The Content-
PlaceHolder
control is a
placeholder for
Content pages
(pages that
inherit from the
Master page) to
populate with
controls.

5. In Solution Explorer, double-click *MasterPage.master* and you will see an empty web page that contains a single ContentPlaceHolder control.

6. Populate the *MasterPage.master* page with content, images, and links by dragging from the Toolbox and dropping onto its surface two Image controls, one Panel control, and four LinkButton controls, as shown in Figure 2-4. Set the properties of each of the controls as follows:

Image controls
Name the first Image control imgLogo and set its ImageURL property to `Images/oreilly_header.gif` to display the O'Reilly tarsier logo. Name the second Image control imgTitle and set its ImageURL property to `Images/oranet_logo.jpg` to display the O'Reilly Network logo.

Panel control
Use the mouse to stretch the Panel control across the page. Set its Backcolor property to `Maroon`.

LinkButton controls
Drop four LinkButton controls onto the Panel control. Name them as shown in Figure 2-4 (via their Text properties). As you are going to click on only one of the links, name the second LinkButton control lnkONDotnet. Set its PostbackUrl property to `ONDotnet.aspx`.

7. Type in the footnote at the bottom of the screen, after the ContentPlaceHolder control. To type the footnote, position your cursor at the end of the ContentPlaceHolder control and press the Enter key. You can then start typing the copyright notice as shown in Figure 2-4.

8. That's it. Your Master page is now created. You will learn how to use it in the next lab.

What about...

...nesting Master Pages?

Nesting a Master page within another Master page is sometimes useful when you want to alter the look and feel of a specific area of your site. For example, suppose the O'Reilly Network wanted to provide unique navigation bars for pages at particular Network sites, such as ONDotnet.com or MozillaDevCenter. Figure 2-5 shows how this might be done with a page that contains two Master Pages, the second nested within the first.

Image Control   LinkButton Control   Image Control
(imgLogo)   (lnkONDotnet)   (imgTitle)   Panel Control

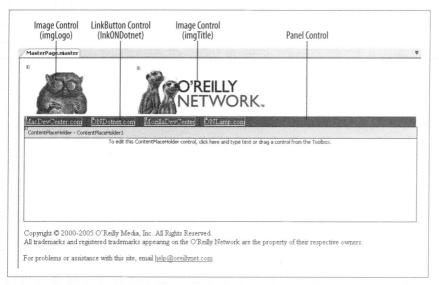

Figure 2-4. Populating the Master page

First Master Page

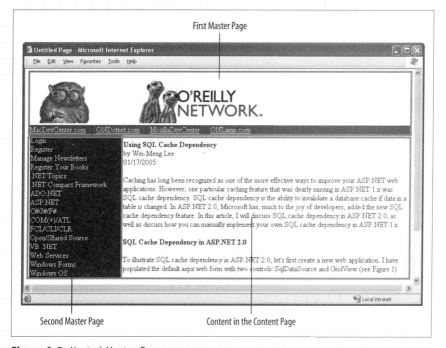

Second Master Page   Content in the Content Page

Figure 2-5. Nested Master Pages

To see how you can nest one Master page inside another, follow these steps:

1. Add a new Master page to the project (*C:\ASPNET20\chap02-MasterPages*) and name it *MasterPage2.master*.

2. This second Master page will consist of a single-row table with two columns. The first column contains a Content control (Content1) that occupies the ContentPlaceHolder control in the first Master page (ContentPlaceHolder1) with text (for simplification, in this example you will use text instead of links) such as Log in, Register, etc. The second column contains a ContentPlaceHolder control (ContentPlaceHolder2) for Content pages to add controls to. Switch to Source View and add the code shown in Example 2-1 to *MasterPage2.master*.

You'll learn more about the Content page in the next lab.

TIP

Visual Studio 2005 does not support visual editing or creation of nested Master Pages. You need to do this work in Source View.

Example 2-1. Creating a nested Master page

```
<%@ Master Language="VB"  MasterPageFile="~/MasterPage.master"
    CodeFile="MasterPage2.master.vb" AutoEventWireup="false"
    Inherits="MasterPage2_master" %>

<asp:Content ID="Content1" ContentPlaceHolderID="ContentPlaceHolder1"
    Runat="Server">
<table>
   <tr>
      <td width=200 bgcolor=black>
      <font color=white>
          Login<br />Register<br />Manage Newsletters<br />
          Register Your Books<br />.NET Topics<br />
          .NET Compact Framework<br />ADO.NET<br />
          ASP.NET<br />C#/J#/F#<br />COM(+)/ATL<br />
          FCL/CLI/CLR<br />Open/Shared Source<br />
          VB .NET<br />Web Services<br />Windows Forms<br />
          Windows OS<br />
      </font>
      </td>
      <td>

          <asp:contentplaceholder id="ContentPlaceHolder2" runat="server">

          </asp:contentplaceholder>
```

Example 2-1. Creating a nested Master page (continued)

```
      </td>
   </tr>
</table>
</asp:Content>
```

3. Figure 2-6 shows the relationship between the two Master Pages.

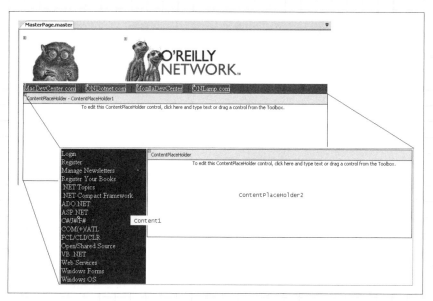

Figure 2-6. The relationship between the two Master Pages

In the next lab, you will learn how to use the Master page you created in this lab to establish a consistent look and feel for your Content pages.

Where can I learn more?

For a guided tour that shows how to build Master Pages using Visual Web Developer 2005 Express, visit *http://beta.asp.net/GuidedTour/s15.aspx*.

Use a Master Page as a Content Page Template

Once you've created a Master page, you can create Content pages for your site that use the Master page as a template.

Using Master Pages and visual inheritance, you can give all your web site Content pages a common look and feel.

How do I do that?

A Content page is a Web Form that uses a Master page.

In this lab, you will add Content pages to your project and give them a consistent look and feel by using the Master page you created in the previous lab, "Create a Master Page for Your Site." You will then add controls to a Content page and see how ASP.NET combines the content of the Master page and Content pages at runtime.

1. First, let's create some pages for your web site. Using the project created in the previous lab, add a new Web Form. Right-click the project name in Solution Explorer and select Add New Item.... On the Add New Item page, select Web Form and use its default name (*Default2.aspx*). Check the "Select master page" checkbox at the bottom of the dialog (see Figure 2-7).

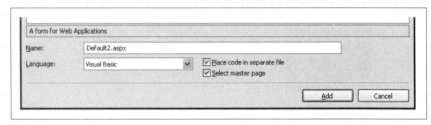

Figure 2-7. Creating a Content page by selecting a Master page

A Content page can have only one Master page.

2. You will be asked to choose a Master page to use for your form. Select *MasterPage.master* (see Figure 2-8).

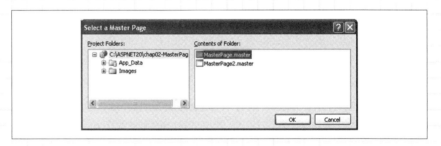

Figure 2-8. Selecting a Master page

3. Click OK and Visual Studio displays the new page, *Default2.aspx*, with the contents of the Master page grayed out (see Figure 2-9), indicating that the content of the Master page cannot be edited in the *Default2.aspx* form. Notice that the page is created with a Content control.

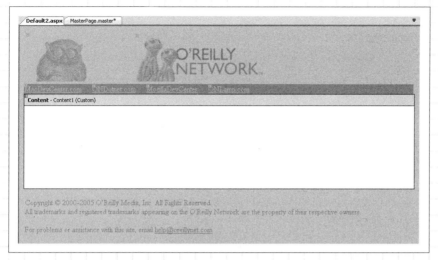

Figure 2-9. Creating a new Content page

4. You can customize the new page, *Default2.aspx*, by adding controls to the Content control. Note that you cannot modify the Master page in this page.

The Content control is the location where you populate the content of the page.

TIP

To edit the Master page, you can either right-click the Master page content and select Edit Master, or simply go to the Solution Explorer and double-click the Master page. Both actions will load the Master page for editing.

---

5. To add content to the Content control, you can directly drag and drop controls onto it. You can also type directly into the Content control. Try adding some text to the Content control (see Figure 2-10).

6. To test the Content page, press F5. Your page should resemble the one shown in Figure 2-11.

TIP

Recall that the Master page contains a ContentPlaceHolder control. You can place content in the ContentPlaceHolder control in the Master page if you want to. If you do so, however, the content within ContentPlaceHolder will appear in the Content page when the page is loaded, unless the Content page overrides it by populating its own Content control.

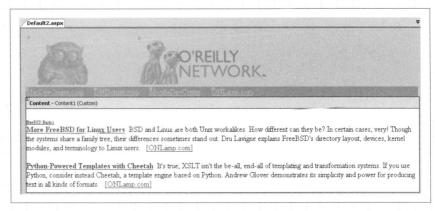

Figure 2-10. Populating the Content page

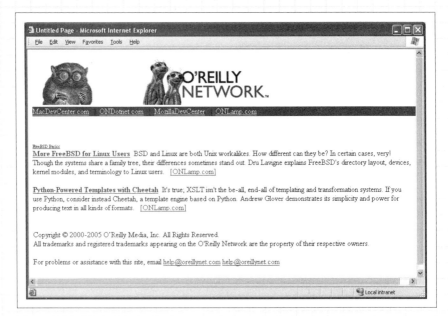

Figure 2-11. Displaying the Content page in Internet Explorer

What just happened?

What you have created is a Web Form (*Default2.aspx*) that inherits from a Master page (*MasterPage.master*). The beauty of a Master page is that you can create the content of a page template once and other Web Forms can then inherit from it. If the content of a Master page is changed, those changes will automatically show up in any page that inherits from it.

Note that if a page uses a nested Master page, such as the *MasterPage2.master*, you won't be able to view the page in Design View (as visual editing of nested Master pages is not supported in Visual Studio 2005). You can only edit a nested Master page in Source View.

To see how a Content page that uses a nested Master page looks, add a new Web Form to the project (name it *SqlArticle.aspx*) and select *MasterPage2.master* as its Master page.

Populate the *SqlArticle.aspx* page by entering the HTML and text shown in Figure 2-12. Note that you have to manually populate the Content control.

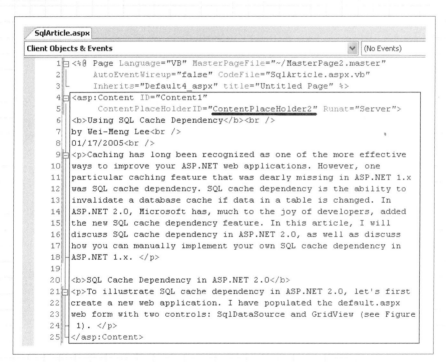

```
SqlArticle.aspx

Client Objects & Events                                    (No Events)

 1  <%@ Page Language="VB" MasterPageFile="~/MasterPage2.master"
 2      AutoEventWireup="false" CodeFile="SqlArticle.aspx.vb"
 3      Inherits="Default4_aspx" title="Untitled Page" %>
 4  <asp:Content ID="Content1"
 5      ContentPlaceHolderID="ContentPlaceHolder2" Runat="Server">
 6  <b>Using SQL Cache Dependency</b><br />
 7  by Wei-Meng Lee<br />
 8  01/17/2005<br />
 9  <p>Caching has long been recognized as one of the more effective
10  ways to improve your ASP.NET web applications. However, one
11  particular caching feature that was dearly missing in ASP.NET 1.x
12  was SQL cache dependency. SQL cache dependency is the ability to
13  invalidate a database cache if data in a table is changed. In
14  ASP.NET 2.0, Microsoft has, much to the joy of developers, added
15  the new SQL cache dependency feature. In this article, I will
16  discuss SQL cache dependency in ASP.NET 2.0, as well as discuss
17  how you can manually implement your own SQL cache dependency in
18  ASP.NET 1.x. </p>
19
20  <b>SQL Cache Dependency in ASP.NET 2.0</b>
21  <p>To illustrate SQL cache dependency in ASP.NET 2.0, let's first
22  create a new web application. I have populated the default.aspx
23  web form with two controls: SqlDataSource and GridView (see Figure
24  1). </p>
25  </asp:Content>
```

Figure 2-12. *Editing a page that uses a nested Master page in Source View*

When the page is loaded in IE (by pressing F5), you will see the content of the two Master Pages combined (see Figure 2–13).

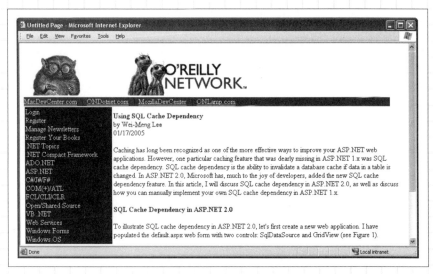

Figure 2-13. Loading a page that uses nested Master Pages

What about...

...converting an existing web page to a Content page?

When you look at the source of a normal Web Form (one that does not use a Master page), you will notice that it contains the usual bits of HTML you expect to find on an ASP.NET page as well as a <form> element:

```
<%@ Page Language="VB" AutoEventWireup="false" CodeFile="Default.aspx.vb"
Inherits="Default_aspx" %>

<!DOCTYPE html PUBLIC "-//W3C//DTD XHTML 1.1//EN" "http://www.w3.org/TR/
xhtml11/DTD/xhtml11.dtd">

<html xmlns="http://www.w3.org/1999/xhtml" >
<head runat="server">
    <title>Untitled Page</title>
</head>
<body>
    <form id="form1" runat="server">
    <div>

    </div>
    </form>
</body>
</html>
```

However, a Content page does not contain the usual elements that make up an ASP.NET page (such as <html>, <body>, or <form>). Instead, you'll see an <asp:Content> element, which represents the Content control and its properties. The <asp:Content> control encapsulates whatever controls (and contents) you drop onto the Content's control.

```
<%@ Page Language="VB" MasterPageFile="~/MasterPage.master"
    AutoEventWireup="false" CodeFile="Default3.aspx.vb"
    Inherits="Default3_aspx" title="Untitled Page"
%>
<asp:Content ID="Content1" ContentPlaceHolderID="ContentPlaceHolder1"
Runat="Server">
...
...
</asp:Content>
```

To convert a Web Form to a Content page, you simply need to add the MasterPageFile attribute to its Page directive and then remove all other HTML elements from the page. Here's a sample Page directive that does the job:

```
<%@ Page Language="VB" MasterPageFile="~/MasterPage.master"
    AutoEventWireup="false" CodeFile="Default.aspx.vb"
    Inherits="Default_aspx" %>
```

The Page directive simply converts the *Default.aspx* page of this lab to a Content page. What about the Content control, which is needed to display the content unique to the page? You can add it in code, like this:

```
<%@ Page Language="VB" MasterPageFile="~/MasterPage.master"
    AutoEventWireup="false" CodeFile="Default.aspx.vb"
    Inherits="Default_aspx" %>

<asp:Content ID="Content1" ContentPlaceHolderID="ContentPlaceHolder1"
    runat="server">
</asp:Content>
```

Or, you can click on the Create Custom Content link in the Context Tasks menu, which you'll find on the right side of the Content control (see Figure 2-14).

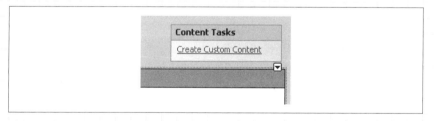

Figure 2-14. Creating a new Content control

TIP

If you don't specify the Content control in code, you will still see the Content control in Design View. You will be unable to add controls to the Content control unless you click on the Create Custom Content link in the Content Tasks menu of the Content control.

...applying a Master page to an entire site?

To require that all pages at a site use a particular Master page by default, just add the <pages> element to the *Web.config* file for the site:

```
<system.web>
    <pages masterPageFile="MasterPage.master" />
    ...
```

A page that does not specify a value for the MasterPageFile attribute in its Page directive will use the *MasterPage.master* Master page by default. To override the default Master page setting in *Web.config*, simply add the MasterPageFile attribute to the Page directive of the web page in question and assign it the name of another file.

...detecting the browser type and switching Master pages on the fly?

If your application targets users with different browsers, you may need to create separate Master pages so each can be optimized for a specific browser. In this case, you need to be able to dynamically switch your Master page during runtime. To do so, add the following code to the PreInit event of the Content page:

```
Protected Sub Page_PreInit(ByVal sender As Object, _
                          ByVal e As System.EventArgs) _
                          Handles Me.PreInit
    If (Request.Browser.IsBrowser("IE")) Then
        MasterPageFile = "MasterPage.master"
    ElseIf (Request.Browser.IsBrowser("Mozilla")) Then
        MasterPageFile = "MasterPage_FireFox.master"
    Else
        MasterPageFile = "MasterPage_Others.master"
    End If
End Sub
```

The preceding code assumes you have three different Master pages: *MasterPage.master* (for IE), *MasterPage_FireFox.master* (for FireFox), and *MasterPage_Others.master* (for all other browsers). The page will check the type of browser requesting the page and then apply the appropriate Master page to it.

Besides switching the Master page programmatically, you can also do this declaratively:

```
<%@ Page Language="VB"
    MasterPageFile="~/MasterPage_Others.master"
    ie:MasterPageFile="~/MasterPage.master"
    mozilla:MasterPageFile="~/MasterPage_FireFox.master"
    ...
```

Where can I learn more?

Scott Guthrie (Product Manager of ASP.NET at Microsoft) has written a blog on how to vary the Master page based on browser type: *http://blogs.msdn.com/scottgu/archive/2004/11/20/267362.aspx*.

Modify a Master Page at Runtime

When a Web Form that uses a Master page is loaded at runtime, it displays the content of the Master page together with its own content. However, there are times when you will want to modify parts of the Master page when a particular web page is loaded. For example, at the O'Reilly Network site (*http://www.oreillynet.com*), pages that belong to the ONDotnet subsite display the ONDotnet logo (a leaping dolphin) in their headers, rather than the generic O'Reilly Network logo (the ever-familiar tarsier). Pages at other subsites, such as Perl.com and ONLamp.com, do likewise.

You can flexibly modify the content of the Master page so that it suits the theme of the page.

How do I do that?

To see how a Master page can be modified on the fly, we'll add a page to our previous project (see "Use a Master Page as a Content Page Template"). This page will use *MasterPage.master* and change the image in the Master page from the O'Reilly Network logo to the ONDotnet logo when it is loaded.

1. Using the project created in the previous lab, add a new Web Form (right-click the project name in Solution Explorer, select Add New Item..., and then select Web Form) and check the "Select master page" checkbox at the bottom of the dialog. Name the Web Form *ONDotnet.aspx*. Click Add.

2. Select *Masterpage.master* as the Master page.

3. Populate the *ONDotnet.aspx* Web Form with text (see Figure 2-15).

4. Switch to Source View and insert the MasterType directive after the Page directive. The MasterType directive allows you to indicate a strongly typed reference to the Master page so that you can programmatically access its content (such as its public properties and methods):

```
<%@ Page Language="VB" MasterPageFile="~/MasterPage.master"
    AutoEventWireup="false" CodeFile="ONDotnet.aspx.vb"
    Inherits="ONDotnet_aspx" title="Untitled Page" %>
<%@ MasterType VirtualPath="~/MasterPage.master" %>
...
```

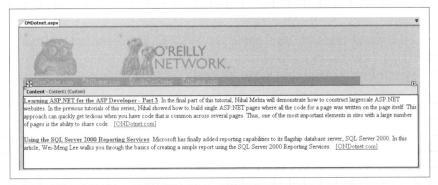

Figure 2-15. The ONDotnet.aspx Web Form with text added

5. In the code-behind of the Master page (*MasterPage.master.vb*), insert the public setLinkColor() method. By adding this public method to the Master page, Content pages will be able to programmatically set the color of the various LinkButton controls:

```vb
Imports System.Drawing
Partial Class MasterPage_master
    Inherits System.Web.UI.MasterPage

    Public Sub setLinkColor(ByVal ctrl As String, _
                            ByVal lnkColor As Color)
        Select Case ctrl
            Case "MacDevCenter"
                lnkMacDevCenter.ForeColor = lnkColor
            Case "ONDotnet"
                lnkONDotnet.ForeColor = lnkColor
            Case "MozillaDevCenter"
                lnkMozillaDevCenter.ForeColor = lnkColor
            Case "ONLamp"
                lnkONLamp.ForeColor = lnkColor
        End Select
    End Sub
End Class
```

You need to use the Public access modifier on the setLinkColor() method, or else the Content page will not be able to call it.

6. In the code-behind of ONDotnet.aspx (*ONDotnet.aspx.vb*), code the following Page_Load event:

```vb
Sub Page_Load(ByVal sender As Object, _
              ByVal e As System.EventArgs) _
              Handles Me.Load
    '---change the link color
    Master.setLinkColor("ONDotnet", Drawing.Color.Yellow)

    '---change the title
    Master.Page.Header.Title = _
        "O'Reilly and Associates Conferences"
```

```
'---change the image
Dim masterImage As Image
masterImage = CType(Master.FindControl("imgTitle"), _
                    Image)
If Not (masterImage Is Nothing) Then
    masterImage.ImageUrl = "Images/ondotnet_logo.gif"
End If
End Sub
```

7. Essentially, you use the Master property to get a reference to the Master page. You first change the color of the ONDotnet.com LinkButton control by invoking the setLinkColor() method. You then change the title of the page by using the Master.Page.Header.Title property. Finally, you change the image of the logo in the Master page by using the FindControl() method.

TIP

Master is a special property exposed by the Web Form as a handler to access the Master page. In fact, every page can access the Master property; however it makes sense only if a page uses a Master page.

---

8. Press F5 to test the application. First load *Default.aspx* and then click the ONDotnet.com link to load *ONDotnet.aspx*. Figure 2-16 shows the differences between the two pages.

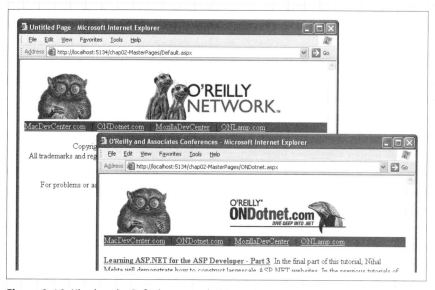

Figure 2-16. Viewing the Default.aspx and ONDotnet.aspx pages

What just happened?

There are two ways you can modify the content of a Master page during runtime:

- Calling the public methods and setting the public properties of the Master page
- Using the FindControl() method (of the Master property) to locate controls on the page, and then calling the methods and setting the properties of those controls

---

WARNING

The Master property is valid only on pages that reference a Master page in the MasterPageFile attribute in the Page directive. If you access the Master property on a page that does not reference a master page, a NullReferenceException is thrown.

Where possible, you should use the first method, which exposes the public methods and properties of the Master page. This approach is a much more efficient way to change controls on a Master page because it uses early binding, and therefore the controls are strongly typed.

Use early binding whenever possible; it makes your development much easier and less error-prone.

To use early binding, the Master page needs to expose its public methods and properties (as in Step 5) so that a Content page can set or access them during runtime. In this lab you have exposed a public method called setLinkColor() in the *MasterPage.master* page. To change the color of a LinkButton in the Master page during runtime, you can call the setLinkColor() method in the Page_Load event of a Content page.

With the second method, you locate the controls you want to modify on the Master page by using the FindControl() method of the Master property, then supplying the name and type of the control you want to modify. Once the control is located, you can change its properties as if it were a local object, as demonstrated in the following code fragment, which locates an image control on the Master page and substitutes a new *.gif* file containing the ONDotnet logo.

```
Dim masterImage As Image
masterImage = CType(Master.FindControl("imgTitle"), _
            Image)
If Not (masterImage Is Nothing) Then
    masterImage.ImageUrl = "Images/ondotnet_logo.gif"
End If
```

This technique uses late binding to access controls on a Master page because you need to explicitly convert the controls you find during runtime to the type that you want.

What about...

...accessing controls that are dynamically created when the Master page loads?

For example, a Master page may display additional late-breaking news by dynamically creating Label controls. The number of new controls generated may vary depending on the urgency of the news.

The advantage of making methods and properties public on a Master page is that you can use early binding, which means you can use IntelliSense to help you with their names and you can rely on the compiler to check their types at compile time.

However, if there are controls that will be created dynamically in the Master page during runtime, exposing public properties is no longer a viable option, since you need to decide what methods and properties to expose at design time.

In this case, you should resort to late binding using the FindControl() method, described earlier in "What just happened?".

Where can I learn more?

To learn more about early and late binding and the advantages and disadvantages of each, visit the following MSDN Help topic: *http://msdn.microsoft.com/library/default.asp?url=/library/en-us/vbcn7/html/vaconearlylatebinding.asp.*

Create a Site Map for Your Web Site

Unless your web site contains only a single web page, you need a way for users to easily navigate between the pages of your site. In ASP.NET 2.0, there are four new controls that make it easy to implement site navigation. These controls are:

SiteMapDataSource

A control that represents a site map. A site map is an XML file that describes the logical structure of a web site and the relationship between its pages. The SiteMapDataSource control is not visible on

The FindControl() method uses late binding, while using public properties has the advantage of early binding and hence is strongly typed.

Your users will never be lost again if you create a site map for your web site!

the page when it is loaded, but its role is to act as a supplier of site information (taken from the site map file) to the SiteMapPath control.

SiteMapPath

A visual control that depicts the path to the current page, "bread crumb" style.

Menu

A visual control that displays information in menu form. The Menu control supports data binding to a site map.

TreeView

A visual control that displays information in a hierarchical structure. The TreeView control supports data binding to a site map.

In the remaining labs in this chapter, you will learn how to use these controls to make it easy for users to navigate your web site. But first, let's take a closer look at the SiteMapDataSource and SiteMapPath controls.

How do I do that?

In this lab, you'll see how you can use the SiteMapPath control together with the *Web.sitemap* file to display navigation paths on your site pages. First, you'll create a web application that uses a Master page. When a Master page is used as a template for all other pages in a site, it's a good place to put a site map and controls that help users find their way around, because that information will be visible on every page a user visits. You'll create a site map file that describes the logical relationship between the pages of your site, and then you'll add a SiteMapPath control to the Master page so users can see where they are in the hierarchy and move "up" and "down" the path to their current page.

1. Launch Visual Studio 2005 and create a new ASP.NET 2.0 web application. Name the project *C:\ASPNET20\Chap02-Navigation*.

2. In Solution Explorer, add a site map to the application by right-clicking the project name and selecting Add New Item → Site Map (see Figure 2-17).

A site map is an XML document describing the logical layout of a web site.

3. Populate the *Web.sitemap* file by opening it and typing in the code shown in Example 2-2.

TIP

Remember to verify that your *Web.sitemap* XML document is well-formed (i.e., the document conforms to the rules of XML). The easiest way to do so is to load the XML document using Internet Explorer. If it is not well-formed, IE will tell you so.

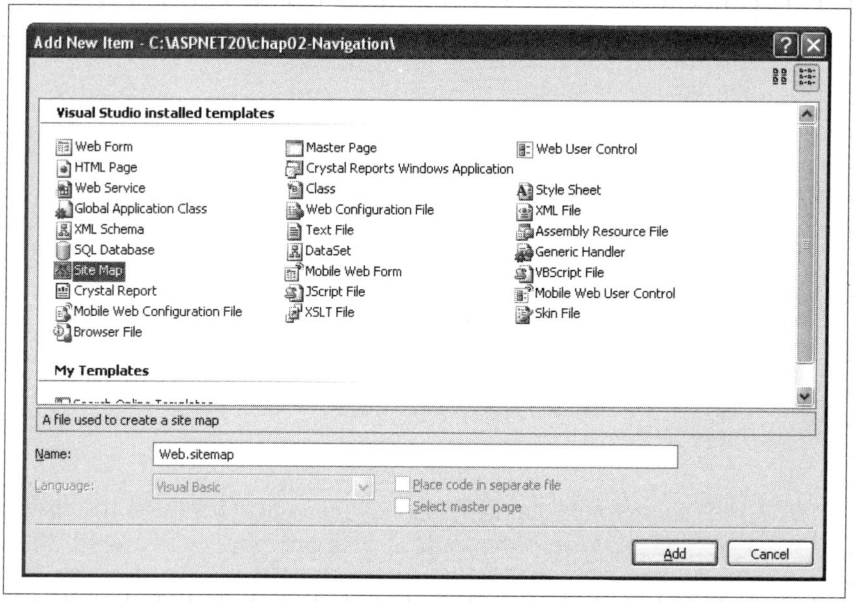

Figure 2-17. Adding a site map to the project

Example 2-2. A Web.sitemap file

```xml
<?xml version="1.0" encoding="utf-8" ?>
<siteMap>
    <siteMapNode url="main.aspx"
        title="Windows Mobile Home"
        description=" Windows Mobile Home " roles="">
        <siteMapNode url="whatiswinmobile.aspx"
           title="What is Windows Mobile"
           description=" What is Windows Mobile " roles="">
        <siteMapNode url="windowsmobileoverview.aspx"
           title=" Windows Mobile Overview"
           description=" Windows Mobile Overview "
           roles="" />
        <siteMapNode url="comparedevices.aspx"
           title="Compare Devices"
           description=" Compare Devices " roles="" />
        <siteMapNode url="software.aspx"
           title="Software Features Tour"
           description=" Software Features Tour "
           roles="" />
        <siteMapNode url="faq.aspx"
           title="Frequently Asked Questions"
           description=" Frequently Asked Questions "
           roles="" />
    </siteMapNode>

    <siteMapNode url="devices.aspx" title="Devices"
        description=" Devices " roles="" />
```

Example 2-2. *A Web.sitemap file (continued)*

```
      <siteMapNode url="downloads.aspx" title="Downloads"
         description=" Downloads " roles="" />
      <siteMapNode url="howto.aspx"
         title="Help and How To"
         description=" Help and How To " roles="" />
      <siteMapNode url="communities.aspx"
         title="Communities"
         description=" Communities " roles="" />
      <siteMapNode url="events.aspx"
         title="News and Events"
         description=" News and Events" roles="" />
      <siteMapNode url="Administrator/Admin.aspx"
         title="Administrator"
         description=" Administrator" roles="" />
   </siteMapNode>
</siteMap>
```

The *Web.sitemap* file simply describes the logical layout of the site. It does not matter where the various files are physically stored. Note that the schema for the document is straightforward; elements are nested to represent their logical groupings.

4. Each <siteMapNode> element has four attributes:

title
> The text to display in each node of a SiteMapPath, TreeView, or Menu control

description
> The Tool Tip text to display when the mouse hovers over a node in a SiteMapPath, TreeView, or Menu control

roles
> The role(s) for which this node is to be displayed

url
> The URL to navigate to when a node in a SiteMapPath, Tree-View, or Menu control is clicked

---

TIP

Note that the value of each url attribute in the <siteMapNode> element must be unique.

---

5. Add a new folder to the project and name it *Images* (right-click the project name in Solution Explorer and select Add Folder → Regular Folder). Copy the images shown in Figure 2-18 into the *C:\ASPNET20\chap02-Navigation\Images* folder. You'll use these on the Master page for this site.

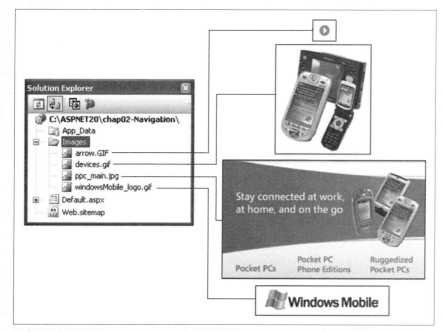

Figure 2-18. The images in the Images folder

6. Next, add a new Master page to your project. Populate the Master page with the controls shown in Figure 2-19. The Master page is the ideal place to locate the SiteMapPath control, because all controls placed on this page are visible in any page that inherits from it. As a result, the "bread crumb" style site navigation path displayed by the SiteMapPath control will be visible in all pages.

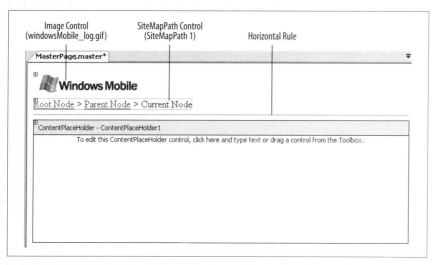

Figure 2-19. Populating the Master page

7. Add a new Web Form to the project and name it *Main.aspx*. Check the "Select master page" option and select the Master page created in the previous step (see Figure 2-20).

Figure 2-20. Selecting a Master page for a Web Form

8. Populate *Main.aspx* with the content shown in Figure 2-21.

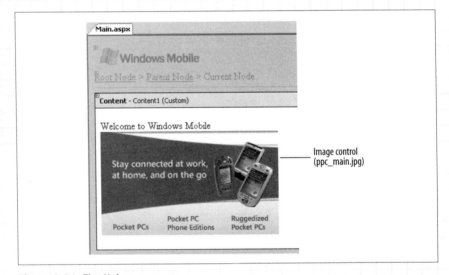

Figure 2-21. The Main.aspx page

9. Next, add another Web Form to the site and name it *Windowsmobileoverview.aspx*. Populate the form with the content shown in Figure 2-22.

10. To test the pages, press F5 and load the *Main.aspx* and *Windowsmobileoverview.aspx* pages. You should be able to see the navigational path shown in Figure 2-23.

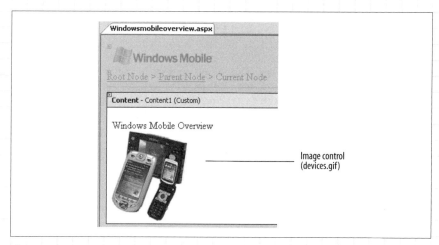

Figure 2-22. The Windowsmobileoverview.aspx page

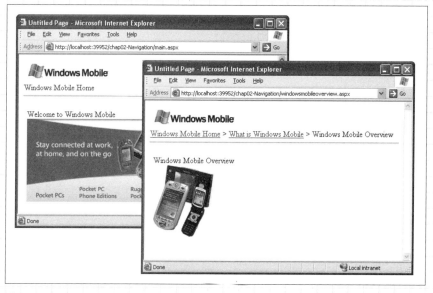

Figure 2-23. Testing the SiteMapPath control

How it works

The SiteMapPath control by default reads the content of the *Web.sitemap* file and displays the site navigation path leading to the currently displayed page.

Note that in ASP.NET 2.0 there is only one possible site map provider: XmlSiteMapProvider. The XmlSiteMapProvider reads site map information from a predefined XML document and, by default, that is the *Web.sitemap* file.

If you need to change the default name of the site map file, you can do so via the *Web.config* file. Example 2-3 shows how you can deregister the default XmlSiteMapProvider and register it again with a different site map name: *My.sitemap* (you can also register a new site map provider, such as one you've written yourself).

Example 2-3. Changing the default site map in Web.config

```
<configuration>
  <system.web>
    <siteMap>
      <providers>
        <remove name="AspNetXmlSiteMapProvider" />
        <add name="AspNetXmlSiteMapProvider"
          type="System.Web.XmlSiteMapProvider,
                System.Web, Version=1.2.3400.0,
                Culture=neutral,
                PublicKeyToken=b03f5f7f11d50a3a"
                siteMapFile="My.sitemap" />
      </providers>
    </siteMap>
  </system.web>
</configuration>
```

Chapter 5 will discuss the provider model that is new in ASP.NET 2.0 in greater detail.

What about...

...customizing the SiteMapPath control?

The default view of the SiteMapPath control displays the navigation path using the string contained in the title attribute of the <siteMapNode> element in the site map file. Each navigation path is separated by the ">" character.

You can customize the look and feel of the SiteMapPath control by adding style information to it. You can customize the SiteMapPath control by switching to Source View of the page that contains the control (in our example it is the Master page).

Example 2-4 shows how you can override the default path-separator character and replace it with an Image control (the image used is saved in the *Images* folder of the application as *arrow.gif*). The code also highlights the current path using a light green background color.

Example 2-4. Customizing the SiteMapPath control

```
<asp:SiteMapPath ID="SiteMapPath2"
    Font-Name="Garamond"
    Font-Size="12pt" RunAt="server">
  <CurrentNodeStyle Height="24px"
    BackColor="LightGreen"
    Font-Bold="true" />
  <NodeStyle Height="24px" />
  <PathSeparatorTemplate>
    <ItemTemplate>
      <asp:Image ID="Image2"
        ImageUrl="~/Images/arrow.gif"
        RunAt="server" />
    </ItemTemplate>
  </PathSeparatorTemplate>
</asp:SiteMapPath>
```

Figure 2-24 shows how the SiteMapPath control looks like after the modification.

Figure 2-24. Customizing the look and feel of the SiteMapPath control

You can also programmatically modify the properties of the SiteMapPath control through the following properties:

PathDirection

> Sets the order in which the paths are displayed. The default is RootToCurrent, which displays the topmost path down to the current path. To display in the reverse order, set this property to CurrentToRoot.

PathSeparator

> Sets the separator to display. Default is ">".

RenderCurrentNodeAsLink

> Displays the current path as a hyperlink. Default is false.

...accessing site map information programmatically?

If you are not using a SiteMapPath control, you can still programmatically access site map information through the Site Map API (found in the System.Web.SiteMap namespace). Example 2-5 (located in the code-behind of a Master page) shows how to display site navigation information programmatically.

Example 2-5. Displaying site information programmatically

```
Partial Class MasterPage_master

Sub Page_Load(ByVal sender As Object, _
            ByVal e As System.EventArgs) _
            Handles Me.Load

    Dim myCurrentNode As SiteMapNode

    '---Gets the current node
    myCurrentNode = SiteMap.CurrentNode

    '---displays the navigational path---
    Dim path As String = myCurrentNode.Title
    While myCurrentNode.ParentNode IsNot Nothing
        myCurrentNode = myCurrentNode.ParentNode
        path = " > " & path
        path = myCurrentNode.Title & path
    End While

    Response.Write(path)
End Sub

End Class
```

Besides the CurrentNode property, additional properties are available for accessing site information, including:

- `SiteMap.CurrentNode.ParentNode`
- `SiteMap.CurrentNode.PreviousSibling`
- `SiteMap.CurrentNode.RootNode`
- `SiteMap.CurrentNode.NextSibling`

...hiding nodes from users who lack proper authorization?

If you examine the *Web.sitemap* file carefully, you will notice the role attribute. In the examples thus far, the role attribute is set to an empty string. By default, the SiteMapDataSource control makes all the nodes information in *Web.sitemap* visible. However, there are times when you would like to restrict the display of certain nodes to a particular group of users. For example, normal users should not be able to see the path to the admin web page, and so the SiteMapDataSource control should allow nodes to be hidden (or trimmed). This feature is known as *security trimming*. The XmlSiteMapProvider disables security trimming by default; to enable security trimming, you need to perform the following steps:

1. Set the securityTrimmingEnabled attribute to `true`. To do so, you can de- and re-register the `AspNetXmlSiteMapProvider` in *Web.config*:

   ```
   <system.web>
     <siteMap>
       <providers>
         <remove name="AspNetXmlSiteMapProvider" />
         <add name="AspNetXmlSiteMapProvider"
             type="System.Web.XmlSiteMapProvider,
             System.Web, Version=1.2.3400.0,
             Culture=neutral,
             PublicKeyToken=b03f5f7f11d50a3a"
             securityTrimmingEnabled="true"
             siteMapFile="Web.sitemap" />
       </providers>
     </siteMap>
   ```

2. Next, specify the node that you want to enable for security trimming. Using the *Web.sitemap* file you have created in this lab, set the roles attribute for the last node to `admin`. In this case, the SiteMapPath control will display the Administrator node (pointing to the page *Admin.aspx* located in the */Administrator* directory) only if the user belongs to the admin role:

   ```
             ...
         <siteMapNode url="Administrator/Admin.aspx"
             title="Administrator"
             description=" Administrator" roles="admin" />
       </siteMapNode>
   ```

3. In the final step, you need to configure the */Administrator* directory to deny access to all users and then fine-tune the access to allow users belonging to the admin role to access the *Admin.aspx* page. You do so by adding a *Web.config* file to the */Administrator* directory that contains the code shown in Example 2-6.

Example 2-6. Web.config for the Administrator directory

```
<configuration xmlns=
    "http://schemas.microsoft.com/.NetConfiguration/v2.0">
    <system.web>
        <compilation debug="false"/>
        <!-- deny all users -->
        <authorization>
            <deny users="*" />
        </authorization>
    </system.web>

    <!-- allow only Admin role users to see Admin.aspx -->
    <location path="Admin.aspx">
        <system.web>
            <authorization>
                <allow roles="Admin" />
            </authorization>
        </system.web>
    </location>
</configuration>
```

See Chapter 5 for more details on roles and membership.

Once you have made these changes, only users in the admin role will be able to see the Administrator node.

Where can I learn more?

For more information on ASP.NET authorization, check out the following MSDN Help topic: *http://msdn.microsoft.com/library/default.asp?url=/library/en-us/cpguide/html/cpconaspnetauthorization.asp.*

To learn more about Site Map Providers, check out the MSDN Help topic "ASP.NET Site Navigation Providers."

If the included AspNetXMLSiteMapProvider does not suit your purpose and you want to store your site map information in a data store other than XML (such as an Oracle database), check out the MSDN Help topic "Implementing a Site Map Provider."

Display Hierarchical Data Using the TreeView Control

At last, a TreeView control that comes right in the box of Visual Studio

If you have ever visited the MSDN Library site, you will no doubt have noticed the tree-like navigational menu on the left side of its home page (see Figure 2-25).

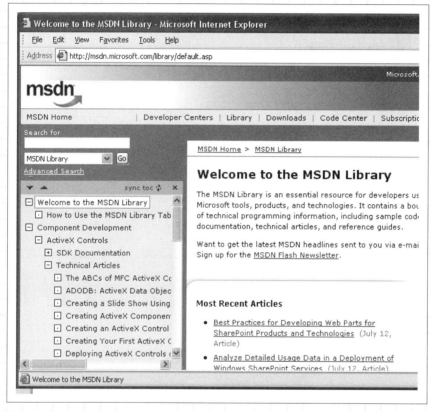

Figure 2-25. The tree-like navigation on the MSDN site

This information is displayed using the TreeView control, which provides an alternative to the SiteMapPath control for navigating your site. Tree maps are great for displaying hierarchical information and, unlike the SiteMapPath control, they let you browse the entire site, not just the path leading to your current page.

How do I do that?

Using the project created in the last lab, let's add a TreeView control to the site. You'll do this by adding the control to your Master page and binding it to your site map so that users can navigate your site by directly clicking the items in the TreeView control.

1. In the *MasterPage.master* Master page, add a 2×1 table (Layout → Insert Table). Add a TreeView control to the left cell of the table and drag the ContentPlaceHolder control into the right cell (see Figure 2-26).

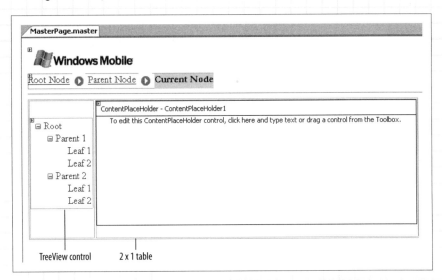

Figure 2-26. Populating the Master page

2. In the TreeView Tasks menu of the TreeView control, select <New data source...> (see Figure 2-27).

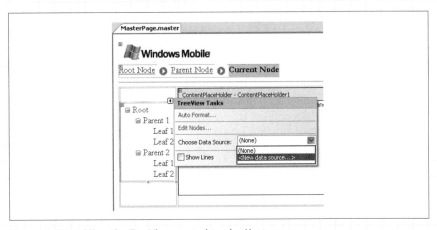

Figure 2-27. Adding the TreeView control to the Master page

3. In the Data Source Configuration Wizard dialog, select Site Map and then click OK (see Figure 2-28).

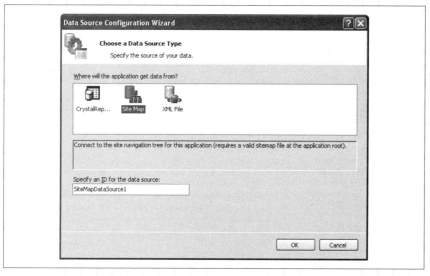

Figure 2-28. Choosing the Site Map as the data source

4. Apply the MSDN theme (via the "Auto Format..." link in the Tree-View Tasks menu shown in Figure 2-29) to the TreeView control, and set the BackColor property of the TreeView control to Gray (#E0E0E0).

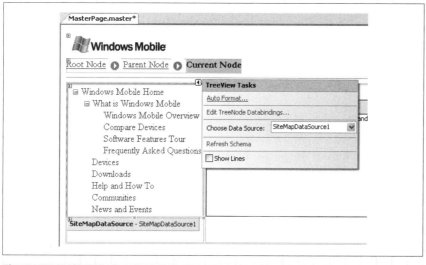

Figure 2-29. The TreeView control

The SiteMapDataSource control represents a site map. As explained in "Create a Site Map for Your Web Site," a site map describes the logical structure of a web site and the relationship between its pages.

TIP

Visual Studio 2005 supports various formatting styles for the Tree-View control. See Figure 2-30 for some samples.

Figure 2-30. The various formatting styles supported for the TreeView

5. The Master page should now look like Figure 2-31.

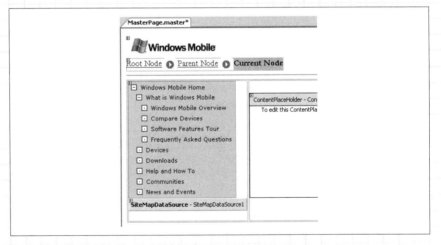

Figure 2-31. The TreeView control in the Master page

6. Press F5 to see how the TreeView control looks. You should now be able to navigate between all the pages in your site by selecting the items in the TreeView control (see Figure 2-32).

Chapter 2: Master Pages and Site Navigation

Figure 2-32. Testing the TreeView control

What about...

...using your own XML document instead of a site map for the Tree-View control?

Apart from using a site map file with the TreeView control, you can also create your own XML document and bind it to the TreeView control. For example, you may want to create an outline of a book and then bind it to the TreeView control so that users can navigate through the book using the TreeView control.

To configure the TreeView control to use an XML file, follow these steps:

1. Add an XML document to the project by right-clicking the project name in Solution Explorer. Select Add New Item..., and then select XML File. Name the file *Book.xml*.

2. Populate *Book.xml* with the XML shown in Example 2-7.

Example 2-7. Book.xml

```xml
<Book>
    <Content Title=".NET Compact Framework Pocket Guide"
            URL="booktop.aspx">
        <Content Title="Part I" URL="PartI.aspx">
            <Content Title="The .NET Framework and Mobile Devices"
                    URL="PartIMain.aspx">
                <Content Title="The .NET CLR" URL="PartI1.aspx" />
                <Content Title="Windows Powered Mobile Devices"
                        URL="PartI2.aspx" />
                <Content Title="Tool and Language Support"
                        URL="PartI3.aspx" />
                <Content Title="Hello, Pocket PC" URL="PartI4.aspx" />
                <Content Title="Debugging the Application"
                        URL="PartI5.aspx" />
                <Content Title="Troubleshooting" URL="PartI6.aspx" />
            </Content>
        </Content>
        <Content Title="Part II" URL="PartIIMain.aspx">
            <Content Title="User Interface Design" URL="PartII.aspx">
                <Content Title="Using the Windows Forms Controls"
                        URL="PartII1.aspx" />
                <Content Title="Design Considerations for Smartphone Applications"
                        URL="PartII2.aspx" />
            </Content>
        </Content>
        <Content Title="Part III" URL="PartIIIMain.aspx">
            <Content Title="Projects" URL="PartIII.apx">
                <Content Title="Project A: Currency Converter"
                        URL="PartIIIA.aspx" />
                <Content Title="Project B: Book Ordering System"
                        URL="PartIIIB.apx" />
                <Content Title="Project C: Bluetooth Chat"
                        URL="PartIIIC.apx" />
            </Content>
        </Content>
        <Content Title="Part IV" URL="PartIVMain.aspx">
            <Content Title="Deploying .NET Compact Framework Applications"
                    URL="PartIV.aspx">
                <Content Title="Packaging CAB Files" URL="PartIV1.aspx" />
                <Content Title="Redistributing the .NET Compact Framework"
                        URL="PartIV2.aspx" />
                <Content Title="Deploying Smartphone Applications"
                        URL="PartIV3.aspx" />
            </Content>
        </Content>
    </Content>
</Book>
```

Note that you can specify an XSLT file to transform the XML document from one format to another. You can also use an XPath expression to filter part of the XML document.

3. You will be prompted to select an XML file to use (see Figure 2-33). Select the newly added *Book.xml* file.

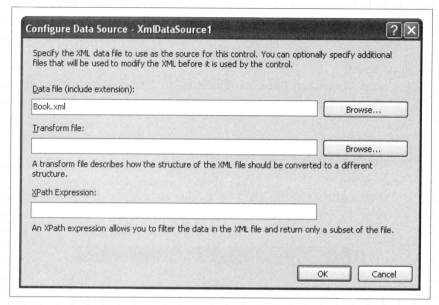

Figure 2-33. Specifying the source of the XmlDataSource

4. The TreeView control should now look like the one shown in Figure 2-34. You need to edit the TreeNode data bindings so that you can display the information you want on the TreeView control. Click on the Edit TreeNode Databindings... link in the TreeView Tasks menu.

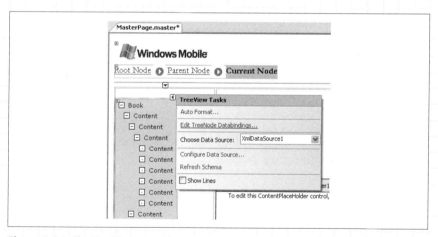

Figure 2-34. The TreeView control

5. In the Available DataBindings box (see Figure 2-35), select the Content item (highlighted) and click Add. Set the DataBinding properties as follows:

DataMember

> The element in the XML document to be used for binding to a node in the TreeView control. Set this property to Content.

NavigateUrlField

> The URL to navigate to when a bound node in the TreeView control is clicked. Set this property to URL.

TextField

> The attribute to be used to display in a node in the TreeView control. Set this property to Title.

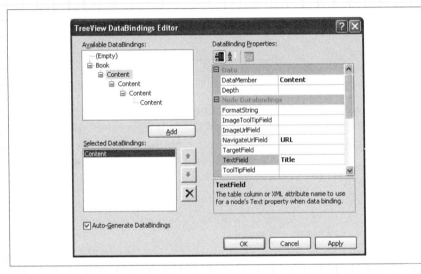

Figure 2-35. Using the TreeView DataBindings Editor

6. Click OK.

7. Press F5 to test the application. The TreeView control will look like the one shown in Figure 2-36.

Where can I learn more?

For alternative TreeView controls in ASP.NET, check out the following:

- *http://www.obout.com/obout/treeview/treeview.asp*
- *http://www.asp.net/ControlGallery/default.aspx?Category= 38&tabindex=2*
- *http://www.telerik.com/Default.aspx?PageId=1828*

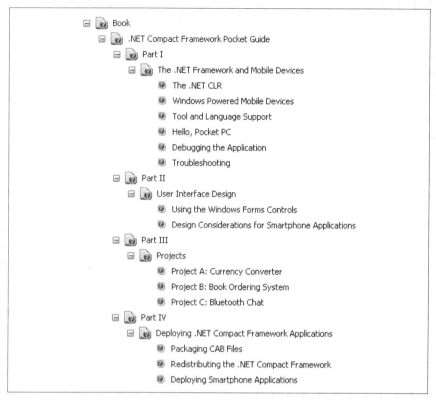

```
☐ 🖼 Book
   ☐ 🖼 .NET Compact Framework Pocket Guide
      ☐ 🖼 Part I
         ☐ 🖼 The .NET Framework and Mobile Devices
               🖼 The .NET CLR
               🖼 Windows Powered Mobile Devices
               🖼 Tool and Language Support
               🖼 Hello, Pocket PC
               🖼 Debugging the Application
               🖼 Troubleshooting
      ☐ 🖼 Part II
         ☐ 🖼 User Interface Design
               🖼 Using the Windows Forms Controls
               🖼 Design Considerations for Smartphone Applications
      ☐ 🖼 Part III
         ☐ 🖼 Projects
               🖼 Project A: Currency Converter
               🖼 Project B: Book Ordering System
               🖼 Project C: Bluetooth Chat
      ☐ 🖼 Part IV
         ☐ 🖼 Deploying .NET Compact Framework Applications
               🖼 Packaging CAB Files
               🖼 Redistributing the .NET Compact Framework
               🖼 Deploying Smartphone Applications
```

Figure 2-36. The TreeView control bound to an XML file

Populate a TreeView Control Programmatically

In other labs in this chapter, you have seen how the TreeView control can be bound to site map files as well as XML documents at design time. However, you can also build your TreeView control dynamically, one node at a time. For example, you might want to display a particular disk directory using the TreeView control, or you may have a site that is changing frequently and hence it is much more efficient to build the tree dynamically.

Instead of statically binding the TreeView control to a site map or XML file, gain flexibility by creating it dynamically during runtime.

In this lab, you will use the TreeView control to display the current application path and its subdirectories.

How do I do that?

In this lab, you will learn how to customize the TreeView control and dynamically populate it with items. Specifically, you will display the current application path and all its subdirectories in the TreeView control.

1. Launch Visual Studio 2005 and create a new ASP.NET 2.0 web application. Name the project *C:\ASPNET20\chap02-DynamicTreeView*.

2. Drag and drop a TreeView control onto the default Web Form.

3. In Solution Explorer, right-click the project name and select Add New Folder → Regular Folder. Name the folder *Images*, since you'll use this folder to store your image files.

4. Add the images shown in Figure 2-37 to the *C:\ASPNET20\chap02-DynamicTreeView\Images* folder.

TIP

The images can be downloaded from this book's support site at *http://www.oreilly.com/catalog/aspnetadn/*.

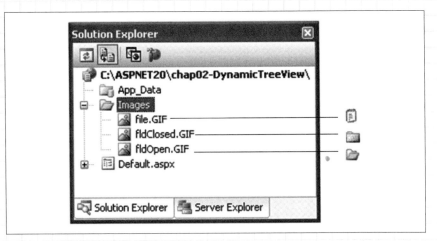

Figure 2-37. The images in the Images folder

5. In the TreeView Tasks window, check the Show Lines checkbox and then click the Customize Line Images… link (see Figure 2-38).

6. In the ASP.NET TreeView Line Image Generator dialog box, set the following properties (see Figure 2-39):
   - CollapseImage: *fldOpen.gif*
   - ExpandImage: *fldClosed.gif*

7. Click OK. When you are prompted to create a new folder called *TreeLineImages*, click Yes. *TreeLineImages* contains a series of images used for displaying the TreeView control. When a TreeView node is expanded, it will display the *fldOpen.gif* image, and when a node is collapsed, the *fldClosed.gif* image.

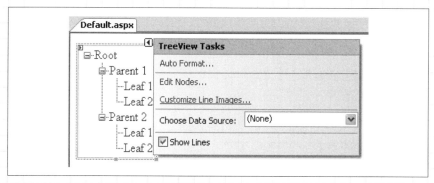

Figure 2-38. Customizing the TreeView control

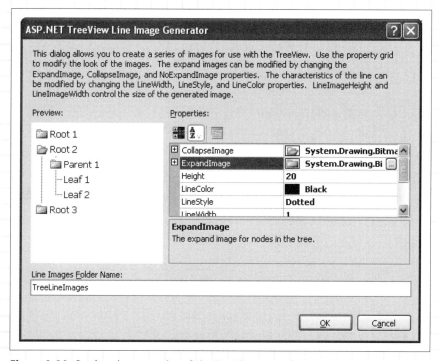

Figure 2-39. Setting the properties of the TreeView control

8. Double-click on the default Web Form to switch to the code-behind.

9. Code the getSubDirectories() method as shown in Example 2-8. This method recursively gets all subdirectories under the current directory and adds the directories as nodes in the TreeView control.

Example 2-8. getSubDirectories() method

```
Public Sub getSubDirectories(ByVal path As String, _
                             ByVal node As TreeNode)
```

Example 2-8. getSubDirectories( ) method (continued)

```
    '---get sub directories under the current one
    Dim dirs As String( ) = Directory.GetDirectories(path)

    '---no subdirectories
    If dirs.Length = 0 Then
        Exit Sub
    Else
        '---for each subdirectory, add to TreeView and
        ' recursively call itself again
        Dim dir As String
        For Each dir In dirs
            '---Add the relatve path to the TreeView control
            Dim newNode As New TreeNode( _
                dir.Substring(dir.LastIndexOf("\") + 1))
            newNode.ToolTip = dir
            node.ChildNodes.Add(newNode)
            '---Find its subdirectories
            getSubDirectories(dir, newNode)
            '---Find files under itself
            getFiles(dir, newNode)
            '---close the current node
            newNode.CollapseAll( )
        Next
    End If
End Sub
```

10. Code the getFiles( ) method as shown in Example 2-9. getFiles( ) lists all the files under the current directory and then adds the files as nodes in the TreeView control.

Example 2-9. getFiles( ) method

```
Public Sub getFiles(ByVal path As String, ByVal node As TreeNode)
    Dim files As String( ) = Directory.GetFiles(path)
    Dim file As String

    '---no files in directory and no subdirectory
    If files.Length = 0 And node.ChildNodes.Count = 0 Then
        Dim newNode As New TreeNode("Directory is empty")
        node.ChildNodes.Add(newNode)
        Exit Sub
    End If
    For Each file In files
        '---Add the file to the TreeView control
        Dim newNode As New TreeNode(file.Substring(path.Length + 1))
        newNode.ToolTip = file
        newNode.ImageUrl = "Images\file.gif"
        node.ChildNodes.Add(newNode)
    Next
End Sub
```

TIP

You can specify the image to use for a node with the ImageUrl property.

11. Finally, add the following code to the Page_Load event so that the TreeView control is populated when the page is loading up:

```
Protected Sub Page_Load(ByVal sender As Object, _
                        ByVal e As System.EventArgs) _
                        Handles Me.Load
    If Not IsPostBack Then
        TreeView1.Nodes.Add(New _
            TreeNode(Request.PhysicalApplicationPath))
        getSubDirectories(Request.PhysicalApplicationPath, _
            TreeView1.Nodes(0))
    End If
End Sub
```

12. To test the application, press F5. You should see a page like the one shown in Figure 2-40.

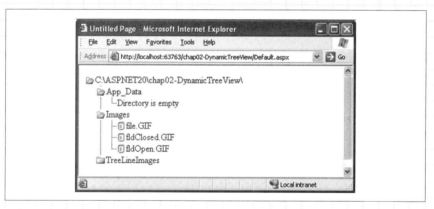

Figure 2-40. Viewing the dynamically generated TreeView control

What about...

...programmatically manipulating the TreeView control?

To programmatically expand or collapse all the nodes, you can use the ExpandAll() and CollapseAll() methods, like this:

```
TreeView1.CollapseAll()
TreeView1.ExpandAll()
```

...customizing the behavior of the individual items in the TreeView control?

There are a few behaviors that you can set for each item in the Tree-View control, some of which are demonstrated in the Source View of a TreeView control in Example 2-10.

Example 2-10. Setting properties of a TreeView control

```
<asp:TreeView ID="TreeView2" runat="server">
   <Nodes>
      <asp:TreeNode SelectAction="Expand"
          Value="Windows" Text="Windows">
         <asp:TreeNode SelectAction="SelectExpand"
             Value="Windows XP" Text="Windows XP">
            <asp:TreeNode ShowCheckBox="True"
                Value="Home Edition" Checked="True"
                NavigateUrl="xphome.aspx"
                Text="Home Edition">
            </asp:TreeNode>
            <asp:TreeNode ShowCheckBox="True"
                Value="Professional"
                NavigateUrl="xpProfessional.aspx"
                Text="Professional">
            </asp:TreeNode>
         </asp:TreeNode>
         <asp:TreeNode Value="Windows 2003 Server"
               NavigateUrl="win2003.aspx"
               Text="Windows Server 2003">
         </asp:TreeNode>
      </asp:TreeNode>
   </Nodes>
</asp:TreeView>
```

When displayed in IE, this TreeView control will look like Figure 2-41.

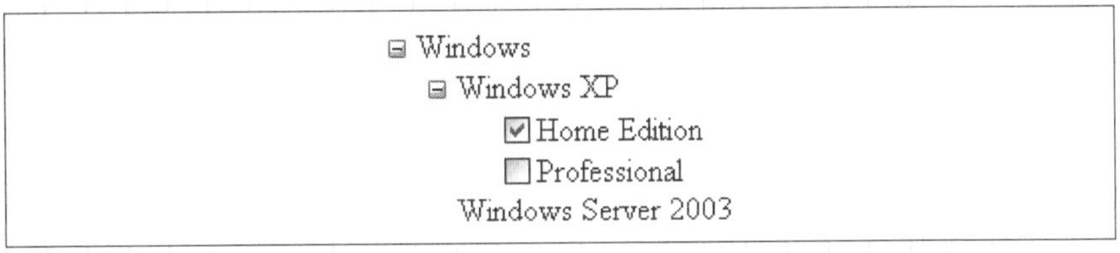

Figure 2-41. The customized TreeView control

If you're able to compare the behavior of the TreeView control with the attributes assigned to its elements in Example 2-10, you should observe the following:

- Clicking on the Windows item will either expand or collapse the tree (SelectAction="Expand"). A postback does not occur.

- Clicking on the Windows XP item will expand and show the items underneath it (if it is collapsed) and a postback will occur (SelectAction="SelectExpand"). You can get the information of the item selected in the Page_Load event via the SelectedNode property of the TreeView control.

- The Home Edition item has a checkbox (ShowCheckBox="True") displayed next to it (Checked="True"). Clicking on the item will cause the *xmhome.aspx* page to be loaded (NavigateUrl="xphome.aspx").

- The Professional item also has a checkbox displayed next to it (ShowCheckBox="True"). Clicking on the item will cause the *xpProfessional.aspx* page to be loaded (NavigateUrl="xpProfessional.aspx").

- Clicking on the Windows Server 2003 item will cause the *win2003.aspx* page to be loaded.

TIP

The default SelectionAction for all TreeView items is Select. To display the target page in a new window, set the Target property.

Where can I learn more?

Check out the MSDN Help topic for the TreeView control for details on all the properties and methods exposed by this versatile control.

Display Drop-Down Menus Using the Menu Control

You can now use the Menu control in ASP.NET 2.0 to menu on the client side. No more client-side script!

Besides using the TreeView control to display site information, you can also use the Menu control to automatically generate a drop-down menu on the browser using client-side script. Sometimes menus are a useful means of navigating a site. For example, Nissan Motors USA (*http://www.nissanusa.com*) uses menus to allow visitors of their site to choose the various vehicle models they want to view.

How do I do that?

In this lab, you will add a Menu control to the Master page created in the earlier lab "Display Hierarchical Data Using the TreeView Control." The user will then be able to use the Menu control to navigate your site.

---

1. Using the project created in the lab "Display Hierarchical Data Using the TreeView Control," add a Menu control (found in the Standard tab of the Toolbox) to the Master page and apply the "Colorful" theme (via the Auto Format... link in the MenuTasks menu) to change its look (see Figure 2-42).

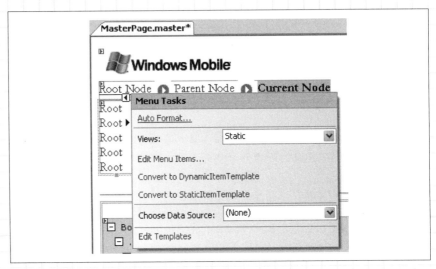

Figure 2-42. Customizing the Menu control

2. In the Menu Tasks of the Menu control, select SiteMapDataSource1 as its data source (see Figure 2-43). The SiteMapDataSource1 control was added when the TreeView control was configured earlier.

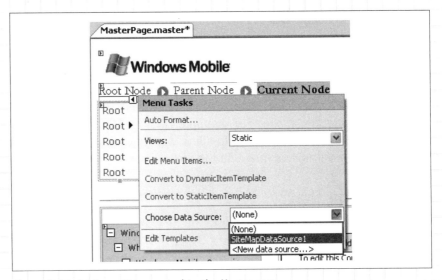

Figure 2-43. Adding a Menu control to the Master page

Chapter 2: Master Pages and Site Navigation

3. To test the Menu control, press F5. You should now be able to navigate the site using the Menu control (see Figure 2-44).

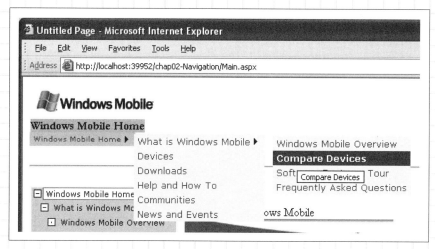

Figure 2-44. Testing the Menu control

4. Note that the Menu control supports two orientations: Horizontal and Vertical. Change the Orientation property of the Menu control from Vertical to Horizontal and observe the changes (see Figure 2-45).

TIP

The default orientation of the Menu control is Vertical.

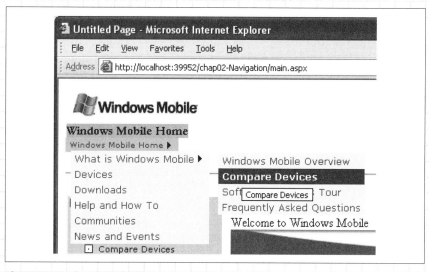

Figure 2-45. Changing the Menu control orientation

What about...

...creating the items in the Menu control declaratively?

Besides binding the Menu control to an XML file or a site map, you can also create the items in the Menu control manually. You can either use the Menu Item Editor (found in the Menu Tasks menu by selecting Edit Menu Items...), as shown in Figure 2-46, or you can add in the items declaratively.

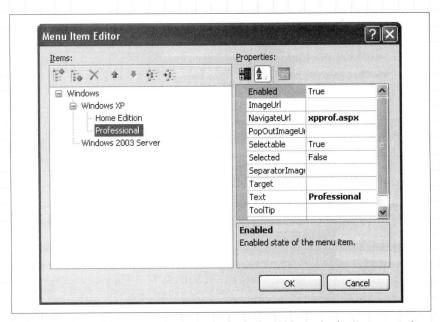

Figure 2-46. Using the Menu Item Editor to manually add items in the Menu control

To declaratively add menu items, drag and drop a Menu control onto the form and switch to Source View. Example 2-11 shows how to implement the menu structure shown in Figure 2-46.

Example 2-11. Adding menu items declaratively

```
<asp:Menu ID="Menu1" Target="newWindow" runat="server">
    <Items>
        <asp:MenuItem Value="Windows" Text="Windows">
            <asp:MenuItem Value="Windows XP" Text="Windows XP">
                <asp:MenuItem Value="Home Edition" Text="Home Edition"
                    navigateurl="xphome.aspx">
                </asp:MenuItem>
                <asp:MenuItem Value="Professional" Text="Professional"
                    navigateurl="xpprof.aspx">
                </asp:MenuItem>
```

Example 2-11. Adding menu items declaratively (continued)

```
            </asp:MenuItem>
            <asp:MenuItem Value="Windows 2003 Server"
                Text="Windows 2003 Server"
                navigateurl="win2003.aspx">
            </asp:MenuItem>
        </asp:MenuItem>
    </Items>
</asp:Menu>
```

TIP

To open a new window when a menu item is selected, set the Target attribute to some value. Note that the Target attribute is supported in both the <Menu> and the <MenuItem> elements. If you specify a target at the menu level, all menu items will default to the specified target, unless you specifically override the target for each individual menu item. If the Target attribute is not set (or set to an empty string), the target will then be the current page.

Note that opening a new window is likely to be confusing to the person browsing the page, unless the menu item is clearly pointing to an external page or site.

Where can I learn more?

To learn how to create menus using client-side scripts, check out the following sites:

- *http://dhtml-menu.com/menu-demos/demo117.html*
- *http://wsabstract.com/javatutors/crossmenu.shtml*
- *http://archive.devx.com/dhtml/articles/td041801/td041801-1.asp*

Web Parts

Web sites today contain a wealth of information, so much that a poorly designed site can easily overwhelm users. To better help users cope, portal web sites today (such as MSN) often organize their data into discrete units that support a degree of personalization. Information is organized into standalone parts, and users can rearrange those parts to suit their individual working styles. Such personalization also lets users hide parts that contain information in which they have no interest. What's more, users can save their settings so that the site will remember their preferences the next time they visit the site. In ASP.NET 2.0, you can now build web portals that offer this kind of modularization of information and personalization using the new Web Parts Framework.

Essentially, the Web Parts Framework contains a set of controls that lets you organize a portal page in a way that allows users of the portal to customize the appearance, content, and behavior of its contents directly from a web browser. The changes are then saved for the user and recalled for subsequent visits. All of this functionality can be implemented without your needing to do much coding.

Figure 3-1 shows the new controls on the WebParts tab of the Toolbox that are the heart and soul of the Web Parts Framework. We'll be discussing these in greater detail throughout the chapter.

Figure 3-2 shows the My MSN page of the Microsoft Network portal (*http://my.msn.com*), which is a good example of the use of Web Parts to organize the content. You can personalize the MSN site by moving around the Web Parts from which it has been built, such as Today on MSN and My favorite links.

In this chapter:
- *Add Web Parts to Your Application*
- *Create a Personalizable Custom Web Part*
- *Let Users Move Web Parts*
- *Let Users Add Web Parts at Runtime*
- *Let Users Edit Web Parts at Runtime*
- *Enable Web Parts to Talk to Each Other*

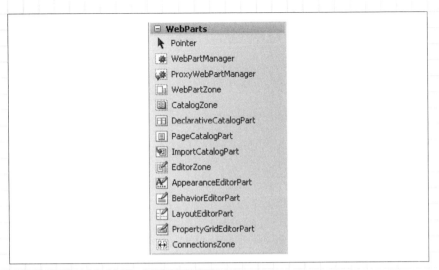

Figure 3-1. The new controls in the WebParts tab in the Toolbox

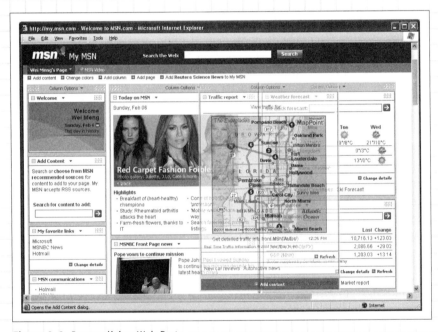

Figure 3-2. Personalizing Web Parts

Add Web Parts to Your Application

Add Web Parts to your page so that positions of the controls can be rearranged by the user.

ASP.NET 2.0 provides a set of ready-made controls to help you develop Web Parts for your portals. You'll find the available controls on the Web-Parts tab of the Toolbox. Let's start with the basics. In this lab, you will learn how to create Web Parts for your ASP.NET web application.

Using Web Parts

In order to use the Web Parts on a portal page, a user must be authenticated.

By default, ASP.NET uses Windows authentication for your web applications, and hence all users need to be authorized to access your machine. However, this is not useful if you want your web application to be accessed by users over the Internet. For this purpose, you need to use Forms authentication. Refer to Chapter 5 for more information on how to enable Forms authentication.

An unauthenticated user who tries to personalize a page using Web Parts will cause a runtime error.

How do I do that?

To understand how Web Parts work, let's build a simple portal page that contains three Web Parts.

There are two ways to add a Web Part to a page:

- By dropping an existing web server control onto the page
- By creating a Web User control from scratch and then dropping that onto the page

Either way, you must first prepare the way for these controls by adding a WebPartManagerControl and one or more WebPartZone controls to the page.

WebPartManager
> Manages all Web Parts controls on a page.

WebPartZone
> Contains and provides overall layout for the Web Part controls that compose the main UI of a page. This control serves as an anchor for Web Part controls.

Let's start by creating a Web Part from a standard web server control.

1. First you need to create a home page for the Web Parts. Launch Visual Studio 2005 and create a new web site project. Name the project *C:\ASPNET20\chap03-Webparts*.

2. Next, drag and drop a WebPartMenuManager control from the Toolbox (under the WebParts tab) onto the default Web Form. The WebPartManager control manages all the Web Parts on a Web Form and must be the first control that you add to the page.

3. To specify where the Web Parts on your page are to be located, insert a 3×1 table onto the form (Layout → Table) and drag and drop a WebPartZone control from the Toolbox (under the WebParts tab) into each of its three cells (see Figure 3-3). Each WebPartZone control will serve as the docking area for one or more Web Parts (more on this in Step 5).

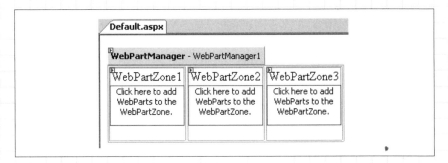

Figure 3-3. Populating the default Web Form

A Web Part zone is an area where Web Parts are anchored. It also defines the default layout and appearance of each Web Part within that zone.

4. Now it's time to add a web server control to the page to give it some functionality. Drag and drop a Calendar control onto WebPartZone1. Apply the Colorful 1 scheme to the Calendar control by selecting it from the Auto Format... link in the Calendar Tasks menu.

When you drop a web server control onto a WebPartZone control, the ASP.NET 2.0 Web Parts Framework wraps it with a special type of control known as a GenericWebPart control, which provides the server control with the basic functionality it needs to become a bona fide Web Part.

5. Switch to Source View for the page (*Default.aspx* in our example), add the <title> attribute to the Calendar control, and set its value to "Today's Date":

```
<asp:Calendar ID="Calendar1"
    title="Today's Date"
    runat="server" BorderWidth="1px"
    Font-Names="Verdana"
...
```

Note that the Calendar control itself does not support the <title> attribute. However, when a control is added to a WebPartZone control, it is wrapped by a GenericWebPart control, which does support the <title> attribute. The value of the <title> attribute will be used as the header for the GenericWebPart control.

6. Your Web Form should now look like the one shown in Figure 3-4.

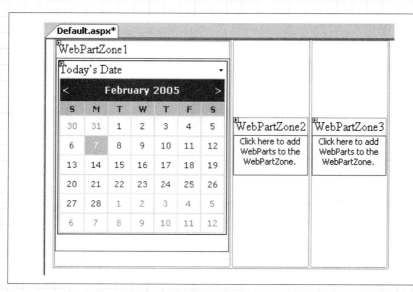

Figure 3-4. The Calendar control as a Web Part

TIP

Note that if you drag and drop more than one control onto a WebPartZone control, the controls will be treated as separate Web Parts, each with its own minimize and close buttons. To combine several controls into one Web Part, you should use a Web User control.

Alternatively, you can also group web server controls within a Placeholder control or a Panel control and then drop it into the WebPartZone control.

---

7. To see how the Calendar control looks in IE, press F5. You will notice an arrow icon in the top-right corner of the Calendar control. Clicking the arrow will reveal two links: Minimize and Close. Click

Minimize to minimize the control. To restore the control to its original state, click the Restore link (see Figure 3-5). To close the Web Part, click the Close link.

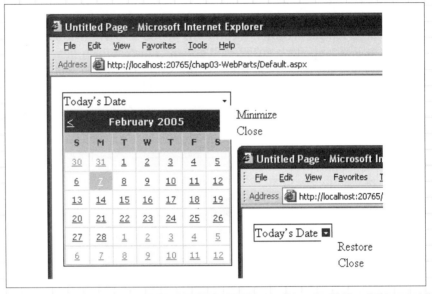

Figure 3-5. The Calendar control

TIP

If you click the Close link, you'll find that you cannot get the Web Part to display again. To open a closed Web Part, refer to the lab "Let Users Add Web Parts at Runtime," later in this chapter.

---

8. Now you've seen how to turn an ordinary web server control into a Web Part. Stop the debugging and return to Visual Studio.

Let's take a look at the second method of adding a Web Part to a portal page: creating a Web User control from scratch and dropping it onto a WebPartZone. The control we're going to build will allow users to search Google.

TIP

A Web User control is a composite control that contains one or more web server controls. Using a Web User control allows you to package multiple web server controls into a single control and then expose public properties and methods so as to customize its behavior.

---

1. First you need to create a new control. Add a new Web User control to your project by right-clicking the project name in Solution Explorer and then selecting Web User Control. Name the Web User control *Google.ascx*.

2. Since we're going to display the Google logo to identify our Web Part, we need to create a folder to store the image. Add a new folder to the project and name it *Images* (right-click the project name in Solution Explorer and select Add Folder → Regular Folder). Save the *Google.gif* image in the *C:\ASPNET\chap03-Webparts\Images* folder (see Figure 3-6).

TIP

The image can be downloaded from this book's support site at *http://www.oreilly.com/catalog/aspnetadn/*.

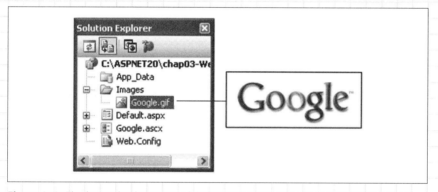

Figure 3-6. The image in the Images folder

3. Now you need to implement your control. First, insert a 2×2 table into the Web User control (Layout → Table) to organize its contents. Add an Image control, a TextBox control, and a Button control to three of the table cells, as shown in Figure 3-7. Associate *Google.gif* with the Image control and add the word "Search" to the Button control.

4. It's time to add the code that will carry out a search when the user enters search terms in the text box and clicks the Search button. Double-click the Search button and type the following code, which will send a search query to Google.com using the terms in the text box:

```
Protected Sub btnSearch_Click(ByVal sender As Object, _
                    ByVal e As System.EventArgs) _
                    Handles btnSearch.Click
```

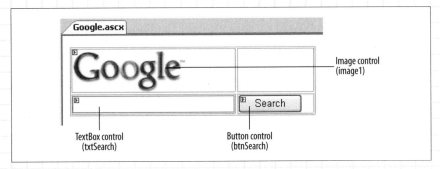

Figure 3-7. Populating the Web User control with the various controls

```
Response.Write(Page.IsValid)
Dim queryStr As String = HttpUtility.UrlEncode(txtSearch.Text)
Response.Redirect("http://www.google.com/search?q=" & queryStr)
End Sub
```

5. You can now drag and drop the *Google.ascx* Web User control from the Solution Explorer onto the WebPartZone2 control in *Default.aspx* (see Figure 3-8).

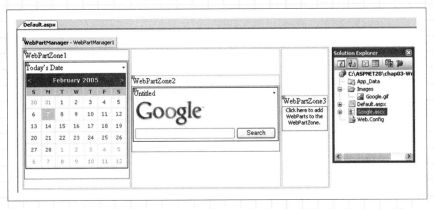

Figure 3-8. Dragging and dropping a Web User control onto a WebPartZone control

6. Note that the Google control is untitled. To add a title, switch to Source View and add the <title> attribute to the newly added Web User control, assigning it the value "Google Search":

```
<uc1:Google title="Google Search" runat="server" ID="Google1" />
```

7. To see how the Web User control looks in IE, press F5. Your portal page should now resemble the one shown in Figure 3-9.

Implementing the IWebPart Interface

To explicitly expose a Web User control as a WebPart control, you need to implement the IWebPart interface and its properties. Doing so will allow your Web User control to access Web Part–specific properties, such as the title of a WebPart control, an icon for the Web Part, and more:

```
Partial Class Google_ascx
    Inherits System.Web.UI.UserControl
    Implements IWebPart
```

If your Web User control implements the IWebPart interface, WebPart properties such as Title and TitleUrl will now appear in the Properties window of the Web User control. Compare this to simply adding a Web User control to a WebPartZone control, which turns it into a GenericWebPart control. For a GenericWebPart control, the Properties window will not display the Web Part–specific properties of the control. The advantage of implementing the IWebPart interface is that a control implementing it has performance advantage over a GenericWebPart control; it also has more advanced properties over those offered by a GenericWebPart control.

To learn how to implement the IWebPart interface, refer to the MSDN Help topic "IWebPart Members."

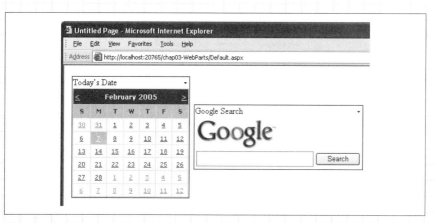

Figure 3-9. Displaying the two Web Parts on the page

What about...

...customizing the look-and-feel of Web Parts?

By default, the look and feel of Web Part controls is determined by the default layout set by the WebPartZone control. By default, Web Parts display their various options (such as Minimize, Close, etc.) as hyperlinks.

Remember, the settings in a WebPartZone control affect the WebPart controls it contains. So you have to set each WebPartZone control in order to adjust the look and feel of its Web Parts.

You adjust the look and feel of Web Parts by altering the properties of the containing WebPartZone control, and you can customize the look of the option links by adding your own images. Let's see how you can do that.

1. First, you'll need some images to use as icons. Add the images shown in Figure 3-10 to the *Images* folder of your project.

TIP

The images can be downloaded from this book's support site at *http://www.oreilly.com/catalog/aspnetadn/*.

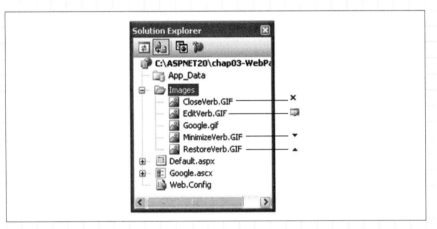

Figure 3-10. The images stored in the Images folder

Settings applied to a WebPartZone control affect all the Web Parts controls contained in that Web Part zone. If a Web Part is moved from one Web Part zone into another, it will assume the behavior of the Web Part zone it is in.

2. Now you'll want to assign each of the images to one of the option links. Select the WebPartZone1 control and view its Properties window. Locate the following properties and set their ImageURL properties as follows:

   - CloseVerb.ImageUrl="Images/CloseVerb.gif"
   - EditVerb.ImageUrl="Images/EditVerb.gif"
   - MinimizeVerb.ImageUrl="Images/MinimizeVerb.gif"
   - RestoreVerb.ImageUrl="Images/RestoreVerb.gif"

3. Apply the Professional scheme to the WebPartZone1 control by clicking on the Auto Format... link in the WebPartZone Tasks menu (see Figure 3-11). Likewise, apply the Color scheme to the WebPartZone2 control.

Figure 3-11. Apply a scheme to the WebPartZone control

4. Press F5 to test the application. You will realize that the Calendar control in the first WebPartZone control has icons displayed next to the Minimize and Close link. In contrast, the Web User control in the second WebPartZone control does not have the icons (see Figure 3-12). This is because you only configured the first WebPartZone control for displaying icons. In the next lab, you will learn how to allow your user to rearrange the various Web Parts on the page.

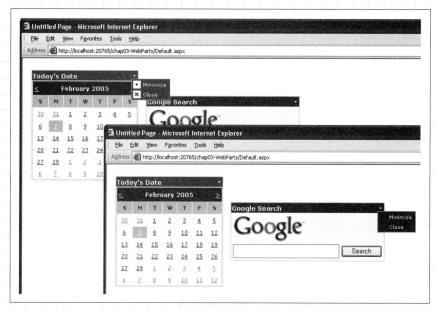

Figure 3-12. Examining the two Web Parts in the two WebPartZone controls

Where can I learn more?

One of the common questions about Web Parts in ASP.NET 2.0 is whether they are compatible with SharePoint Portal Server. The current version of SharePoint Portal Server is not compatible with the ASP.NET 2.0 Web Parts Framework. However, the next release of SharePoint Portal Server will use the new ASP.NET 2.0 Web Parts Framework, and hence Web Parts created with ASP.NET 2.0 could be reused by the new SharePoint Portal Server.

To learn how to develop Web Parts for SharePoint Portal Server 2003 in .NET, check out the following article: *http://www.devx.com/dotnet/Article/17518.*

Create a Personalizable Custom Web Part

Learn how to create a person-alizable custom Web Part and see how it can be exported to a file.

In the previous lab, "Add Web Parts to Your Application," you have seen how to create a Web Part by using either a web server control or a Web User control. In this lab, you will learn another way of creating Web Parts: using a custom control. By using a custom control you gain the flexibility to design your own UI for the Web Part. But more importantly, by inheriting from the WebPart class you also are able to perform tasks that would not ordinarily be available, such as exporting a Web Part to a file. Also, you will learn how you can create personalizable Web Parts that are able to persist information in the Web Part for each specific user.

TIP

Personalizable Web Parts are also applicable to a Web User control.

How do I do that?

In this lab, you will add a custom Web Control Library to the solution created in the previous lab. The Web Control Library project template allows you to create a custom web control, and in this lab you will learn how to convert this control into a Web Part control. This custom control will consume a translation web service that translates words from English to French. The control will also save the last word (to be translated) so that when the user visits the page again, that word will be displayed.

1. First, you'll need to create the Web Control Library. Launch Visual Studio 2005 and add a new Web Control Library project (File → Add → New Project) to the project created in the last lab (*C:\ ASPNET20\chap03-Webparts*). Name the project *C:\ASPNET20\ chap03-TranslationWebPart* (see Figure 3-13).

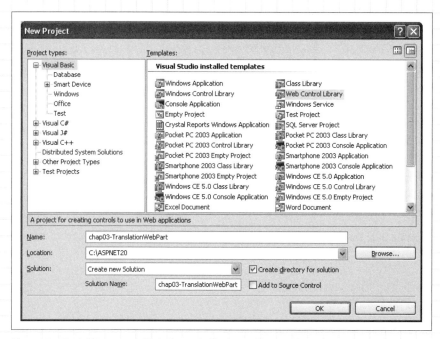

Figure 3-13. Adding a new Web Control Library project to the current project

2. Add a Web Reference (right-click the *chap03-TranslationWebPart* project name in Solution Explorer and select Add Web Reference...) to point to the Translation Web service at *http://www.webservicex.com/ TranslateService.asmx?WSDL*. This step makes the translation service available to your project as a web service.

3. To help keep the bits of the project organized in your head, rename the source file for the project from the default name, *WebCustomControl1.vb*, to *TranslationWebPart.vb*.

4. The Solution Explorer window for your project should now look like Figure 3-14.

5. Provide the implementation for this control by replacing the default content of *TranslationWebPart.vb* with the code shown in Example 3-1.

Figure 3-14. The Solution Explorer with the two projects

Example 3-1. TranslationWebPart.vb

```vb
Imports System.Web.UI.WebControls.WebParts

Public Class TranslationWebPart
    Inherits WebPart

    Private pStrText As String = Nothing
    Private txtStringToTranslate As TextBox

    Private lblTranslatedString As Label

    Public Sub New()
        Me.AllowClose = True
    End Sub

    <Personalizable(), WebBrowsable()> _
    Public Property strToTranslate() As String
        Get
            Return pStrText
        End Get
        Set(ByVal value As String)
            pStrText = value
        End Set
    End Property

    Protected Overrides Sub CreateChildControls()
        Controls.Clear()
```

Example 3-1. TranslationWebPart.vb (continued)

```vb
        '---display a textbox
        txtStringToTranslate = New TextBox()
        txtStringToTranslate.Text = Me.strToTranslate
        Me.Controls.Add(txtStringToTranslate)

        '---display a button
        Dim btnTranslate As New Button()
        btnTranslate.Text = "Translate"
        AddHandler btnTranslate.Click, AddressOf Me.btnTranslate_Click
        Me.Controls.Add(btnTranslate)

        '---display a label
        lblTranslatedString = New Label()
        lblTranslatedString.BackColor = _
          System.Drawing.Color.Yellow
        Me.Controls.Add(lblTranslatedString)
        ChildControlsCreated = True
    End Sub

    Private Sub btnTranslate_Click(ByVal sender As Object, _
                         ByVal e As EventArgs)
        '---display the translated sentence
        If txtStringToTranslate.Text <> String.Empty Then
            Me.strToTranslate = txtStringToTranslate.Text
            txtStringToTranslate.Text = String.Empty

            '---access the web service
            Dim ws As New com.webservicex.www.TranslateService
            lblTranslatedString.Text = "<br/>" & Me.strToTranslate & "-->" & _
            ws.Translate(com.webservicex.www.Language.EnglishTOFrench, _
            Me.strToTranslate)
        End If
    End Sub
End Class
```

6. Specifically, you are creating a custom Web Part control that looks like Figure 3-15. The custom Web Part control will allow users to enter a string in English so that it can be translated into French. The translated text would then be displayed in a label control.

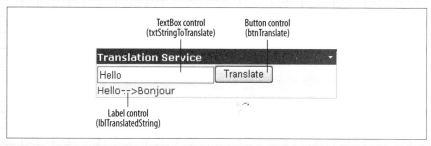

Figure 3-15. Creating the custom control

7. To use the custom control, you need to compile the custom control into a DLL. Right-click the *chap03-TranslationWebPart* project name in Solution Explorer and select Build.

8. It's time to put your new control to work. First, return to the *Default.aspx* page in the *chap03-WebParts* project you created in the last lab, "Add Web Parts to Your Application."

9. To make the control readily available for use with your projects, let's add it to the Toolbox. To do so, right-click the Standard tab within the Toolbox and select Choose Items... (see Figure 3-16).

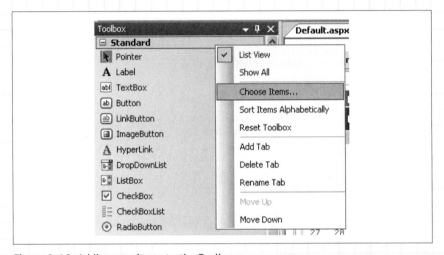

Figure 3-16. Adding new items to the Toolbox

10. In the Choose Toolbox Items dialog, click the Browse... button. Locate the *chap03-TranslationWebPart.dll* file in the *C:\ASPNET20\ chap03-TranslationWebPart\bin* folder. Click OK and then OK again.

11. You should now be able to see the custom control in the Toolbox (see Figure 3-17).

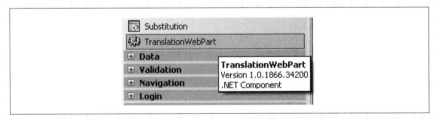

Figure 3-17. The TranslationWebPart control in the Toolbox

12. To use the control, drag and drop the TranslationWebPart control from the Toolbox onto WebPartZone2 on the *Default.aspx* page of your project (see Figure 3-18).

13. Your Web Part lacks a title, as you'll notice. To fix that, switch to Source View for the page, and under WebPartZone2, locate the <cc1: TranslationWebPart> element. Add the <title> attribute as follows:

```
<ZoneTemplate>
    <uc1:Google ID="Google1" title="Google Search" runat="server" />
    <cc1:TranslationWebPart runat="server" ID="TranslationWebPart1"
        title="Translation Service" />
</ZoneTemplate>
```

14. To see the results of your work, switch back to Design View, and your page should now look like Figure 3-18.

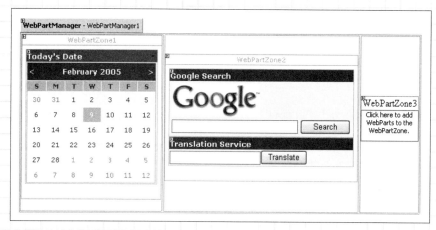

Figure 3-18. Adding a custom Web Part control to WebPartZone2

15. Press F5 to test the application. You will now be able to use the custom Web Part you have created and perform a translation from English to French. Try typing in the word "Hello" and observe the result, which should resemble Figure 3-19. You can also minimize and close the Web Part just like any other Web Part.

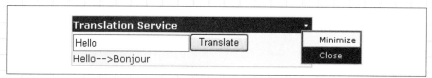

Figure 3-19. Using the custom Web Part

What just happened?

What you have just done is create a new custom Web Part control. If you observe the property definition for strToTranslate, you will notice that there are two attributes prefixing it:

```
<Personalizable(), WebBrowsable()> _
Public Property strToTranslate() As String
...
```

The Personalizable attribute allows you to persist information contained within the Web Part so that it can be personalized for each user. There are two scopes you can set for the Personalizable attribute: User (default) and Shared. In this example, you use the default User scope for personalization; hence, each time a user enters text into the text box, that text will be saved. In other words, the Web Part will remember the last word typed into the text box for each individual user.

The other personalization scope, Shared, saves this information but makes it visible to all users. To use shared personalization, use the PersonalizationScope.Shared enumeration within the Personalizable attribute:

```
<Personalizable(PersonalizationScope.Shared), WebBrowsable()> _
Public Property strToTranslate() As String
...
```

In doing so, all users will be able to see the text (typed in by the last user) to be translated.

You will learn more about the use of the <WebBrowsable> attribute in the lab "Let Users Edit Web Parts at Runtime," later in this chapter.

What about...

...exporting a Web Part control?

You can export a Web Part to a file so that it can be shared among users by, say, exchanging email. To see how to export a Web Part, try following these steps:

1. Go to *Default.aspx* and switch to Source View. Locate the Translation Web Part and add the ExportMode attribute, as shown in the following snippet:

```
<cc1:TranslationWebPart title="Translation Service"
    ExportMode=All
    runat="server" ID="TranslationWebPart1" />
```

Testing Per-User Personalization

So far, you have been using the default Windows authentication for your project and hence you won't be able to see how per-user personalization actually works for different users. To test per-user personalization for different users, follow these steps:

1. Add two user accounts to your web site through the ASP.NET Web Site Administration Tool (WebSite → ASP.NET Configuration). Refer to Chapter 5 for more information on how to add new users to your web site.

2. Add a *Login.aspx* page to your web site and populate it with the Login control.

3. Modify *Web.config* to disallow anonymous users:

```
<authenication mode="Forms" />
<authorization>
   <deny users="?"/>
</authorization>
```

4. Select *Default.aspx* in Solution Explorer and press F5. You will be redirected to *Login.aspx*. Log in using the first user account. Type in some text in the custom Web Part control's text box and click the Translate button.

5. Load *Login.aspx* again and this time log in using the other user account. As usual, type in some text in the custom Web Part control and click the Translate button.

6. If you now load *Login.aspx* again and log in using the first user account, you will notice that the text box in the custom Web Part control will display the text that you last entered for the first user.

TIP

You can export a Web Part only if the custom control inherits from the WebPart class.

---

2. You also need to add the <webParts> element into *web.config*:

```
<system.web>
   <webParts enableExport="true" />
   ...
```

3. Press F5 to test the application. In the Translation Web Part, click on the arrow in the top-right corner and select Export (see Figure 3-20).

4. When you test the application, you will see a warning that this Web Part may contain confidential information (see Figure 3-21).

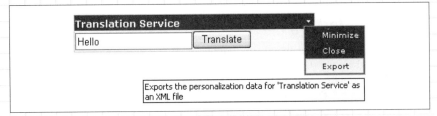

Figure 3-20. Exporting a Web Part

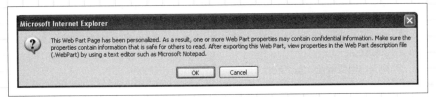

Figure 3-21. The warning dialog before saving a Web Part

Controlling the Export of Sensitive Data

The ExportMode attribute can take either of the following values: All, None, and NonSensitiveData. The default export mode is None. The NonSensitive-Data mode will persist only data that is not marked as sensitive (through the isSensitive parameter in the <Personalizable> attribute).

To mark data in a Web Part as sensitive, specify True for the second parameter of the <Personalizable> attribute:

```
<Personalizable(PersonalizationScope.User, True), _
             WebBrowsable()> _
Public Property strToTranslate() As String
  ...
```

5. Click OK and then in the next dialog box, click the Save button to save the Web Part to a file.

6. Use the default name of *TranslationService.WebPart* and click the Save button to save the Web Part to the Desktop.

7. To examine the state of the saved Web Part, use Notepad and load the *TranslationService.WebPart* file. You should see code that resembles the XML in Example 3-2.

Example 3-2. TranslationService.WebPart content

```
<webParts>
  <webPart>
    <metaData>
```

Example 3-2. TranslationService.WebPart content (continued)

```
      <type name="chap03_TranslationWebPart.TranslationWebPart" />
      <importErrorMessage>Cannot import this Web Part.</importErrorMessage>
    </metaData>
    <data>
      <properties>
        <property name="AllowClose">True</property>
        <property name="Width" />
        <property name="strToTranslate">Hello</property>
        <property name="AllowMinimize">True</property>
        <property name="AllowConnect">True</property>
        <property name="ChromeType">Default</property>
        <property name="TitleIconImageUrl" />
        <property name="Description" />
        <property name="Hidden">False</property>
        <property name="TitleUrl" />
        <property name="AllowEdit">True</property>
        <property name="Height" />
        <property name="HelpUrl" />
        <property name="Title">Translation Service</property>
        <property name="CatalogIconImageUrl" />
        <property name="Direction">NotSet</property>
        <property name="ChromeState">Normal</property>
        <property name="AllowZoneChange">True</property>
        <property name="AllowHide">True</property>
        <property name="HelpMode">Navigate</property>
        <property name="ExportMode">All</property>
      </properties>
    </data>
  </webPart>
</webParts>
```

Note that the word "Hello" persisted in the *.WebPart* file.

Where can I learn more?

To learn more about creating custom controls, check out the following links:

- *http://www.ondotnet.com/pub/a/dotnet/excerpt/progaspdotnet_14/ index2.html*

- *http://samples.gotdotnet.com/quickstart/aspplus/doc/ webctrlauthoring.aspx*

Let Users Move Web Parts

So far we have been discussing how to create Web Parts and how to configure them to look good and nice. But we have not really touched on the most important feature of Web Parts—that is, how to let users move the Web Parts from one zone to another.

Let your users rearrange the positions of the Web Parts on your portal to their liking.

How do I do that?

In this lab, you will learn how to use the ASP.NET 2.0 Web Parts Framework to enable users to move Web Parts directly in the web browser. First you'll add a pair of radio buttons to the page so you can turn the feature on and off, and then you'll observe the behavior of the Web Parts as you move them from one zone to another.

1. Using the project created in the previous lab (*C:\ASPNET20\chap03-Webparts*), add a RadioButtonList control onto the form (see Figure 3-22) and populate it with two items: a radio button named Browse Display Mode and another one named Design Display Mode. Also, check the AutoPostBack checkbox in the RadioButtonList control Tasks menu:

   ```
   <asp:RadioButtonList ID="rblMode" runat="server" AutoPostBack="True">
       <asp:ListItem>Browse Display Mode</asp:ListItem>
       <asp:ListItem>Design Display Mode</asp:ListItem>
   </asp:RadioButtonList>
   ```

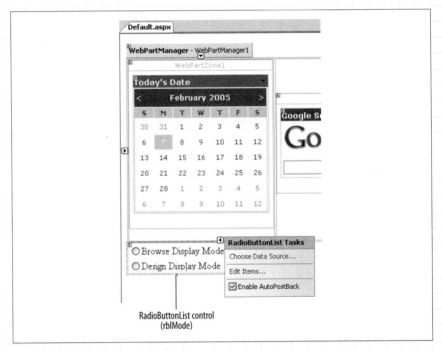

Figure 3-22. Adding a RadioButtonList control to the form

2. Double-click the RadioButtonList control to switch to its code-behind page, and then enter the following code. The WebPartManager control manages the display mode of all the Web Parts on the

page. By default, all Web Parts under its control are set to browse display mode (BrowseDisplayMode). To allow users to move Web Parts, you need to set the display mode to design display mode (DesignDisplayMode).

```
Protected Sub rblMode_SelectedIndexChanged( _
            ByVal sender As Object, _
            ByVal e As System.EventArgs) _
            Handles rblMode.SelectedIndexChanged
    Select Case rblMode.SelectedIndex
        Case 0 : WebPartManager1.DisplayMode = _
                    WebPartManager.BrowseDisplayMode
        Case 1 : WebPartManager1.DisplayMode = _
                    WebPartManager.DesignDisplayMode
    End Select
End Sub
```

3. Press F5 to test the application. When the page is loaded, click the Design Display Mode button and notice that the outlines of the three WebPartZone controls are displayed. You can now drag a Web Part by its title bar from one zone to another (see Figure 3-23).

Figure 3-23. Moving Web Parts from one zone to another

You can change the default header text (WebPartZone1, WebPartZone2, etc.) of each WebPartZone control by setting its HeaderText property.

4. If you drag the Google Search Web Part onto the first Web Part zone, the result will look like Figure 3-24. Note that now the Google Search Web Part uses the scheme set by the WebPartZone1 control.

Also, notice that the Minimize and Close links each now have an icon.

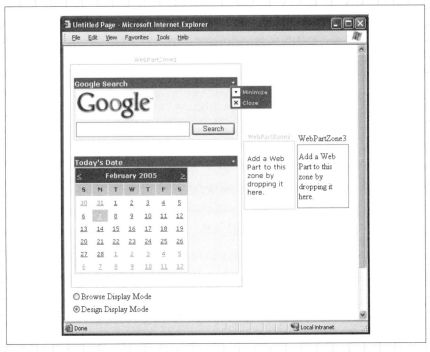

Figure 3-24. The Google Search Web Part now takes on the scheme defined in WebPartZone1

5. When you are done moving the Web Part control, click on the Browse Display Mode option so that the page is set again to browse mode.

What just happened?

What you have just seen is how to configure a Web Part so it can be moved from one Web Part zone to another, and you've observed how the look and feel and behavior of the Web Part itself change when you do that. All of this is handled by the WebPartManager control. When you click on the Browse Display Mode button, the display mode of the WebPartManager control is set to WebPartManager.DesignDisplayMode:

```
Case 1 : WebPartManager1.DisplayMode = _
            WebPartManager.DesignDisplayMode
```

When you are done moving the Web Parts and want to finalize the positioning of the Web Parts on the page, you can simply set it back to browse mode:

```
Case 0 : WebPartManager1.DisplayMode = _
         WebPartManager.BrowseDisplayMode
```

Now, if you close IE and press F5 in Visual Studio again, you will notice that the Web Parts remain in their most recent position. The Web Parts Framework is able to "remember" where you previously positioned them. So how is this done?

Actually, the positional information of each Web Part is stored in a table called the aspnet_PersonalizationPerUser table, found in the ASPNETDB.MDF database (SQL Express 2005) located in the *App_Data* folder of your project. Table 3-1 shows a record in the aspnet_ PersonalizationPerUser table.

When I run the application on my system, the Id can be traced to the username "WINXP2\ Wei-Meng Lee" in the aspnet_Users table, also located within the ASNETDB.MDF database.

Table 3-1. A record in the aspnet_PersonalizationPerUser table

Field	Value
Id	{94CACA48-36D3-4F64-A6AB-BD5352FF4522}
PathId	{BF32CB1F-DEB7-4384-B3DB-5D9B45F59FF9}
UserId	{F9D14F92-540B-4A64-A4B2-75DB80857E78}
PageSettings	<Binary>
LastUpdatedDate	2/7/2005 8:48:58 PM

If you wish to restore the Web Parts to their original position, simply delete the row (corresponding to a particular user) in the aspnet_PersonalizationPerUser table.

What about...

...restoring a Web Part after it has been closed?

In the process of trying out the labs, you may have clicked on the Close button on a Web Part. If you did this, you might have had difficulty getting the page back. But fear not, the Web Parts are not gone forever; you just need to know how to get them back. There are two ways of restoring a closed Web Part:

• Delete the relevant row in the aspnet_PersonalizationPerUser table, as outlined earlier.

• Use the PageCatalogPart control, to be discussed in the lab "Let Users Add Web Parts at Runtime."

You can always disable the Close link of a Web Part by setting the Visible attribute within the CloseVerb property to `false`.

Where can I learn more?

To learn how to write your own custom personalization provider, check out the following articles:

- *http://msdn.microsoft.com/library/default.asp?url=/library/en-us/ dnaspnet/html/asp02182004.asp*

- *http://msdn.microsoft.com/library/default.asp?url=/library/en-us/ dnaspnet/html/asp04212004.asp?frame=true*

Let Users Add Web Parts at Runtime

In addition to the Web Parts already visible when the user loads the page, you can provide users with a list of other available Web Parts they can selectively add to the page. For example, in My MSN, you can choose from a list of available content that you can add to your page (see Figure 3-25).

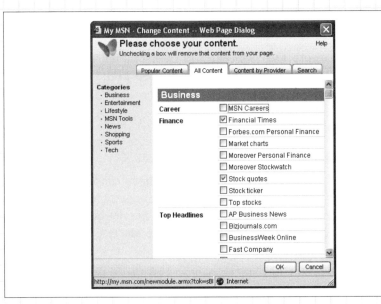

Figure 3-25. Adding additional content in http://my.msn.com

To let users add Web Parts to the page, you will use the DeclarativeCatalogPart, PageCatalogPart, and ImportCatalogPart controls.

How do I do that?

In this lab, you will learn how to use the CatalogZone control to list Web Parts available for users to add when they're running your application. You will use the CatalogZone control and the three related CatalogPart controls—DeclarativeCatalogZone, PageCatalogZone, and ImportCatalog-Zone—so that users can look for and add Web Parts from a variety of sources.

Here is a quick overview of the controls you will use in this lab:

CatalogZone

> Contains CatalogPart controls (DeclarativeCatalogPart, PageCatalog-Part, and ImportCatalogPart). This control is used to create a catalog of Web Part controls so that users can select controls to add to a page.

DeclarativeCatalogPart

> Enables developers to add a catalog of Web Part controls to a web page so that users can choose to add them to a page.

PageCatalogPart

> Provides a page catalog of Web Part controls that a user has closed on a Web Parts page, and that the user can add back to the page.

ImportCatalogPart

> Imports Web Part controls, so that the control can be added to a web page with preassigned settings

For this lab, let's continue to use the project we've used throughout this chapter (*C:\ASPNET20\chap03-Webparts*).

1. Drag and drop a CatalogZone control from the WebParts tab of the Toolbox onto the form (see Figure 3-26). The CatalogZone control is the primary control for hosting CatalogPart controls (more on this in Step 2) on a Web page.

2. Now you'll add the controls that make it possible for users to pick and choose the parts they use from various lists. Drag and drop a DeclarativeCatalogPart, a PageCatalogPart, and an ImportCatalogPart from the WebParts tab of the Toolbox onto the CatalogZone control. The CatalogZone control should now look like the one shown in Figure 3-27.

   The DeclarativeCatalogPart control allows developers to add a catalog of Web Parts to a web page. Users can then select the Web Parts they want to use and add them to Web Part zones on the page. The PageCatalogPart control provides a catalog of Web Parts that a user has closed so that the user can add them back to the page, if desired.

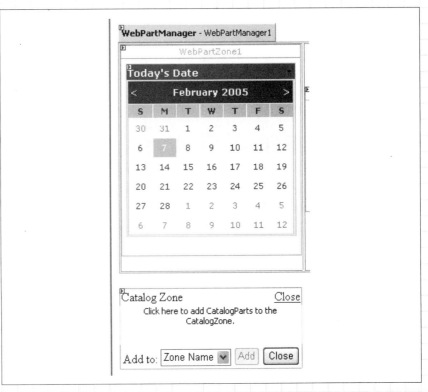

Figure 3-26. Adding the CatalogZone control onto the default form

The ImportCatalogPart control allows users to import saved Web Parts into the page.

3. The CatalogZone needs a look and feel, so apply the Classic scheme via the Auto Format... link on the CatalogZone Tasks menu.

4. In the radio button list control at the bottom of the form, add a new item (shown in bold):

```
<asp:RadioButtonList ID="rblMode" runat="server" AutoPostBack="True">
    <asp:ListItem>Browse Display Mode</asp:ListItem>
    <asp:ListItem>Design Display Mode</asp:ListItem>
    <asp:ListItem>Catalog Display Mode</asp:ListItem>
</asp:RadioButtonList>
```

5. In the code-behind of the radio button list control, add the following line (in bold) to the SelectedIndexChanged event. This will cause the CatalogZone control to be displayed when the Catalog Display Mode item in the radio button list control is clicked:

```
Protected Sub rblMode_SelectedIndexChanged( _
            ByVal sender As Object, _
            ByVal e As System.EventArgs) _
```

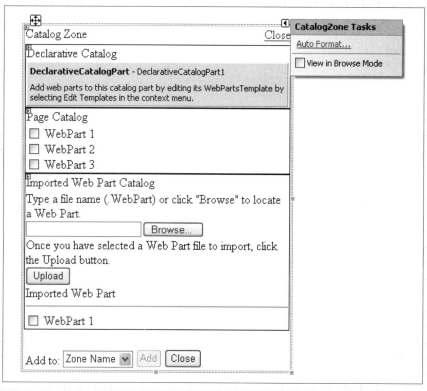

Figure 3-27. The CatalogZone control

```
                Handles rblMode.SelectedIndexChanged
        Select Case rblMode.SelectedIndex
            Case 0 : WebPartManager1.DisplayMode = _
                        WebPartManager.BrowseDisplayMode
            Case 1 : WebPartManager1.DisplayMode = _
                        WebPartManager.DesignDisplayMode
            Case 2 : WebPartManager1.DisplayMode = _
                        WebPartManager.CatalogDisplayMode
        End Select
    End Sub
```

6. In the DeclarativeCatalogPart Tasks menu, click on the Edit Templates link (see Figure 3-28). You will add a Google Search Web Part into the DeclarativeCatalogPart control so that users will have the option to add Google Search Web Parts to their page.

7. Drag and drop the *Google.ascx* file from Solution Explorer onto the DeclarativeCatalogPart control (see Figure 3-29). This will enable the Google Search Web Part to be available in the DeclarativeCatalog-Part control, allowing users to add additional Google Search Web Parts to the page during runtime.

Figure 3-28. Editing the DeclarativeCatalogPart control

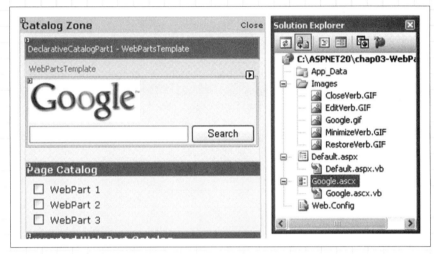

Figure 3-29. Adding the Google Search Web User control onto the DeclarativeCatalogPart control

8. Right-click the Google Search Web User control in the Declarative-CatalogZone control and then select Properties. Set the title property to Google Search, so that this user-friendly name will be displayed in the DeclarativeCatalogPart control during runtime.

9. Press F5 to test the application. Click on the Catalog Display Mode option. You should now be able to see the CatalogZone control.

TIP

The default name displayed for the DeclarativeCatalogPart control is Declarative Catalog. This name might not be very obvious to your users as to its purposes. You can change the name by right-clicking it in Visual Studio and selecting Properties. Set the Title property to something like "Available Web Parts."

---

10. The contents of the DeclarativeCatalogPart are always displayed (see Figure 3-30). To add the Google Search Web Part, click the

---

checkbox next to Google Search, select the Web Part zone to add into (WebPartZone2 in this case), and click Add.

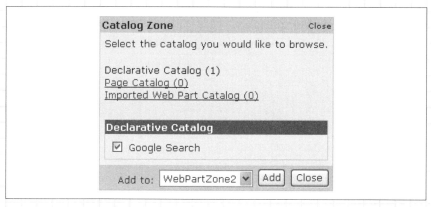

Figure 3-30. The CatalogZone control in action

11. Figure 3-31 shows what happens when you add the Google Search Web Part to WebPartZone2.

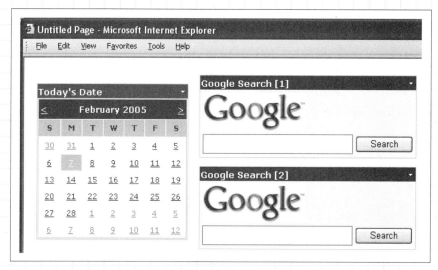

Figure 3-31. Adding the Google Search Web Part to WebPartZone2

12. Now, close all three Web Parts on the page by clicking the Close link at the top-right corner of each one. You will discover how you can get them back onto the page again.

13. Click on the Catalog Display Mode option again. This time, click the Page Catalog link in the CatalogZone control (see Figure 3-32). You

should see that the PageCatalogPart control now shows the three Web Parts you have just closed.

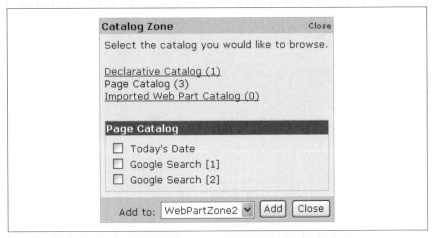

Figure 3-32. Viewing the page catalog

14. To add the closed Web Parts back into the page, check the Web Parts you want to add, select the Web Part zone to add into, and then click Add.

15. Finally, click on the Imported Web Part Catalog link in the Catalog-Zone control. You can click the Browse… button to locate a saved Web Part. Click the Upload button to upload the Web Part.

16. Select the Web Part zone to add to and click Add to add the selected Web Part to the page (see Figure 3–33).

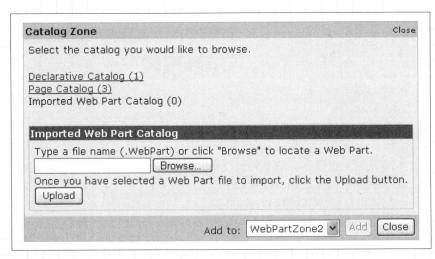

Figure 3-33. Importing saved Web Parts

What about...

...exporting a Web Part?

Your user might like a particular Web Part on your site and want to customize the Web Part so that she can share it with her colleagues. In this case, you need to allow the user to export the Web Parts on your page.

To make a Web Part exportable, you need to create a custom control that inherits from WebPart. Refer to the lab "Create a Personalizable Custom Web Part," earlier in this chapter, for information on how to export a Web Part.

Where can I learn more?

For more information on the CatalogPart controls, refer to the MSDN Help topic "CatalogPart Class."

Let Users Edit Web Parts at Runtime

Let users customize the look and feel of the Web Parts at your site.

In addition to giving users the power to move Web Parts around on your portal pages, you can empower them to change the appearance of the Web Parts themselves. In this lab, you will learn how to use the EditorPart controls (`AppearanceEditorPart`, `BehaviorEditorPart`, `LayoutEditorPart`, and `PropertyGridEditorPart`) to allow users to change the look and feel of their Web Parts.

Here is a quick overview of the EditorPart controls you'll use in this lab:

`AppearanceEditorPart`
    Provides an editor control that enables end users to edit several user interface properties (such as title, width, and height) on a Web Part control

`BehaviorEditorPart`
    Provides an editor control that enables end users to edit several user interface properties (such as the display of the Edit, Close, and Minimize buttons) on a Web Part control

`LayoutEditorPart`
    Provides an editor control that enables end users to edit several layout-oriented user interface properties on a Web Part control

`PropertyGridEditorPart`
    Provides an editor control that enables end users to edit custom properties on a Web Part control

How do I do that?

In this lab, you will learn how to let users change the look and behavior of every Web Part on the page. You will add an EditorZone control to the page to contain the four EditorPart controls: `AppearanceEditorPart`, `BehaviorEditorPart`, `LayoutEditorPart`, and `PropertyGridEditorPart`. These four controls allow users to make a variety of changes to the look and feel of Web Parts on the page. For example, users can change the title of a Web Part, as well as selectively enable and disable the various buttons (such as Close, Edit, and Minimize) on a Web Part.

1. Using the project created in the last lab (*C:\ASPNET20\chap03-Webparts*), drag and drop the EditorZone control onto the form (see Figure 3-34). The EditorZone control serves as the primary control for hosting EditorPart controls on a web page (more on this in Step 2).

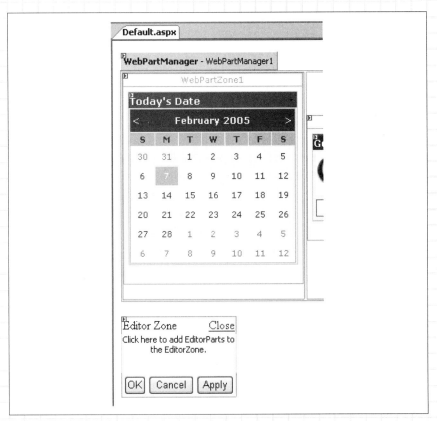

Figure 3-34. Adding an EditorZone control onto the default form

2. To edit the Web Parts, you need to populate the EditorZone control with the three EditorPart controls. Drag and drop the AppearanceEditorPart, BehaviorEditPart, PropertyGridEditorPart, and LayoutEditorPart controls onto the EditorZone control. Apply the Colorful scheme to the EditorZone control (via the "Auto Format…" link in the EditorZone Tasks menu). The EditorZone control should now look like Figure 3-35.

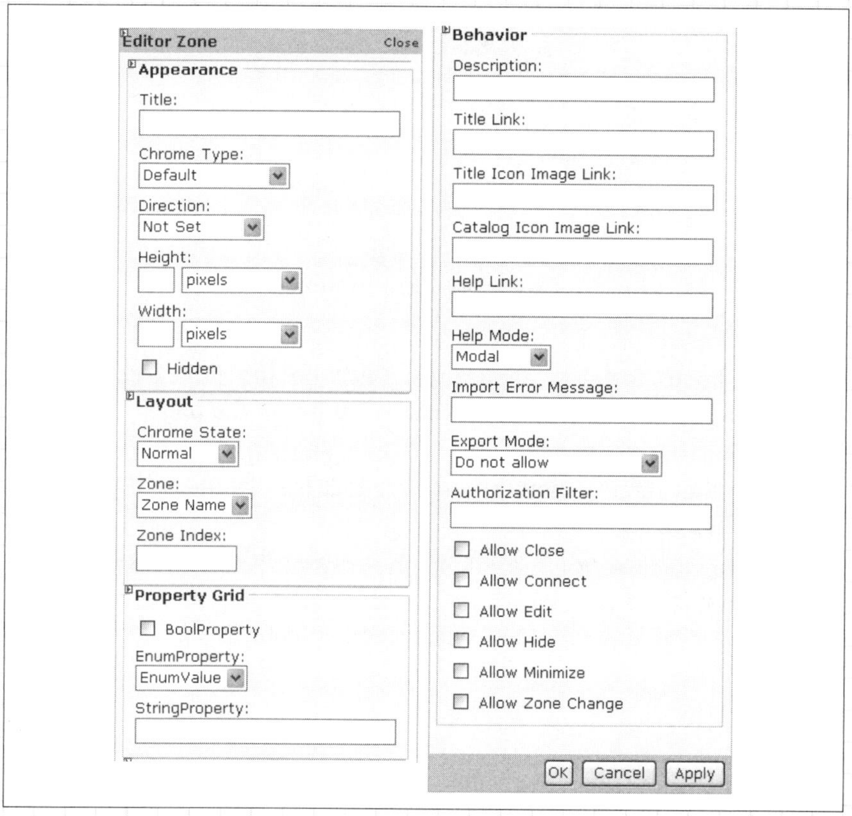

Figure 3-35. The EditorZone control with AppearanceEditorPart, BehaviorEditorPart, LayoutEditorPart, and PropertyGridEditorPart controls (images split for easy presentation on this page)

3. In the radio button list control at the bottom of the form, add a new item (shown in bold) so that the user can choose the option to edit the Web Parts on the page:

```
<asp:RadioButtonList ID="rblMode" runat="server" AutoPostBack="True">
    <asp:ListItem>Browse Display Mode</asp:ListItem>
    <asp:ListItem>Design Display Mode</asp:ListItem>
    <asp:ListItem>Catalog Display Mode</asp:ListItem>
    <asp:ListItem>Edit Display Mode</asp:ListItem>
</asp:RadioButtonList>
```

4. In the code-behind of the radio button list control, add the following line (shown in bold) to the SelectedIndexChanged event of the radio button list control. This will cause the EditorZone control to be displayed when the Catalog Display Mode item in the radio button list control is clicked:

```
Protected Sub rblMode_SelectedIndexChanged( _
            ByVal sender As Object, _
            ByVal e As System.EventArgs) _
            Handles rblMode.SelectedIndexChanged
    Select Case rblMode.SelectedIndex
        Case 0 : WebPartManager1.DisplayMode = _
                    WebPartManager.BrowseDisplayMode
        Case 1 : WebPartManager1.DisplayMode = _
                    WebPartManager.DesignDisplayMode
        Case 2 : WebPartManager1.DisplayMode = _
                    WebPartManager.CatalogDisplayMode
        Case 3 : WebPartManager1.DisplayMode = _
                    WebPartManager.EditDisplayMode
    End Select
End Sub
```

5. Press F5 to test the application. Click on the Edit Display Mode option. Note that there are no visual changes to the page.

6. Examine the top right corner of the Calendar Web Part. You will notice that there is now a new Edit link (see Figure 3-36). Click on the Edit link.

7. You should now see the EditorZone control. You can customize the appearance of the Web Part by modifying the properties in the AppearanceEditorPart and LayoutEditorPart controls (see Figure 3-37). Click OK.

TIP

Note that the PropertyGridEditorPart control is not displayed for this Web Part. You will learn more about the PropertyGridEditorPart control in the "What about..." section for this lab.

What about...

...displaying the PropertyGridEditorPart control?

Notice that in this lab the PropertyGridEditorPart control is not displayed when you switch the page to edit mode. So what is the use for this control? Let's explore this.

For the PropertyGridEditorPart control to appear, a Web Part must have public properties that are browsable (through the WebBrowsable

Untitled Page - Microsoft Internet Explorer
File Edit View Favorites Tools Help
WebPartZone1
Today's Date
February 2005
S M T W T F S
30 31 1 2 3 4 5
6 7 8 9 10 11 12
13 14 15 16 17 18 19
20 21 22 23 24 25 26
27 28 1 2 3 4 5
6 7 8 9 10 11 12
Minimize
Close
Edit
Edits 'Today's Date'
Google Search [1]
Google Search [2]

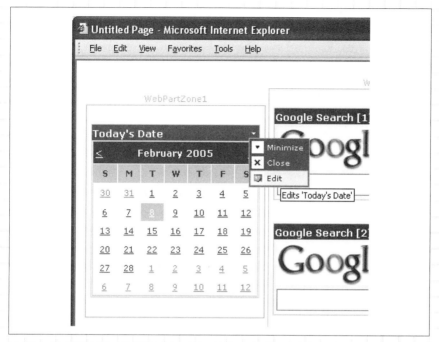

Figure 3-36. Editing a Web Part

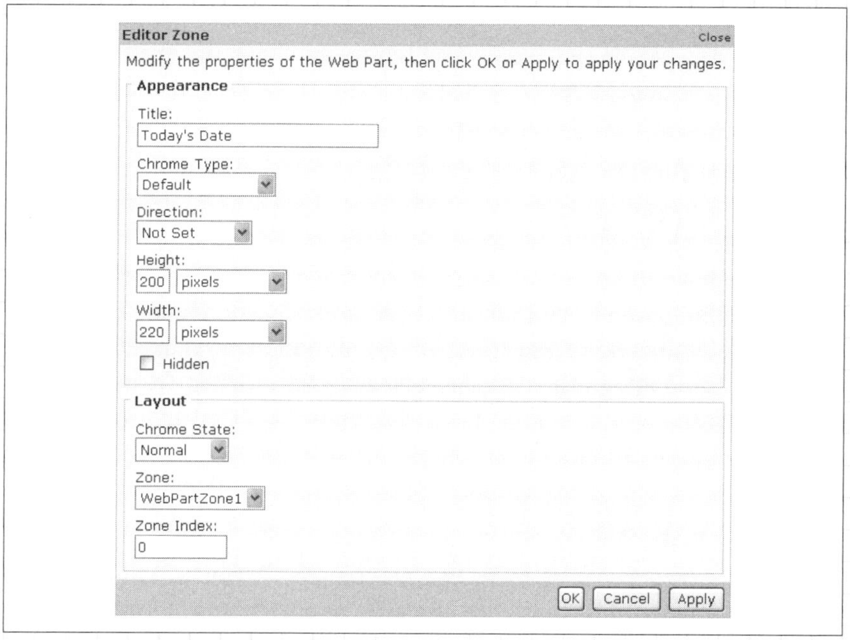

Editor Zone
Close
Modify the properties of the Web Part, then click OK or Apply to apply your changes.
Appearance
Title:
Today's Date
Chrome Type:
Default
Direction:
Not Set
Height:
200
pixels
Width:
220
pixels
Hidden
Layout
Chrome State:
Normal
Zone:
WebPartZone1
Zone Index:
0
OK
Cancel
Apply

Figure 3-37. Customizing the look and feel of a Web Part

attribute) and personalizable (through the Personalizable attribute). Web User controls do not support these properties, and hence only controls that inherit from WebPart can use the PropertyGridEditorPart control.

If you now edit the Translation Service Web Part, you will notice that the PropertyGridEditorPart control appears (see Figure 3-38). This is because the Translation Service Web Part has public and browsable properties:

```
<Personalizable(), WebBrowsable()> _
Public Property strToTranslate() As String
...
```

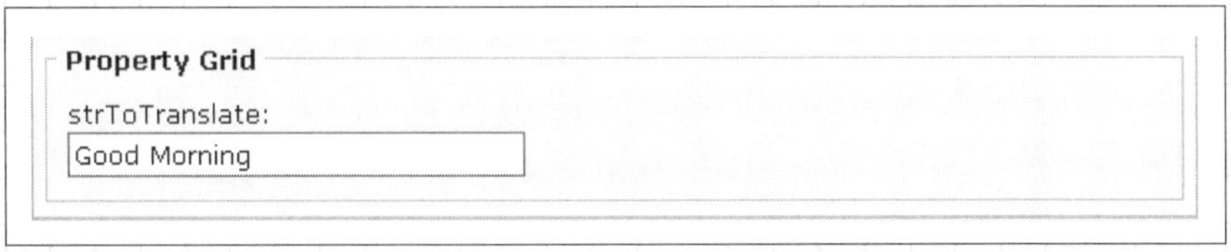

Figure 3-38. The PropertyGridEditorPart control

You can set a value for the public strToTranslate properties so that the next time the Translation Service Web Part is loaded, the value is shown by default.

Where can I learn more?

Check out the MSDN Help topic on "EditorPart Class" for more information on the various EditorPart controls.

Learn how the various Web Parts on a page can communicate with each other.

Enable Web Parts to Talk to Each Other

The various Web Parts on a page are not standalone islands of information. You can enable them to talk to each other by connecting them. This is useful in cases where you need to pass information obtained from one Web Part to another. For example, you may enter a Zip Code to obtain address information in a Web Part. The same Zip Code may be sent to another Web Part so that it can retrieve weather information.

How do I do that?

To illustrate how two Web Parts can be connected, you will first create a new Web User control that contains a Calendar control. When the user clicks a date in the Calendar control, the date selected will be sent to and displayed by the text box in the Google Web User control that you created in the "Add Web Parts to Your Application" lab.

1. Using the project created in the previous lab (*C:\ASPNET20\chap03-Webparts*), add a new class to the project (right-click the project name in Solution Explorer and select Add New Item..., then select Class) and name it *ISelectedDate.vb*.

2. Code the *ISelectedDate.vb* class as follows. The ISelectedDate interface would be implemented by both the connection provider (the *CalendarUC.ascx*) and provider consumer (*Google.ascx*). This interface serves as a contract for the communication between the provider and consumer:

```
Imports Microsoft.VisualBasic

Public Interface ISelectedDate
    ReadOnly Property SelectedDate() As Date
End Interface
```

3. Add a new Web User control to the project by right-clicking the project name (*C:\ASPNET20\chap03-Webparts*) in Solution Explorer, selecting Add New Item..., and then selecting Web User Control.

4. Name the Web User control project *CalendarUC.ascx*.

5. Populate *CalendarUC.ascx* with a Calendar control and apply the Simple scheme (via the Auto Format... link in the Calendar Tasks menu). The *CalendarUC.ascx* should now look like Figure 3-39.

Communications between Web Parts is based on the provider and consumer model. To ensure that a Web Part can receive data from another Web Part, the Web Part that is providing data must publish a contract specifying the type of data it is publishing. The Web Part consuming the data can then use this contract to obtain the data.

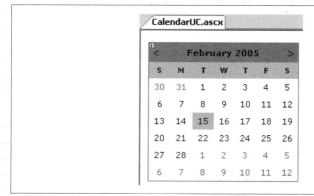

Figure 3-39. CalendarUC.ascx

6. Double-click on *CalendarUC.ascx* to switch to its code-behind, and add the following code to configure the Web User control as a provider:

```
Partial Class CalendarUC_ascx
    Inherits System.Web.UI.UserControl
    Implements ISelectedDate
```

```
Public ReadOnly Property SelectedDate() As Date _
      Implements ISelectedDate.SelectedDate
   Get
        Return Calendar1.SelectedDate.Date
   End Get
End Property

<ConnectionProvider("SelectedDate", "SelectedDate")> _
Public Function GetSelectedDate() As ISelectedDate
     Return Me
  End Function
End Class
```

The first parameter to the ConnectionProvider attribute assigns a
friendly name to the provider connection point. The second parameter assigns a unique ID to the provider connection point.

7. Essentially, you are implementing the ISelectedDate interface and
creating a provider connection point by using the ConnectionProvider attribute. You also implemented the SelectedDate property to
return the selected date in the Calendar control.

8. In the *Google.ascx* user control, add the following lines of code that
are shown in bold:

```
Partial Class Google_ascx
    Inherits System.Web.UI.UserControl

    Protected Sub btnSearch_Click(ByVal sender As Object, _
                                  ByVal e As System.EventArgs) _
                                  Handles btnSearch.Click
       Response.Write(Page.IsValid)
       Dim queryStr As String = HttpUtility.UrlEncode(txtSearch.Text)
       Response.Redirect("http://www.google.com/search?q=" & queryStr)
    End Sub

    Private _selectedDate As ISelectedDate

    <ConnectionConsumer("SelectedDate", "SelectedDate")> _
    Sub setSearchText(ByVal SearchText As ISelectedDate)
       Me._selectedDate = SearchText
    End Sub

    Protected Sub Page_PreRender(ByVal sender As Object, _
                                 ByVal e As System.EventArgs) _
                                 Handles Me.PreRender
       If _selectedDate IsNot Nothing Then
          txtSearch.Text +=
                        _selectedDate.SelectedDate.ToShortDateString
       End If
    End Sub
End Class
```

The first parameter to the ConnectionConsumer attribute assigns a friendly name to the consumer connection point. The second parameter assigns a unique ID to the consumer connection point.

9. Essentially, you are using the ConnectionConsumer attribute to define a consumer connection point, and allowing it to act as a receiver of the ISelectedDate interface. The date that is received is then appended to the text box in *Google.ascx* in the PreRender event of the Page class.

10. Add the *CalendarUC.ascx* Web User control to WebPartZone2 in *Default.aspx*. Ensure that they are named as shown in Figure 3-40 (the Google Web Part was added in the previous lab). Also, add the title attribute for the Calender Web User control:

```
<ZoneTemplate>
    <uc1:Google title="Google Search" runat="server"
                ID="Google1" />
    <uc3:CalendarUC title="Calendar Web Part" runat="server"
                    ID="CalendarUC1" />
</ZoneTemplate>
```

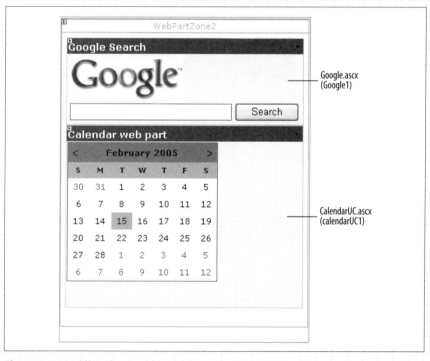

Figure 3-40. Adding the provider and consumer Web Parts to the page

11. To wire up the provider and consumer Web Parts, add the following static connections in *Default.aspx* under the WebPartManager control:

```
<asp:WebPartManager ID="WebPartManager1" runat="server">
    <StaticConnections>
        <asp:WebPartConnection ID="Connection"
            ProviderID="CalendarUC1"
            ProviderConnectionPointID="SelectedDate"
            ConsumerID="Google1"
            ConsumerConnectionPointID="SelectedDate" />
    </StaticConnections>
</asp:WebPartManager>
```

12. Press F5 to test the application. When you select a date in the Calendar control, notice that the text box in the Google Web Part will display the selected date (see Figure 3-41).

Figure 3-41. Connecting two Web Parts

What about...

...creating connections on the fly while the application is running?

In this lab, you learned how to statically connect two Web Parts together at design time. What happens if you need to connect a new Web Part (newly added to the page, for example) to another provider? In this case, you need to dynamically allow the user (not the developer) to create the connection.

The following steps will show how you can use the ConnectionsZone control to link two Web Parts together during runtime. The nice feature of this control is that there isn't much you need to do; it simply does the work for you.

1. Add the Google Web User control (*Google.ascx*) into WebPartZone2. There should now be two Google Search Web Parts and one Calendar Web Part (see Figure 3-42).

Figure 3-42. The Web Parts in WebPartZone2

2. Drag and drop the ConnectionsZone control (found under the Web-Parts tab in the Toolbox) onto *Default.aspx*. Apply the Classic scheme (see Figure 3-43) to the ConnectionsZone control (via the Auto Format... link in the ConnectionsZone Tasks menu).

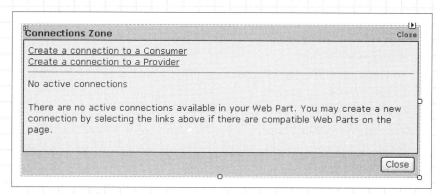

Figure 3-43. Applying the Classic scheme to the ConnectionsZone control

3. In the code-behind, add the following line (shown in bold) to the SelectedIndexChanged event of the radio button list control (see Figure 3-44). This will cause the ConnectionsZone control to be displayed when the Connect Display Mode item in the radio button list control is clicked:

```
Protected Sub rblMode_SelectedIndexChanged( _
            ByVal sender As Object, _
            ByVal e As System.EventArgs) _
            Handles rblMode.SelectedIndexChanged
    Select Case rblMode.SelectedIndex
        Case 0 : WebPartManager1.DisplayMode = _
                    WebPartManager.BrowseDisplayMode
        Case 1 : WebPartManager1.DisplayMode = _
                    WebPartManager.DesignDisplayMode
        Case 2 : WebPartManager1.DisplayMode = _
                    WebPartManager.CatalogDisplayMode
        Case 3 : WebPartManager1.DisplayMode = _
                    WebPartManager.EditDisplayMode
        Case 4 : WebPartManager1.DisplayMode = _
                    WebPartManager.ConnectDisplayMode
    End Select
End Sub
```

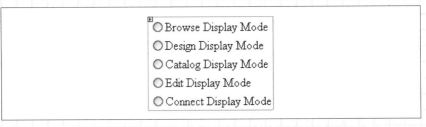

Figure 3-44. Adding the Connect Display Mode item to the radio button list control

4. To test the page, press F5. Click on the Connect Display Mode option in the radio button list control. Note that there is no visual change to the page.

5. Click on the top-right corner of the Google Search [2] Web Part. You will see that there is now a Connect link (see Figure 3-45). Click on the Connect link.

6. You will now see the Connections Zone (see Figure 3-46). Click on the "Create a connection to a Provider" link to connect the Google Search Web Part to another Web Part.

7. You can now select a provider connection for this Web Part. In the From: drop-down listbox, select "Calendar Web Part." Click Connect (see Figure 3-47).

Chapter 3: Web Parts

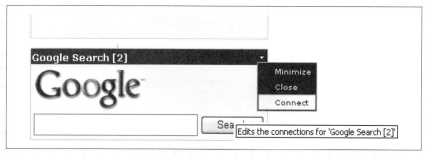

Figure 3-45. Configuring connection for a Web Part

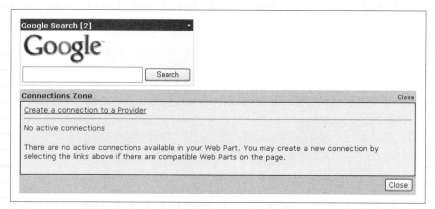

Figure 3-46. Creating a connection for a Web Part

Figure 3-47. Selecting a provider connection

8. You will now notice that the two Google Search Web Parts are connected to the Calendar Web Part (see Figure 3-48).

9. To dislodge the connection, click on the Disconnect button in the Connections Zone (see Figure 3-49).

Figure 3-48. Connecting the two Google Search Web Parts to the Calendar Web Part

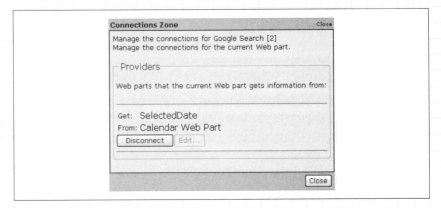

Figure 3-49. Disconnecting a connection

Where can I learn more?

To learn more about how Web Parts and cross-page connections work, check out the following useful discussion: *http://www.nikhilk.net/ CrossPageConnections.aspx.*

Data Access

Data access is one of the most common tasks that you're likely to perform when you write web applications. This is made evident by the number of new data controls that ship with Visual Studio 2005. Most visible in ASP.NET 2.0 is the new GridView control, which is a much improved version of the venerable DataGrid control (the older DataGrid control is still supported in ASP.NET 2.0, though). In addition, ASP.NET 2.0 ships with several new data source controls that make it easier to consume a variety of data sources.

In this chapter, you will learn how to use the various new data controls—GridView, DetailsView, and DataList—together with new data source controls such as SqlDataSource, ObjectDataSource, and XmlDataSource. With each of these controls, data access is now much easier than before, and you can spend your time writing business logic instead of data access plumbing.

Display Data in a Table

If you've done serious ASP.NET programming you've probably used the DataGrid control. DataGrid is a very powerful and flexible control for displaying structured data from a data source such as a database. However, when it comes to manipulating the content of a DataGrid control, such as editing the rows or simply sorting the columns of a table, you need to write a moderate amount of code to customize it.

This is where the GridView control comes in handy. Instead of requiring you to write code to perform such common functions as editing or displaying rows in multiple pages, the GridView control now accomplishes the same tasks as the DataGrid control, but with much less coding and work.

The GridView control can be found in the Toolbox under the Data tab (see Figure 4-1).

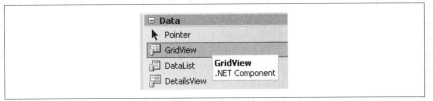

Figure 4-1. The GridView control

How do I do that?

To see how powerful and configurable the GridView control is, let's create a page that contains a drop-down listbox and a GridView control. We'll use the pubs sample database (that comes with SQL Server 2000) together with SQL Server 2005 Express to populate the drop-down listbox with a list of the states where the authors in the database live. When a user selects a state, the GridView control will display the names of all the authors who live there.

TIP

SQL Server 2005 Express does not ship with the pubs and North-wind sample databases, but you can install them by downloading their installation scripts at *http://www.microsoft.com/downloads/search.aspx?displaylang=en*.

Once the scripts are installed on your system, go to the Visual Studio 2005 command prompt (Start → Programs → Microsoft Visual Studio 2005 → Visual Studio Tools → Visual Studio 2005 Command Prompt) and type in the following to install the pubs and Northwind databases (assuming your installation scripts are stored in *C:*):

```
C:\>sqlcmd -S .\SQLEXPRESS -i instpubs.sql
C:\>sqlcmd -S .\SQLEXPRESS -i instnwnd.sql
```

---

1. Launch Visual Studio 2005 and create a new web site project. Name the project *C:\ASPNET20\Chap04-GridView*.

2. Drag and drop the DropDownList control from the Toolbox into the default Web Form.

3. On the DropDownList Tasks menu, click the Choose Data Source... link to select a data source to populate the items in the control (see Figure 4-2).

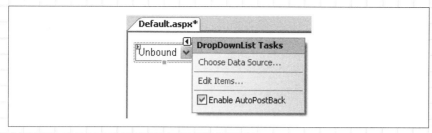

Figure 4-2. Configuring the DropDownList control

4. The Data Source Configuration Wizard dialog will appear. In the "Select a data source" drop-down list, select <New data source…> to create a new connection to a data source (see Figure 4-3).

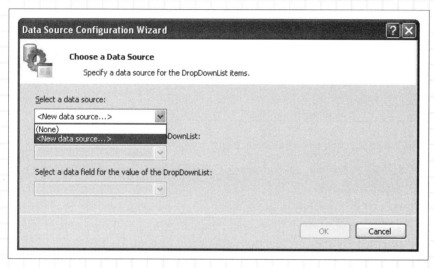

Figure 4-3. Creating a new data source

5. In the "Where will the application get data from" section, select Database and click OK (see Figure 4-4). Use the default name SqlDataSource1 as the ID for the data source.

TIP

The Database data source type can connect to any SQL database (such as Oracle), not just SQL Server.

You use the SqlDataSource control to declaratively establish a connection to a SQL data source without writing any code. In the days of

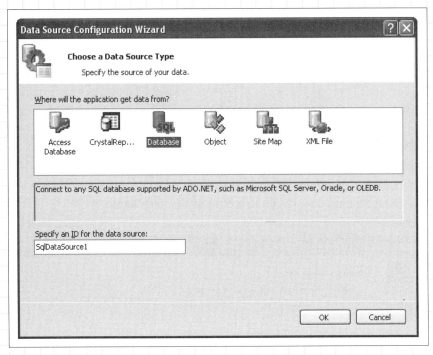

Figure 4-4. Selecting a new data source type

ASP.NET 1.x, you had to write elaborate code to access data sources using ADO.NET.

In ASP.NET 2.0, you now have data source controls that encapsulate all the logic needed to access a data source. (I will discuss the rest of the data source controls throughout this chapter.)

6. Click the New Connection... button to establish a connection to the database you want to use (see Figure 4-5).

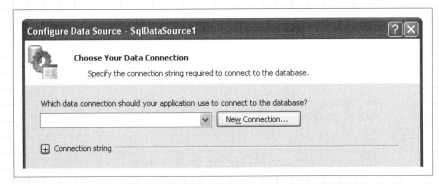

Figure 4-5. Creating a new data connection

7. You will be asked to select the type of data source you want to connect to. Select SQL Server to connect to a SQL Server 2005 Express database (see Figure 4-6). Click Continue.

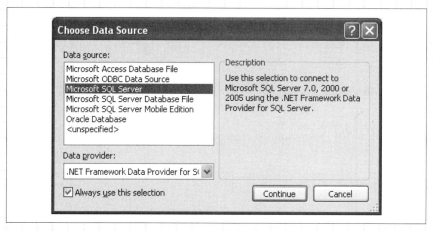

Figure 4-6. Specifying the new data connection properties

8. Specify the database server information as well as the database to use (see Figure 4-7). For this example, use the pubs database. Click the Test Connection button to verify that the connection can be established. Click OK.

9. You should now see the data connection that you have selected (*winxp2\sqlexpress.pubs.dbo*). Click Next (see Figure 4-8).

10. You will be asked if you want to save the database connection in the application configuration file (*Web.config*). This is the preferred option because it allows you to modify your database server settings without modifying your code. This is especially useful after you have deployed your application. To save the connection string in *Web.config*, use the suggested pubsConnectionString and ensure that the "Yes, save this connection as:" checkbox is selected. Click Next (see Figure 4-9).

TIP

It is a good practice to save your connection string in the *Web.config* file so that any changes to the database can be modified easily.

---

11. You can now select the database fields you want to use. You can either specify a custom SQL statement (or use a stored procedure), or make use of the checkboxes to select the fields you want. For this

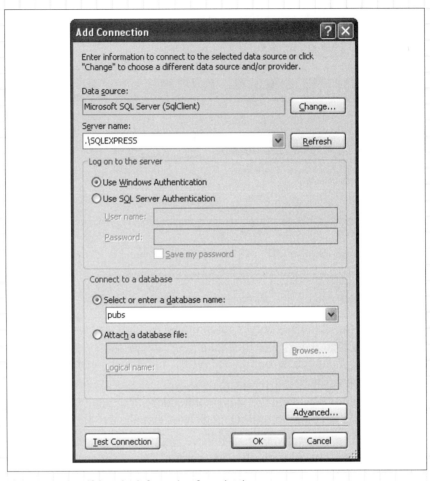

Figure 4-7. Specifying the information for a database server

example, select the "Specify columns from a table or view" radio button and select the authors table. Select the state and "Return only unique rows" checkboxes. Click Next (see Figure 4-10).

12. You can now test your query. Click Test Query to see the results returned from your selection. Click Finish (see Figure 4-11). You should now see a list of states.

13. Finally, configure the DropDownList control to use the data source that you have just created. Select SqlDataSource1 as the data source and select state as the field to display, as well as the value to use for the DropDownList control. Click OK (see Figure 4-12).

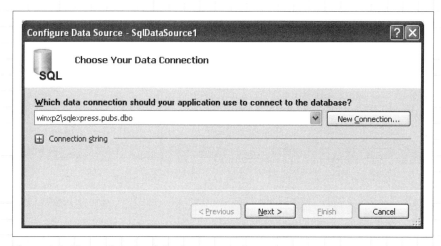

Figure 4-8. The newly created database connection

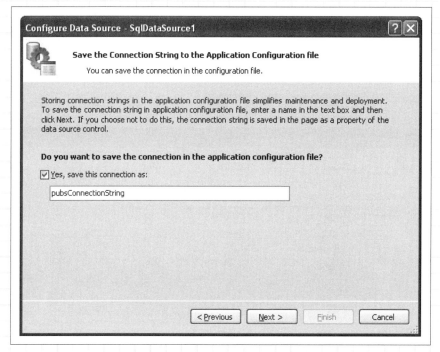

Figure 4-9. Saving the connection string in Web.config

14. Your page should now look like Figure 4-13. A SqlDataSource control is created for you.

15. Press F5 to test the application. You should see the DropDownList control displaying a list of states that all the authors live in (see Figure 4-14).

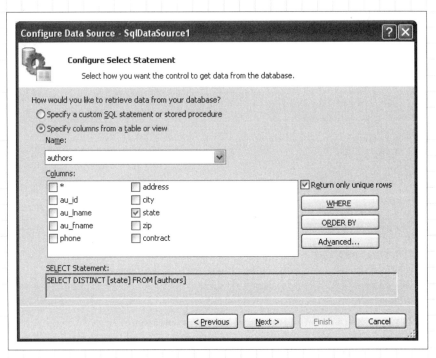

Figure 4-10. Configuring the Select statement

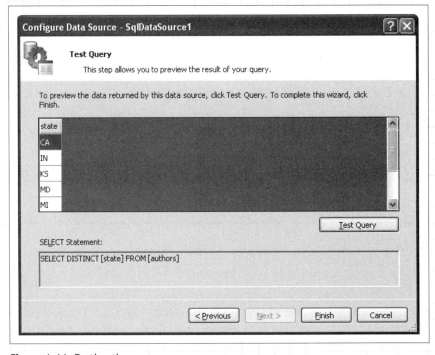

Figure 4-11. Testing the query

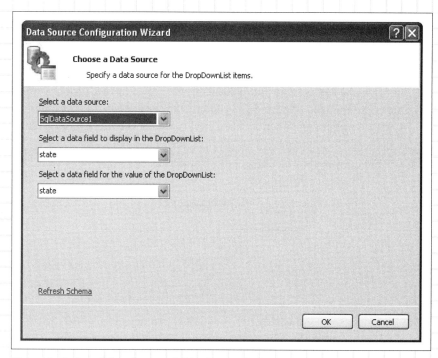

Figure 4-12. Specifying the data field value for display and binding

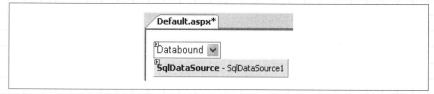

Figure 4-13. The SqlDataSource control

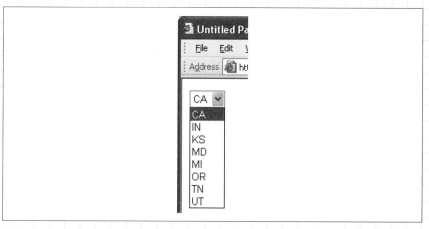

Figure 4-14. Listing all the states in the DropDownList control

In the next series of steps, you will add a GridView control to the Web Form so that when a state is selected from the DropDownList control, all of the authors that live in that selected state will be displayed in an orderly way.

Remember to set the AutoPostBack property of the ListBox control so that a postback is performed when an item within the ListBox is selected.

1. First, check the Enable AutoPostBack checkbox in the DropDownList Tasks menu (see Figure 4-15). Doing so will cause a postback to occur whenever the item in the DropDownList control is changed, so that the GridView control can display the related records.

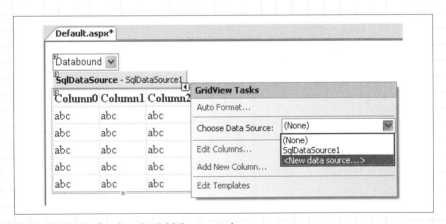

Figure 4-15. Enabling a postback to occur when the item in the DropDownList control is changed

2. Next, drag and drop a GridView control (found in the Toolbox under the Data tab) onto the form.

3. In the GridView Tasks menu, select a new data source (see Figure 4-16). You will configure a new SqlDataSource control to retrieve rows from the pubs table based on the selection in the Drop-DownList control.

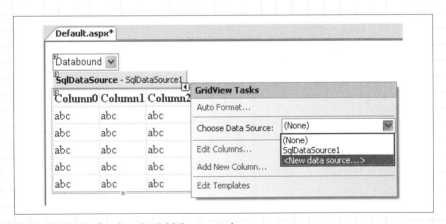

Figure 4-16. Configuring the GridView control

4. You will be asked to choose the data source type (choose `Database`) as well as the database connection to use (use the one configured earlier, `pubsConnectionString`).

5. You should now see the window shown in Figure 4-17. Check the "Specify columns from a table or view" option and select the asterisk (*) checkbox. You will display all the fields in the authors table. Click the WHERE button to customize the SQL statement to retrieve only authors from a particular state.

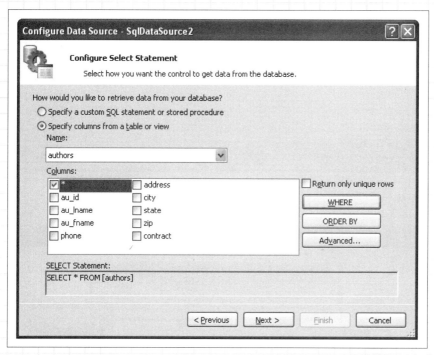

Figure 4-17. Specifying an SQL statement for use with the control

6. In the Add WHERE Clause window, select the options as shown in Figure 4-18. Basically, you specify that the state field (in the SQL statement) must match the value of the DropDownList control. Click Add and the following SQL expression will be shown in the "WHERE clause" box:

    ```
    SELECT * FROM [authors] WHERE ([state] = @state)
    ```

7. Click OK in the Add WHERE Clause window. You can now test the connection. Click Test Query and you will be prompted to give a value to the state field. Enter `CA` to see a list of authors from California (see Figure 4-19).

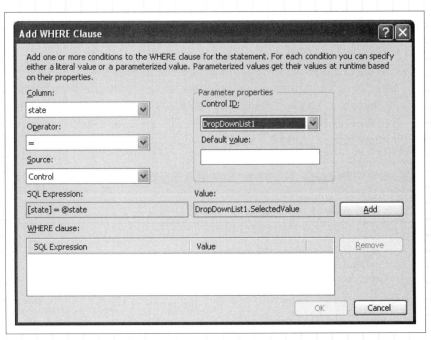

Figure 4-18. Specifying a parameter in the SQL statement

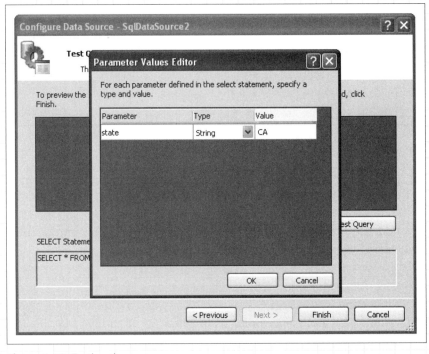

Figure 4-19. Testing the query

8. Click Finish to complete the configuration (see Figure 4-20). A new SqlDataSource control (SqlDataSource2) will be created.

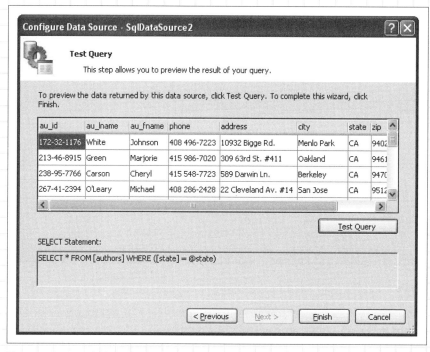

Figure 4-20. Retrieving the list of authors from California

9. Press F5 to test your application. When you select a state from the DropDownList control, the GridView control should display the list of authors who live in that state (see Figure 4-21).

What about...

...configuring the DropDownList control declaratively?

By all means! One of the nice features of ASP.NET 2.0 is that, within the *Web.config* files, you can declaratively execute all the cool things you can do with its wizards. In fact, after a while, you may find that configuring the controls declaratively is a much more efficient way of developing your application.

So, instead of using the wizard to create a database connection string for you, you can simply add the <connectionStrings> element to your *Web.config* file. The following connection string, pubsConnectionString,

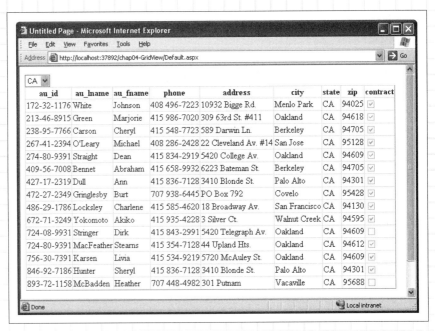

Figure 4-21. The GridView control in action

connects to SQL Server Express 2005 on the local computer and uses integrated security to access the pubs database:

```xml
<?xml version="1.0"?>
<configuration
  xmlns="http://schemas.microsoft.com/.NetConfiguration/
  v2.0">
   <appSettings/>
      <connectionStrings>
         <add name="pubsConnectionString" connectionString=
                   "Data Source=.\SQLEXPRESS;Initial
                   Catalog=pubs; Integrated
                   Security=True" providerName=
                   "System.Data.SqlClient"/>
      </connectionStrings>
      <system.web>
      ...
      ...
      </system.web>
</configuration>
```

To establish a connection to the pubs database, you can use the SqlDataSource control. You can configure the SqlDataSource control to use the connection string defined in *Web.config* by specifying the following in the Source View of the form:

```
<asp:SqlDataSource
    ID="SqlDataSource1" runat="server"
```

```
    SelectCommand="SELECT DISTINCT [state] FROM [authors]"
    ConnectionString=
        "<%$ ConnectionStrings:pubsConnectionString %>">
</asp:SqlDataSource>
```
To display the records in the pubs database, bind a DropDownList control to
the SqlDataSource control through the DataSourceID attribute:
```
<asp:DropDownList ID="DropDownList1" runat="server"
    DataSourceID="SqlDataSource1"
    DataTextField="state"
    DataValueField="state">
</asp:DropDownList
```
You can also bind the SqlDataSource and DropDownList controls pro-
grammatically, like this:
```
DropDownList1.DataSource = SqlDataSource1
DropDownList1.DataBind( )
```

...formatting the GridView control to give it a professional look?

Most certainly. The GridView control comes with a few themes that you
can apply. To apply a theme to the GridView control, select the Auto Format... link in the GridView Tasks menu (see Figure 4-22).

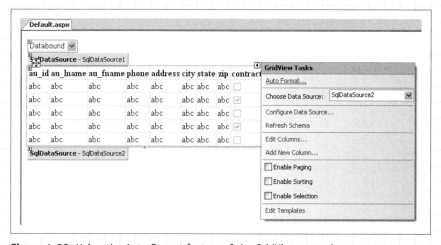

Figure 4-22. Using the Auto Format feature of the GridView control

Figures 4-23 and 4-24 show the Professional and Sand & Sky themes
applied to the GridView control.

Where can I learn more?

We have barely touched the surface of the GridView control. Be sure to
check out the MSDN Help topic on "GridView Class" for the list of properties and methods exposed by the GridView control.

au_id	au_lname	au_fname	phone	address	city	state	zip	contract
172-32-1176	White	Johnson	408 496-7223	10932 Bigge Rd.	Menlo Park	CA	94025	☑
213-46-8915	Green	Marjorie	415 986-7020	309 63rd St. #411	Oakland	CA	94618	☑
238-95-7766	Carson	Cheryl	415 548-7723	589 Darwin Ln.	Berkeley	CA	94705	☑
267-41-2394	O'Leary	Michael	408 286-2428	22 Cleveland Av. #14	San Jose	CA	95128	☑
274-80-9391	Straight	Dean	415 834-2919	5420 College Av.	Oakland	CA	94609	☑
409-56-7008	Bennet	Abraham	415 658-9932	6223 Bateman St.	Berkeley	CA	94705	☑
427-17-2319	Dull	Ann	415 836-7128	3410 Blonde St.	Palo Alto	CA	94301	☑
472-27-2349	Gringlesby	Burt	707 938-6445	PO Box 792	Covelo	CA	95428	☑
486-29-1786	Locksley	Charlene	415 585-4620	18 Broadway Av.	San Francisco	CA	94130	☑
672-71-3249	Yokomoto	Akiko	415 935-4228	3 Silver Ct.	Walnut Creek	CA	94595	☑
724-08-9931	Stringer	Dirk	415 843-2991	5420 Telegraph Av.	Oakland	CA	94609	☐
724-80-9391	MacFeather	Stearns	415 354-7128	44 Upland Hts.	Oakland	CA	94612	☑
756-30-7391	Karsen	Livia	415 534-9219	5720 McAuley St.	Oakland	CA	94609	☑
846-92-7186	Hunter	Sheryl	415 836-7128	3410 Blonde St.	Palo Alto	CA	94301	☑
893-72-1158	McBadden	Heather	707 448-4982	301 Putnam	Vacaville	CA	95688	☐

Figure 4-23. The Professional theme applied to the GridView control

au_id	au_lname	au_fname	phone	address	city	state	zip	contract
172-32-1176	White	Johnson	408 496-7223	10932 Bigge Rd.	Menlo Park	CA	94025	☑
213-46-8915	Green	Marjorie	415 986-7020	309 63rd St. #411	Oakland	CA	94618	☑
238-95-7766	Carson	Cheryl	415 548-7723	589 Darwin Ln.	Berkeley	CA	94705	☑
267-41-2394	O'Leary	Michael	408 286-2428	22 Cleveland Av. #14	San Jose	CA	95128	☑
274-80-9391	Straight	Dean	415 834-2919	5420 College Av.	Oakland	CA	94609	☑
409-56-7008	Bennet	Abraham	415 658-9932	6223 Bateman St.	Berkeley	CA	94705	☑
427-17-2319	Dull	Ann	415 836-7128	3410 Blonde St.	Palo Alto	CA	94301	☑
472-27-2349	Gringlesby	Burt	707 938-6445	PO Box 792	Covelo	CA	95428	☑
486-29-1786	Locksley	Charlene	415 585-4620	18 Broadway Av.	San Francisco	CA	94130	☑
672-71-3249	Yokomoto	Akiko	415 935-4228	3 Silver Ct.	Walnut Creek	CA	94595	☑
724-08-9931	Stringer	Dirk	415 843-2991	5420 Telegraph Av.	Oakland	CA	94609	☐
724-80-9391	MacFeather	Stearns	415 354-7128	44 Upland Hts.	Oakland	CA	94612	☑
756-30-7391	Karsen	Livia	415 534-9219	5720 McAuley St.	Oakland	CA	94609	☑
846-92-7186	Hunter	Sheryl	415 836-7128	3410 Blonde St.	Palo Alto	CA	94301	☑
893-72-1158	McBadden	Heather	707 448-4982	301 Putnam	Vacaville	CA	95688	☐

Figure 4-24. The Sand & Sky theme applied to the GridView control

Sort and View Records on Multiple Pages

Want to make the GridView control display records in multiple pages? Tick a checkbox and consider it done!

By default, the GridView control will display all the records in its data set on a single page. If you have a large number of records to display, this is not a very elegant way to display your data. For example, you might want to display all the employees in your company. If you have large list of names to display, it is much neater and more efficient to display the list in multiple pages. You might also want the names to be displayed in alphabetical order, or to allow the user to jump to a particular page.

You can now perform all of these functions in the GridView control by simply selecting some checkboxes. There is no need to write lengthy code to do any of these mundane tasks.

How do I do that?

To see how easy it is to configure the GridView control to display records in multiple pages and to allow sorting of fields, you will use the Grid-View control created in the last lab and configure it to perform these additional functions.

1. Using the project created in the last lab, you will now configure the GridView control so that the data is displayed in multiple pages.

2. In the GridView Tasks menu of the GridView control, select the following checkboxes (see Figure 4-25):

   Enable Paging
   Displays the data in multiple pages

   Enable Sorting
   Allows the data to be sorted by fields

   Enable Selection
   Enables rows to be selected

TIP

The Enable Selection option is useful when you need to explicitly select a row in the GridView control. For example, you might want to select a row in the GridView control so that the detailed information in the row can be displayed in another GridView control.

If a GridView is configured to allow selection, the SelectedIndex-Changed event of the GridView control will be fired when the user selects a row in the control.

---

3. The GridView control will now look like the one shown in Figure 4-26.

4. To make the GridView control look nicer, apply the Sand & Sky theme (via the Auto Format... link in the GridView Tasks menu).

5. Press F5 to test the application (see Figure 4-27). You can now sort the rows by field (by clicking on the field name in the GridView

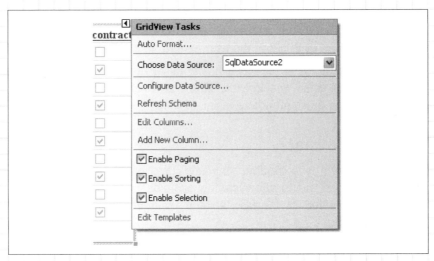

Figure 4-25. Enabling paging, sorting, and selecting for the GridView control

	au_id	au_lname	au_fname	phone	address	city	state	zip	contract
Select	abc	abc	abc	abc	abc	abc	abc	abc	☐
Select	abc	abc	abc	abc	abc	abc	abc	abc	☑
Select	abc	abc	abc	abc	abc	abc	abc	abc	☐
Select	abc	abc	abc	abc	abc	abc	abc	abc	☑
Select	abc	abc	abc	abc	abc	abc	abc	abc	☐
Select	abc	abc	abc	abc	abc	abc	abc	abc	☑
Select	abc	abc	abc	abc	abc	abc	abc	abc	☐
Select	abc	abc	abc	abc	abc	abc	abc	abc	☑
Select	abc	abc	abc	abc	abc	abc	abc	abc	☐
Select	abc	abc	abc	abc	abc	abc	abc	abc	☑

1 2

Figure 4-26. The GridView control after the configuration

control), select a particular row (by clicking on the Select link), as well as display the data in multiple pages.

TIP

GridView supports client-side paging and sorting, all without needing to refresh the page. To do so, set the EnableSortingAndPaging-Callbacks property of the GridView control to True. This feature uses the Client Callback manager, which is new in ASP.NET 2.0.

For more information on the Client Callback manager, see Chapter 6.

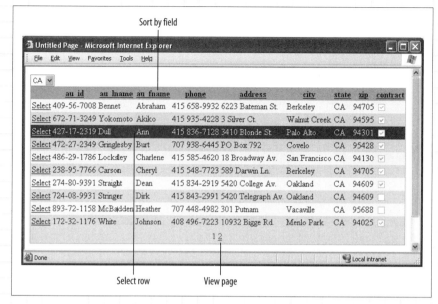

Figure 4-27. The GridView control with sortable fields, selectable rows, and multiple pages

What about...

...modifying the Paging UI of the GridView control?

The Paging UI of the GridView control refers to the links that are displayed to allow users to navigate from one page to another. If your GridView control is going to display multiple pages, you can customize the texts displayed in the Paging UI. The Mode property (within the PagerSettings property) of the GridView control allows you to display pages in different formats. The Mode property can take any one of the following values:

NextPrevious
  Displays the Next and Previous symbols; e.g., < >

Numeric
  Displays the page number; e.g., 1 2 3 4 ...

NextPreviousFirstLast
  Displays the Next, Previous, First and Last symbols; e.g., << < > >>

NumericFirstLast
  Displays the page number as well as the First and Last symbols; e.g.,
  << ... 4 5 6 ... >>

The PagerSettings property also exposes the following properties:

- FirstPageText
- NextPageText
- PageButtonCount
- Position
- PreviousPageText

Figure 4-28 shows how the various properties configure the paging UI of the GridView control.

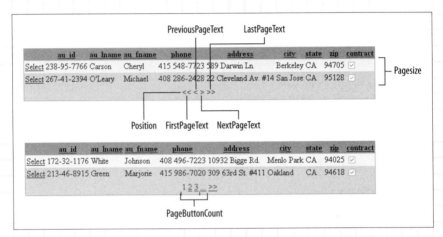

Figure 4-28. The properties in the GridView control affecting the paging UI

In addition, you can use images for navigation purposes using the following properties (simply set these properties to point to the path containing the images to be used):

- FirstPageImageUrl
- LastPageImageUrl
- PreviousPageImageUrl
- NextPageImageUrl

Where can I learn more?

If you want to learn how paging and sorting works in the old DataGrid, check out the DataGrid Girl site (*http://datagridgirl.com/*), a popular site that covers all things DataGrid. Who knows, after visiting that site you might be even be more impressed with the GridView control!

Edit and Delete Records

Apart from simply displaying records in the GridView control, you can also allow users to edit or delete records directly while they're being viewed. Unlike the old DataGrid, the new GridView control makes editing and deleting records very simple. And with the wizards to help you configure the GridView control, your life as a developer could not be simpler.

Let users edit and delete records in the GridView control.

How do I do that?

In the previous lab, you saw how GridView binds to the SqlDataSource control. You have also seen how rows can be sorted automatically without requiring you to write code to do it and how records can be displayed in multiple pages. In this lab, you'll go one step further. You will see how you can configure the GridView control for editing and deleting records.

1. Using the project built in the previous lab, you will now configure the SqlDataSource2 control (which was bound to the GridView control) so that it supports the editing and deletion of records.

2. In the SqlDataSource Tasks menu of SqlDataSource2, click the Configure Data Source... link (see Figure 4-29).

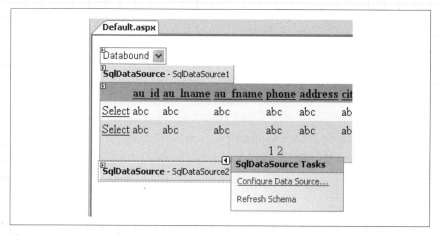

Figure 4-29. Configuring the SqlDataSource2 control

3. Click Next in the following window and then, in the Configure Select Statement window, click on Advanced.... Check the "Generate Insert, Update, and Delete statements" checkbox to generate the appropriate SQL statements to perform modifications to the table (see Figure 4-30). To prevent concurrency conflicts, check the "Use optimistic concurrency" checkbox, too. Click OK.

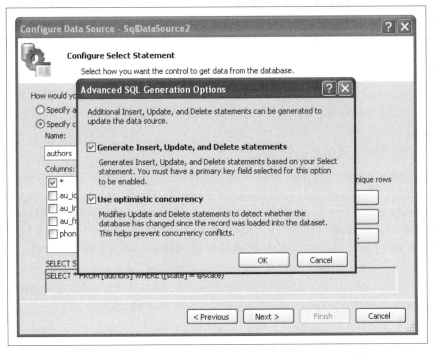

Figure 4-30. Generating the appropriate SQL statements to perform modifications to the table

4. Back in the Configure Select Statement window, click Next and then Finish in the next window.

5. To allow the GridView control to support editing and deleting of records, select the Enable Editing and Enable Deleting checkboxes in the GridView Tasks menu (see Figure 4-31).

6. Press F5 to test the application. You will now be able to edit or delete records (see Figure 4-32) by clicking the Edit and Update links.

What about...

...resolving concurrency conflicts?

Recall that in Figure 4-30 you checked the "Use optimistic concurrency" checkbox. By selecting this checkbox, the SqlDataSource control will detect any changes to the table before an update is performed. Consider a case in which two users are both trying to update the same record. If one user has updated the record, the other user will detect that the original values have been changed when he tries to update the same record, and the update will not be successful.

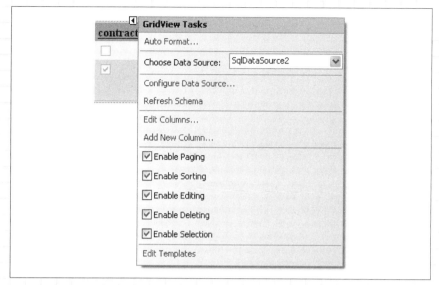

Figure 4-31. Checking the Enable Editing and Enable Deleting checkboxes

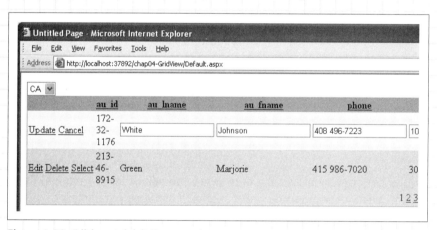

Figure 4-32. Editing and deleting records

If you switch to Source View, you will notice that the SqlDataSource control has acquired a number of new elements and attributes. In particular, the DeleteCommand, InsertCommand, and UpdateCommand attributes take care of the tasks of deleting, inserting, and editing records in the database. Their syntax is shown in Example 4-1.

Example 4-1. DeleteCommand, InsertCommand, and UpdateCommand

```
DeleteCommand="DELETE FROM [authors]
        WHERE [au_id] = @original_au_id
        AND [au_lname] = @original_au_lname
        AND [au_fname] = @original_au_fname
```

Example 4-1. DeleteCommand, InsertCommand, and UpdateCommand (continued)

```
                   AND [phone] = @original_phone
                   AND [address] = @original_address
                   AND [city] = @original_city
                   AND [state] = @original_state
                   AND [zip] = @original_zip
                   AND [contract] = @original_contract"

InsertCommand="INSERT INTO [authors] ([au_id], [au_lname],
                   [au_fname], [phone], [address], [city],
                   [state], [zip], [contract]) VALUES (@au_id,
                   @au_lname, @au_fname, @phone, @address,
                   @city, @state, @zip, @contract)"

UpdateCommand="UPDATE [authors] SET [au_lname] = @au_lname,
                   [au_fname] = @au_fname, [phone] = @phone,
                   [address] = @address, [city] = @city,
                   [state] = @state, [zip] = @zip,
                   [contract] = @contract
                   WHERE
                   [au_id] = @original_au_id
                   AND [au_lname] = @original_au_lname
                   AND [au_fname] = @original_au_fname
                   AND [phone] = @original_phone
                   AND [address] = @original_address
                   AND [city] = @original_city
                   AND [state] = @original_state
                   AND [zip] = @original_zip
                   AND [contract] = @original_contract"

ConflictDetection="CompareAllValues"
```

The SQL statements are structured so that they can detect concurrency issues. As an example, consider the UpdateCommand statement. An update can be performed successfully only when the values for the original fields are the same (checked using the @original_fieldname parameter).

To implement the "First-One Wins" strategy, you need to set the Conflict-Detection attribute to CompareAllValues.

The update conflict resolution strategy in which the first user to update a record wins is called "First-One Wins."

The <updateParameters> element keeps track of the old values of each field:

```
<UpdateParameters>
  <asp:Parameter Type="String" Name="au_lname" />
  <asp:Parameter Type="String" Name="au_fname" />
  <asp:Parameter Type="String" Name="phone" />
  <asp:Parameter Type="String" Name="address" />
  <asp:Parameter Type="String" Name="city" />
  <asp:Parameter Type="String" Name="state" />
  <asp:Parameter Type="String" Name="zip" />
  <asp:Parameter Type="Boolean" Name="contract" />
  <asp:Parameter Type="String" Name="original_au_id" />
```

```
        <asp:Parameter Type="String" Name="original_au_lname" />
        <asp:Parameter Type="String" Name="original_au_fname" />
        <asp:Parameter Type="String" Name="original_phone" />
        <asp:Parameter Type="String" Name="original_address" />
        <asp:Parameter Type="String" Name="original_city" />
        <asp:Parameter Type="String" Name="original_state" />
        <asp:Parameter Type="String" Name="original_zip" />
        <asp:Parameter Type="Boolean" Name="original_contract" />
    </UpdateParameters>
```

Note that the old value of each parameter is prefixed with the string "original_". You can change this value by setting the OldValuesParameterFormatString property of the SqlDataSource control.

...handling errors in updating?

If you try to update a record in the GridView control and an error occurs, you can trap this error via the RowUpdated event, like this:

```
Protected Sub GridView1_RowUpdated(_
                ByVal sender As Object, _
                ByVal e As System.Web.UI.WebControls. _
                        GridViewUpdatedEventArgs) _
                Handles GridView1.RowUpdated
    If e.Exception IsNot Nothing Then
        Response.Write("Error in updating record.")
        e.ExceptionHandled = True
    End If
End Sub
```

Where can I learn more?

To learn how to handle concurrency issues in .NET, check out the article at *http://www.15seconds.com/issue/030604.htm*.

To learn how to service the event fired by the GridView control before a record is deleted, check out the MSDN Help topic "GridView.RowDeleting Event."

Display One Record at a Time

Besides the GridView control, there is another new control that is similar to it but presents a slightly different view. Instead of displaying multiple records on one page, the DetailsView control displays one record at a time. The DetailsView control is located in the Toolbox on the Data tab (see Figure 4-33).

The GridView control comes with the companion DetailsView control, which displays one record at a time.

How do I do that?

To see how the DetailsView control differs from the GridView control, you will replace the GridView control created in the previous lab with a

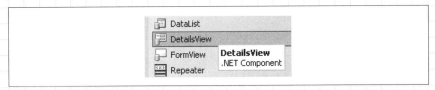

Figure 4-33. The DetailsView control

DetailsView control. You will also see how the DetailsView control allows new records to be inserted into the database, which is not allowed in the GridView control.

1. Using the project created in the previous lab, replace the GridView control with the DetailsView control in the default form.

2. Apply the Mocha theme to the DetailsView control (via the Auto Format... link in the DetailsView Tasks menu).

3. In the DetailsView Tasks menu, select SqlDataSource2 as its data source and select the following checkboxes (see Figure 4-34):

   - Enable Paging
   - Enable Inserting
   - Enable Editing
   - Enable Deleting

   The checkboxes available are dependent on how the data source is configured. For example, Enable Editing and Enable Deleting are available only if the data source that is being used supports them. If you have configured your data source to support Inserting as well, there is also an Enable Inserting checkbox.

4. Press F5 to test the application. Figure 4-35 shows the DetailsView in action. You can also edit and insert new records.

TIP

By default the GridView and DetailsView controls use the field name of the table as header text. For example, you see au_id and au_fname used as the header for both the GridView and DetailsView controls in this and previous labs.

To customize the header text of a DetailsView control, click on the Edit Fields... link in the DetailsView Tasks menu and then configure it in the Fields dialog (see Figure 4-36) via the HeaderText property.

To customize the header text of a GridView control, click on the Edit Columns... link in the GridView Tasks menu and then configure it in the Fields dialog via the HeaderText property.

Chapter 4: Data Access

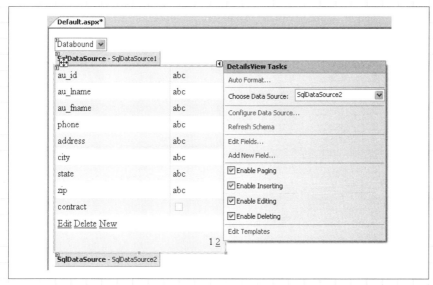

Figure 4-34. Enabling the DetailsView control for paging, inserting, editing, and deleting

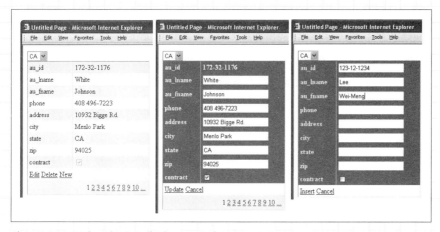

Figure 4-35. Using the DetailsView control

What about...

...creating a Master/Detail view of records in a table?

The GridView and DetailsView controls together make a good pair of controls for displaying a Master/Detail view of records. For example, the GridView control could display all the employee IDs, and clicking on a particular employee ID could trigger the DetailsView control to display the details of the selected employee.

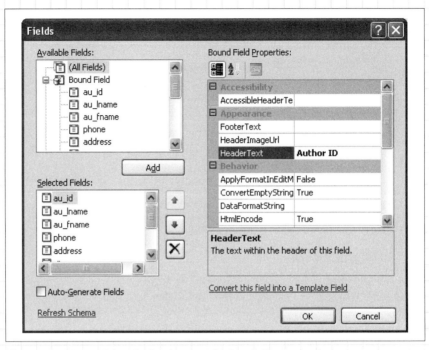

Figure 4-36. Customizing the header text of a DetailsView control

To create a Master/Detail view, follow these steps:

1. Add a new Web Form to the project and name it *Default2.aspx*.

2. Add a 2 × 1 table to the Web Form (Layout → Insert Table), and add a GridView control to the left cell of the table and a DetailsView control to the right cell of the table (see Figure 4-37).

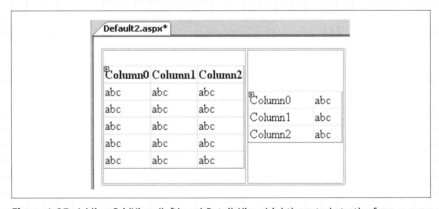

Figure 4-37. Adding GridView (left) and DetailsView (right) controls to the form

3. Configure the GridView control to bind to a new SqlDataSource control and retrieve the au_id field from the authors table in the pubs database (see the lab "Display Data in a Table" for detailed instruction on how to do this). The Source View of the GridView control and the newly created SqlDataSource control now looks like Example 4-2.

TIP

For this example, I strongly suggest you download the sample code from *http://www.oreilly.com/catalog/aspnetadn/*.

Example 4-2. Source View of the GridView and SqlDataSource controls

```
<asp:GridView ID="GridView1" runat="server"
    Width="158px"
    DataSourceID="SqlDataSource1"
    AutoGenerateColumns="False"
    DataKeyNames="au_id"
    AllowPaging="True"
    PageSize="4"
    AllowSorting="True">
  <Columns>
    <asp:CommandField ShowSelectButton="True">
    </asp:CommandField>
    <asp:BoundField ReadOnly="True"
        HeaderText="au_id"
        DataField="au_id"
        SortExpression="au_id">
    </asp:BoundField>
  </Columns>
</asp:GridView>

<asp:SqlDataSource ID="SqlDataSource1" runat="server"
    SelectCommand="SELECT [au_id] FROM [authors]"
    ConnectionString="<%$ ConnectionStrings:
                        pubsConnectionString %>">
</asp:SqlDataSource>
```

4. Configure the DetailsView control to bind to a new SqlDataSource control and retrieve all the fields from the authors table in the pubs database. In particular, the au_id field is dependent on the record selected in the GridView control (see Figure 4-38).

5. The Source View of the DetailsView control and the newly created SqlDataSource control should now look like the source shown in Example 4-3.

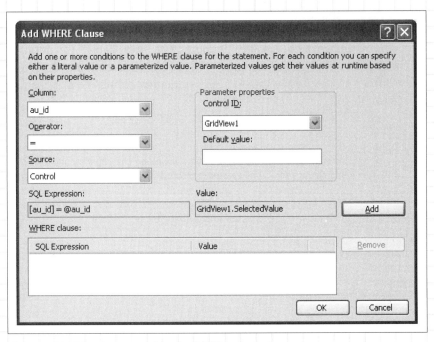

Figure 4-38. Selecting a record in the GridView control

Example 4-3. Source view of the DetailsView and SqlDataSource controls

```
<asp:DetailsView ID="DetailsView1" runat="server"
    Height="50px" Width="286px"
    DataSourceID="SqlDataSource2"
    AutoGenerateRows="False"
    DataKeyNames="au_id">
  <Fields>
    <asp:BoundField ReadOnly="True" HeaderText="au_id"
        DataField="au_id" SortExpression="au_id">
    </asp:BoundField>
    <asp:BoundField HeaderText="au_lname" DataField="au_lname"
        SortExpression="au_lname">
    </asp:BoundField>
    <asp:BoundField HeaderText="au_fname" DataField="au_fname"
        SortExpression="au_fname">
    </asp:BoundField>
    <asp:BoundField HeaderText="phone" DataField="phone"
        SortExpression="phone">
    </asp:BoundField>
    <asp:BoundField HeaderText="address" DataField="address"
        SortExpression="address">
    </asp:BoundField>
    <asp:BoundField HeaderText="city" DataField="city"
        SortExpression="city">
    </asp:BoundField>
    <asp:BoundField HeaderText="state" DataField="state"
        SortExpression="state">
```

Example 4-3. Source view of the DetailsView and SqlDataSource controls (continued)

```
        </asp:BoundField>
        <asp:BoundField HeaderText="zip" DataField="zip"
            SortExpression="zip">
        </asp:BoundField>
        <asp:CheckBoxField HeaderText="contract"
            SortExpression="contract" DataField="contract">
        </asp:CheckBoxField>
    </Fields>
</asp:DetailsView>

<asp:SqlDataSource ID="SqlDataSource2" runat="server"
    SelectCommand="SELECT * FROM
        [authors] WHERE ([au_id] = @au_id)"
    ConnectionString="<%$ ConnectionStrings:
        pubsConnectionString %>">
    <SelectParameters>
        <asp:ControlParameter Name="au_id" ControlID="GridView1"
            PropertyName="SelectedValue"
            Type="String" />
    </SelectParameters>
</asp:SqlDataSource>
```

6. Apply the Sand & Sky theme to both the GridView and DetailsView controls.

7. Press F5 to test the application. You should now be able to select a record in the GridView control and see the details of the selected record in the DetailsView control (see Figure 4-39).

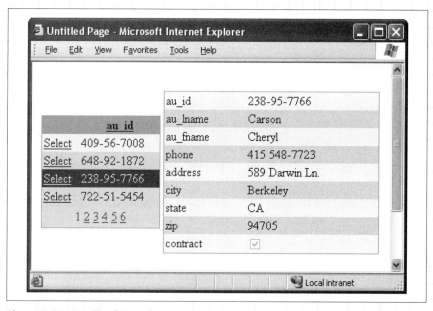

Figure 4-39. Details of the selected record

Where can I learn more?

One particular operation with the GridView and DetailsView control that you should take note of is deletion. You wouldn't want the user to delete a record mistakenly without giving him a second chance. The GridView and DetailsView will gladly delete the record without any warning (if you have enabled deleting). Before a record is deleted, it is your duty to ensure that the user is asked to confirm his action. You can do so via a client-side script. To learn more about writing this kind of script, check out the following sites:

- *http://msdn.microsoft.com/library/default.asp?url=/library/en-us/ dndive/html/data01102002.asp*
- *http://www.dotnetbips.com/displayarticle.aspx?id=108*
- *http://www.dotnetjunkies.com/Article/17F2328F-ECB8-478F-A393- 3D0E0F024EC0.dcik*

To learn more about the DetailsView control, check out the MSDN Help topic "DetailsView class."

Cache the Data Source Control

To improve the performance of your application, you should cache the data source control if you are using one.

Performing database access is a time-consuming operation; therefore, it is important that you reduce the number of times you connect to the database. The SqlDataSource control (as well as the AccessDataSource control) supports caching of data. Caching of the data source controls is useful in cases when your data does not change often—for example, when you have pages displaying product listings and information.

How do I do that?

In general, the more static your data, the longer the time you should cache your data.

To see how to enable caching of data source controls in your application, you will build an application in this lab that uses a SqlDataSource control to retrieve rows from the authors table in the pubs database and then uses the GridView control to display them. The SqlDataSource control will be cached for 60 seconds before the cache is invalidated.

1. Launch Visual Studio 2005 and create a new web site project. Name the project *C:\ASPNET20\chap04-DataSourceCache*.

2. Drag and drop a GridView control onto the default Web Form and configure it to use a SqlDataSource control to connect to the pubs database in SQL Server 2005 Express (see the lab "Display Data in a Table" for detailed instructions on how to do this). In particular, the

au_id, au_fname, and au_lname fields are retrieved. The Source View of the GridView and SqlDataSource control looks like Example 4-4.

Example 4-4. Source View of the GridView and SqlDataSource controls

```
<asp:GridView ID="GridView1" runat="server"
    DataSourceID="SqlDataSource1"
    AutoGenerateColumns="False"
    DataKeyNames="au_id">
  <Columns>
    <asp:BoundField ReadOnly="True" HeaderText="au_id"
        DataField="au_id" SortExpression="au_id">
    </asp:BoundField>
    <asp:BoundField HeaderText="au_lname"
        DataField="au_lname" SortExpression="au_lname">
    </asp:BoundField>
    <asp:BoundField HeaderText="au_fname"
        DataField="au_fname" SortExpression="au_fname">
    </asp:BoundField>
  </Columns>
</asp:GridView>

<asp:SqlDataSource ID="SqlDataSource1" runat="server"
    SelectCommand="SELECT [au_id], [au_lname],
                  [au_fname] FROM [authors]"
    ConnectionString="<%$ ConnectionStrings:
                        pubsConnectionString %>">
</asp:SqlDataSource>
```

3. To enable caching of the SqlDataSource control, set the CacheDuration (in seconds) and EnableCaching attributes, as shown in the following code snippet:

```
<asp:SqlDataSource ID="SqlDataSource1" runat="server"
    SelectCommand="SELECT [au_id], [au_lname],
                  [au_fname] FROM [authors]"
    ConnectionString="<%$ ConnectionStrings:pubsConnectionString %>"
    CacheDuration="60"
    EnableCaching="True"
    CacheExpirationPolicy="Absolute" >
</asp:SqlDataSource>
```

4. Press F5 to test the application. To verify that the data in the SqlDataSource control is cached, modify one of the rows in the authors table and refresh the page. You will notice that the data in the GridView control is not updated until approximately one minute (60 seconds) later.

The default cache expiration policy is that of absolute, which means that the data cached by the data source control will expire *x* seconds (as specified in the CacheDuration attribute) after the data source has been loaded.

What about...

...sliding cache policy?

In the sliding cache policy, the cache will expire if a request is not made within a specified duration. For example, the following code specifies that the cache will have a sliding duration of one minute. If a request is made 59 seconds after the cache is accessed, the validity of the cache would be reset to another minute. Sliding expiration policy is useful whenever you have a large number of items to cache, since this policy enables you to keep only the most frequently accessed items in memory.

```
<asp:SqlDataSource ID="SqlDataSource1" runat="server"
    SelectCommand="SELECT [au_id], [au_lname],
                   [au_fname] FROM [authors]"
    ConnectionString="<%$ ConnectionStrings:pubsConnectionString %>"
    CacheDuration="60"
    EnableCaching="True"
    CacheExpirationPolicy="Sliding" >
</asp:SqlDataSource>
```

Where can I learn more?

For a good discussion on implementing page caching in ASP.NET using absolute expiration, check out the article at:

> http://msdn.microsoft.com/library/default.asp?url=/library/en-us/ dnpatterns/html/ImpPageCacheInASP.asp.

You will also learn how to cache fragments of a page in Chapter 6.

Cache Using Dependency

Instead of just invalidating a database cache based on a specific duration, it is much more effective to invalidate a cache if a change is detected in the database.

Specifying duration for a cache is not always a practical approach. For example, you may cache the data from a database for 10 minutes, but due to unforeseen circumstances (such as price fluctuations of stocks reacting to sudden happenings in world events) the data in the database may be updated more than once during the 10-minute interval. In such cases, it would be much better if the cache duration is dependent on the changes of data in the database.

In ASP.NET 2.0, a new SQL Cache Dependency is available that allows you to invalidate your cache whenever certain types of changes are made to the database. You can now be assured that your database cache is always up to date whenever your database changes.

How do I do that?

To use SQL Cache Dependency, you first need to prepare your database (SQL Server 2000 in this example) and its tables for change notification (so that your ASP.NET application can be notified of the changes in the database). You do this by running a utility called *aspnet_regsql.exe* on the databases and tables that you want to enable for SQL Cache Dependency. Once the database is ready, you will then build an application and use the GridView and SqlDataSource controls to test out SQL Cache Dependency.

TIP

You need not perform Steps 1–4 if you are using SQL Server 2005.

---

1. To use the *aspnet_regsql.exe* utility, go to the command prompt and change to the following directory: *C:\WINDOWS\Microsoft.NET\ Framework\<version>*.
2. The *aspnet_regsql.exe* utility is a mixed-mode (both graphical and command-based) tool that helps you configure your SQL Server database for use with your ASP.NET application. To see the various options available with it, use:

```
C:\WINDOWS\Microsoft.NET\Framework\version>aspnet_regsql /?
```

Parameters of the aspnet_regsql Utility

Here is the summary of the options used for the *aspnet_regsql* utility in this lab:

-S

    SQL server instance

-E

    Authenticate with current Windows credentials

-d

    Database name

-t

    Table name

-ed

    Enable database

-et

    Enable table

---

3. There are two steps you need to take to enable SQL Cache Dependency:

   a. Enable the database.

   b. Enable the table(s).

4. To enable a database, use the –ed option (see the sidebar "Parameters of the aspnet_regsql Utility"):

   ```
   C:\WINDOWS\Microsoft.NET\Framework\version>aspnet_regsql
       -S localhost -E -d Pubs -ed
   ```

5. To enable the table(s), use the –et option:

   ```
   C:\WINDOWS\Microsoft.NET\Framework\version>aspnet_regsql
       -S localhost -E -t Authors -d Pubs -et
   ```

   Steps 3 and 4 create a new table in your database: AspNet_SqlCacheTablesForChangeNotification (shown in Figure 4-40).

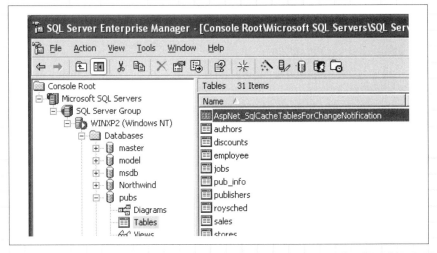

Figure 4-40. The newly created AspNet_SqlCacheTablesForChangeNotification table

The AspNet_SqlCacheTablesForChangeNotification table has three fields, shown in Figure 4-41, and contains the last modification date of the table you are monitoring (through the notificationCreated field), as well as the total number of changes. Each time your table is modified, the value in the changeId field is incremented; it is this table that is tracked by ASP.NET for SQL Cache Dependency.

SQL Server knows when to increment the AspNet_SqlCacheTablesForChangeNotification table because a trigger called AspNet_SqlCacheNotification_Trigger was installed by *aspnet_regsql* during the enabling process, and this trigger is invoked whenever the table is modified (see Figure 4-42).

Figure 4-41. The content of the AspNet_SqlCacheTablesForChangeNotification table

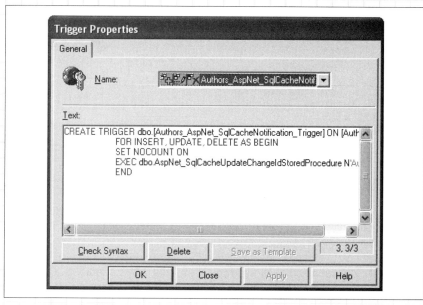

Figure 4-42. The AspNet_SqlCacheNotification_Trigger trigger installed by aspnet_regsql

6. Now that the database has been enabled, to test SQL Cache Dependency, launch Visual Studio 2005 and create a new web site project. Name the project *C:\ASPNET20\Chap04-SQLCacheDep*.

7. Add the *Web.config* file to the project by right-clicking the project name in Solution Explorer and then selecting Add New Item…. Select Web Configuration File.

8. The next step is to add a database connection string in your application. To do so, you need to first modify the *Web.config* file (note the added code in bold in Example 4-5).

Example 4-5. Modifying Web.config to support SQL Cache Dependency

```
<?xml version="1.0"?>
<configuration xmlns="http://schemas.microsoft.com/.NetConfiguration/v2.0">
  <appSettings/>
  <connectionStrings>
    <add name="PubsDatabase"
        connectionString="Server=(local);Integrated Security=True;
        Database=pubs;Persist Security Info=True"
```

Example 4-5. *Modifying Web.config to support SQL Cache Dependency (continued)*

```
        providerName="System.Data.SqlClient" />
  </connectionStrings>

  <system.web>
    <compilation debug="true"/>
    <authentication mode="Windows"/>
    <caching>
      <sqlCacheDependency enabled="true">
        <databases>
          <add
            name="Pubs"
            connectionStringName="PubsDatabase"
            pollTime="10000" />
        </databases>
      </sqlCacheDependency>
    </caching>
  </system.web>
</configuration>
```

TIP

If you are using SQL Server 2005, you do not need to add in the
<caching> element (and its child elements) in *Web.config*.

---

9. In the *Web.config* file in Example 4-5, you have specified a connection string that connects to the pubs database. You have also specified the use of SQL Server caching and indicated a polling time of 10 seconds (unit is in milliseconds). This is the time the ASP.NET runtime (a background thread that is spun off for this purpose) polls the database (specifically, the AspNet_SqlCacheTablesForChangeNotification table) for changes. As this table is small, this process is very efficient and will not slow down the system. Hence, it would be good to specify a low number so that the application is always displaying the most up to date data.

10. Populate the default Web Form with a GridView control. Configure the GridView control to use a SqlDataSource control. In particular, the SqlDataSource control will use the connection string stored in *Web.config*. The Source View of the GridView should now look something like this:

```
<asp:GridView ID="GridView1" runat="server"
    DataSourceID="SqlDataSource1"
    AutoGenerateColumns="False"
    DataKeyNames="au_id">
    ...
    ...
```

```
</asp:GridView>
<asp:SqlDataSource ID="SqlDataSource1" runat="server"
    SelectCommand="SELECT * FROM [authors]"
    ConnectionString="<%$ ConnectionStrings:PubsDatabase %>">
</asp:SqlDataSource>
```

TIP

Refer to the lab "Display Data in a Table," earlier in this chapter, if you are not sure how to configure the GridView control to use a Sql-DataSource control.

---

11. The default Web Form should now look like Figure 4-43.

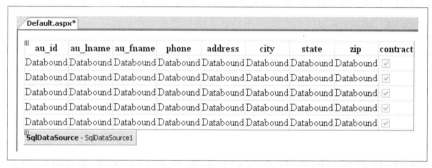

Figure 4-43. The GridView and SqlDataSource controls

12. Switch to Source View and modify the SqlDataSource control to enable SQL Cache Dependency:

```
<asp:SqlDataSource ID="SqlDataSource1" runat="server"
    EnableCaching="true" SqlCacheDependency="Pubs:Authors"
    SelectCommand="SELECT * FROM [authors]"
    ConnectionString="<%$ ConnectionStrings:PubsDatabase %>">
</asp:SqlDataSource>
```

Level of Caching in SQL Server 7, 2000, and 2005

In SQL Server 7 and 2000, a change in a record in a table invalidates the cache, regardless of the number of pages being cached. In SQL Server 2005, page-level caching is supported, thereby invalidating only the page that is affected by the change.

In SQL Server 2005, there is no need for ASP.NET to constantly poll the database. Instead, SQL Server 2005 automatically notifies ASP.NET whenever a particular row of data has been modified. SQL Server 2005 does this by using the Notification Delivery Services, which directly interacts with IIS to notify ASP.NET of updates to specific rows.

TIP

The SqlCacheDependency attribute has the format of *database*:
table for SQL Server 2000 polling. If you are using SQL Server
2005, the SqlCacheDependency attribute should be set to
CommandNotification.

---

13. Press F5 to test the application. Modify the data in the authors table
    (using tools such as SQL Enterprise Manager or Query Analyzer), and
    refresh the web browser. You will notice that the data in the
    GridView will be updated every 10 seconds (approximately) only if
    there are changes in the authors table.

What about...

...page output caching?

You can use page output caching together with SQL Cache Dependency.
For example, suppose a Web Form has a GridView control bound to a
SqlDataSource control. You can specify output caching by using the Out-
putCache directive:

```
<%@ OutputCache  Duration="15000"  VaryByParam="none"
     SqlDependency ="Pubs:Authors" %>
```

Assuming that the SQL Cache Dependency is set to 10 seconds, the
GridView will be refreshed every 10 seconds (if there are changes).
Alternatively, the page will expire every 15 seconds, and any changes
would also be reflected when the page gets refreshed every 15 seconds.

...programmatically enabling a database and its tables for SQL Cache Dependency?

You have seen how to configure SQL Cache Dependency using the
aspnet_regsql.exe utility. Besides using the tool, you can programmatically enable a database and table(s) for notification by using the Sql-
CacheDependencyAdmin class.

The code in Example 4-6 shows how to enable a database and its tables
for notifications.

Example 4-6. Enabling a database and its tables for notifications

```
Public Sub EnableNotification(ByVal tableName As String)
    Dim connStr As String = "Server=.\SQLEXPRESS;Integrated
        Security=True;Database=pubs;Persist Security
        Info=True"
    Dim mustEnable As Boolean = True
    Try
```

```
        Dim tablesEnabled( ) As String
        '---Retrieve all tables enabled for notifications--
        tablesEnabled = _
            SqlCacheDependencyAdmin. _
            GetTablesEnabledForNotifications(connStr)
        If (tablesEnabled IsNot Nothing) Then
            Dim table As String
            Response.Write("<b>Tables Enabled For " & _
                           "Notification</b><br/>")
            For Each table In tablesEnabled
                Response.Write(table & "<br>")
                If (table.ToString.Equals(tableName)) Then
                    mustEnable = False
                End If
            Next
        End If
    Catch ex As Exception
        mustEnable = True
    End Try
    If mustEnable Then
        '--enables the database for notification
        SqlCacheDependencyAdmin.EnableNotifications(connStr)
        '--enables the table for notification
        SqlCacheDependencyAdmin. _
            EnableTableForNotifications(connStr, tableName)
        Response.Write(tableName & "<br>")
    End If
End Sub
```

The SqlCacheDependencyAdmin class performs administrative tasks on a SQL Server so that you can enable SQL Cache Dependency. The GetTablesEnabledForNotifications( ) method retrieves all the tables already enabled for notification in the database (as indicated in the connection string) and returns the table names as an array of strings. You then loop through the array of table names to see if the table that you need to enable for notification is found. If the name is in the list, that means the table is already enabled; otherwise, you need to enable it for notifications.

You need to first enable a database and then enable the table for SQL Cache Dependency to work. So, use the EnableNotifications( ) method to enable the database first, and then use the EnableTableForNotifications( ) method to enable the individual tables.

Where can I learn more?

To see how you can implement your own SQL Cache Dependency in .NET 1.1 applications, check out my O'Reilly Network article at *http://www.ondotnet.com/pub/a/dotnet/2005/01/17/sqlcachedependency.html*.

To learn how you can use caching in ASP.NET 1.x and 2.0 applications, check out my DevX.com article at *http://www.devx.com/asp/Article/21751*.

For a good discussion on the differences in how SQL Server 2000 and SQL Server 2005 handle SQL Cache Dependency, check out this link: *http://beta.asp.net/GuidedTour/s20.aspx*.

Encrypt Connection Strings

Protect your connection strings in Web.config from peering eyes by encrypting them!

Instead of saving your database connection string within your application, it is often much better (and easier to maintain) to have your connection strings stored in the *Web.config* file. In ASP.NET 2.0, Microsoft has taken this further by allowing you to encrypt the connection string that you store in *Web.config*.

How do I do that?

To see how you can encrypt the connection strings stored in *Web.config*, you will configure a GridView control to bind to a SqlDataSource control. The connection string used by the SqlDataSource control would be saved in the *Web.config* file. You will then encrypt the connection strings using the two Protection Configuration Providers available in .NET 2.0.

1. Launch Visual Studio 2005 and create a new web site project. Name the project *C:\ASPNET20\chap04-EncryptConfig*.

2. Populate the default form with a GridView control and configure it to use a SqlDataSource control. Configure the SqlDataSource control to connect to the pubs database and use the authors table. In particular, ensure that the connection string is stored in *Web.config*.

TIP

Refer back to the lab "Display Data in a Table" if you are not sure how to configure the GridView control to use a SqlDataSource control.

---

3. The default form should now look like Figure 4-44.

4. The *Web.config* file will now contain the following connection string:

```
<configuration
    xmlns="http://schemas.microsoft.com/.NetConfiguration/v2.0">
    <appSettings/>
    <connectionStrings>
        <add name="pubsConnectionString" connectionString="Data
                Source=.\SQLEXPRESS;Initial Catalog=pubs;
                Integrated Security=True"
            providerName="System.Data.SqlClient" />
```

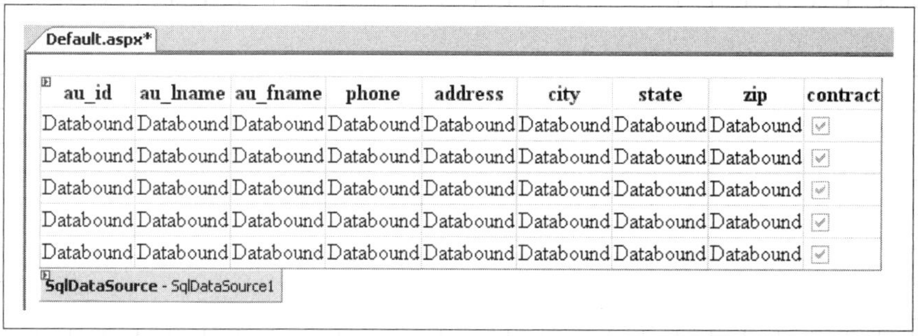

Figure 4-44. The GridView and SqlDataSource control

```
</connectionStrings>
<system.web>
...
```

5. Switch to the code-behind of the default form and add in the
Encrypt() method. The Encrypt() method first retrieves the *Web.config*
file and then applies encryption to the specified section of the file
(<connectionStrings>, in this case) using the Protection Configuration
Provider indicated (passed in via the protectionProvider parameter).

```
Imports System.Configuration
Imports System.Web.Security

    Public Sub Encrypt(ByVal protectionProvider As String)
        '---open the web.config file
        Dim config As Configuration = _
            System.Web.Configuration. _
                WebConfigurationManager.OpenWebConfiguration( _
            Request.ApplicationPath)
        '---indicate the section to protect
        Dim section As ConfigurationSection = _
            config.Sections("connectionStrings")
        '---specify the protection provider
        section.SectionInformation.ProtectSection(protectionProvider)
        '---Apple the protection and update
        config.Save()
    End Sub
```

6. Also, add the Decrypt() method to decrypt the encrypted connection
strings in *Web.config*:

```
    Public Sub Decrypt()
        Dim config As Configuration = _
            System.Web.Configuration. _
                WebConfigurationManager.OpenWebConfiguration( _
            Request.ApplicationPath)
        Dim section As ConfigurationSection = _
            config.Sections("connectionStrings")
        section.SectionInformation.UnProtectSection()
        config.Save()
    End Sub
```

7. Two protection configuration providers are available for your use:

   - DataProtectionConfigurationProvider
   - RSAProtectedConfigurationProvider

   To test the Encrypt( ) method, call it in the Form_Load event:

```
Protected Sub Page_Load(ByVal sender As Object, _
                        ByVal e As System.EventArgs) _
                        Handles Me.Load
    Encrypt("DataProtectionConfigurationProvider")
    '--or--
    ' Encrypt("RSAProtectedConfigurationProvider")
End Sub
```

8. If you use the DataProtectionConfigurationProvider, your connection string will now look like Example 4-7.

Example 4-7. Connection string with DataProtectionConfigurationProvider

```
<configuration xmlns="http://schemas.microsoft.com/.NetConfiguration/v2.0">
    <protectedData>
        <protectedDataSections>
            <add name="connectionStrings"
                provider="DataProtectionConfigurationProvider"
                inheritedByChildren="False" />
        </protectedDataSections>
    </protectedData>
    <appSettings/>
            <connectionStrings>
        <EncryptedData>
            <CipherData>
                <CipherValue>AQAAANCMnd...........WaWSpYkRgVTirQ=</CipherValue>
            </CipherData>
```

Example 4-7. Connection string with DataProtectionConfigurationProvider (continued)

```
        </EncryptedData>
      </connectionStrings>
   <system.web>
...
```

9. If you use the `RSAProtectedConfigurationProvider`, your connection string will now look like Example 4-8.

Example 4-8. Connection string with RSAProtectedConfigurationProvider

```
...
<configuration xmlns="http://schemas.microsoft.com/.NetConfiguration/v2.0">
   <protectedData>
      <protectedDataSections>
         <add name="connectionStrings"
              provider="RSAProtectedConfigurationProvider"
              inheritedByChildren="False" />
      </protectedDataSections>
   </protectedData>
   <appSettings/>
      <connectionStrings>
         <EncryptedData Type="http://www.w3.org/2001/04/xmlenc#Element"
            xmlns="http://www.w3.org/2001/04/xmlenc#">
            <EncryptionMethod
               Algorithm="http://www.w3.org/2001/04/xmlenc#tripledes-cbc" />
            <KeyInfo xmlns="http://www.w3.org/2000/09/xmldsig#">
               <EncryptedKey xmlns="http://www.w3.org/2001/04/xmlenc#">
                  <EncryptionMethod Algorithm="http://www.w3.org/2001/04/
                     xmlenc#rsa-1_5" />
                  <KeyInfo xmlns="http://www.w3.org/2000/09/xmldsig#">
                     <KeyName>RSA Key</KeyName>
                  </KeyInfo>
                  <CipherData>
                     <CipherValue>XzI2CV8F1Pd........oVf1DnuM=</CipherValue>
                  </CipherData>
               </EncryptedKey>
            </KeyInfo>
            <CipherData>
               <CipherValue>O39jWP/......XIvitvOKBQ==</CipherValue>
            </CipherData>
         </EncryptedData>
      </connectionStrings>
      <system.web>
...
```

10. The really nice thing about encrypting the *Web.config* file is that the process of decrypting the required connection string is totally transparent to the developer. Controls and code that need to access the connection string will automatically know how to encrypt the encrypted information. However, if you want to decrypt the *Web.config* file so

that you can make modifications to it, simply call the Decrypt()
method.

11. You can check whether a section is protected by using the IsPro-
tected property, like this (you can use this block of code in the Page_
Load event, for example):

```
If Not section.SectionInformation.IsProtected Then
    section.SectionInformation.ProtectSection(protectionProvider)
    config.Save()
End If
```

Self-Contained Protection

Notice that the <protectedData> section added to *Web.config* contains information needed to decrypt the connection strings.

More importantly, `<protectedData>` doesn't contain the decryption key. For
example, if you use the Windows `DataProtectionConfigurationProvider`,
the decryption key is autogenerated and saved in the Windows Local Security Authority (LSA).

What about...

...programmatically adding a new connection string to an encrypted Web.config file?

The following AddConnString() method shows how you can add a new
connection string to the *Web.config* file.

```
Public Sub AddConnString()
    '---add a connection string to Web.config
    Dim config As Configuration = _
        System.Web.Configuration. _
            WebConfigurationManager.OpenWebConfiguration( _
        Request.ApplicationPath)
    config.ConnectionStrings.ConnectionStrings.Add _
       (New ConnectionStringSettings("NorthwindConnectionString", _
        "server=.\SQLEXPRESS;database=northwind;integrated security=true"))
    config.Save()
End Sub
```

...protecting other sections in Web.config?

You can encrypt almost any section in *Web.config*, with the exception of
sections accessed by parts of the unmanaged code in ASP.NET, such as
`<httpRuntime>` and `<processModel>`.

...retrieving connection strings programmatically?

It can be done. To programmatically retrieve a connection string from *Web.config*, use the following code:

```
Dim connect As String = _
   ConfigurationManager.ConnectionStrings _
   ("NorthwindConnectionString").ConnectionString
Response.Write(connect)
```

Where can I learn more?

To learn more about the ProtectedConfigurationProvider class, check out the MSDN Help topic "ProtectedConfigurationProvider Class."

To understand how Windows Data Protection works, check out *http:// msdn.microsoft.com/library/default.asp?url=/library/en-us/dnsecure/html/ windataprotection-dpapi.asp*.

For an introduction to the cryptography classes in .NET, check out my article at *http://msdn.microsoft.com/library/default.asp?url=/library/en-us/dnhcvs03/html/vs0311.asp*.

Connect to a Business Object

A well-designed system uses different tiers for different operations (such as a three-tier architecture). For example, programmers frequently encapsulate their business logic in classes separate from those that handle interactions with the user. In ASP.NET 2.0, you can expose your data-aware classes to data-bound controls (such as the GridView) through the ObjectDataSource control. Doing so will allow changes to be made to either layer (business logic or UI) without affecting the other.

Unless you are writing a simple web application, you should really encapsulate all your business logic into components and then bind your UI controls (such as the GridView) to the business objects.

How do I do that?

To illustrate how you can bind a GridView control to an object through the ObjectDataSource control, you will create a class that encapsulates your data access logic and then use an ObjectDataSource control to bind to it. You will then bind the GridView control to the ObjectDataSource control. When you're finished, you'll have a three-tier application.

1. Launch Visual Studio 2005 and create a new web site project. Name the project *C:\ASPNET20\chap04-ObjectDataSource*.

2. Add a new *App_Code* folder to your project by right-clicking the project name in Solution Explorer and then selecting Add Folder → App_Code Folder (see Figure 4-45).

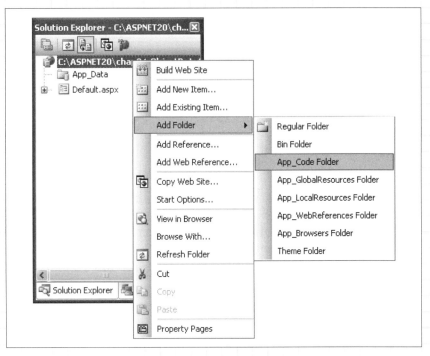

Figure 4-45. Adding an App_Code folder to the project.

3. Add a *Web.config* file to the project by right-clicking the project name in Solution Explorer and then selecting Add New Item → Web Configuration File.

4. Add the following connection string to *Web.config*:

```
<connectionStrings>
    <add name="pubsConnectionString" connectionString="Data
        Source=.\SQLEXPRESS;Initial Catalog=pubs;
        Integrated Security=True"
        providerName="System.Data.SqlClient" />
</connectionStrings>
```

5. Right-click the *App_Code* folder and select Add New Item…. Select Class and name it *Authors.vb*.

6. Code *Authors.vb* as shown in Example 4-9. The Authors class contains a single method—getAuthors( )—which returns a data set.

Example 4-9. Authors.vb

```
Imports System.Data.SqlClient
Imports System.Data
Imports Microsoft.VisualBasic
```

Example 4-9. Authors.vb (continued)

```
Public Class Authors
    Public Function getAuthors() As DataSet
        Dim conn As New SqlConnection( _
            ConfigurationManager.ConnectionStrings _
            ("pubsConnectionString").ConnectionString)
        Dim adapter As New SqlDataAdapter( _
            "SELECT au_id, au_fname, au_lname FROM Authors", conn)
        Dim ds As New DataSet
        adapter.Fill(ds, "Authors")
        Return ds
    End Function
End Class
```

TIP

Remember to save the *Authors.vb* file before proceeding to the next step.

---

7. Add a GridView control to the default Web Form. In the GridView Tasks menu, select <New data source...> (see Figure 4-46).

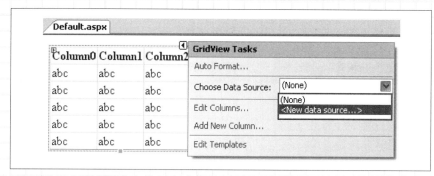

Figure 4-46. Selecting a new data source

8. Choose Object as the data source in the window that opens (see Figure 4-47). Use the default ID of ObjectDataSource1 for the data source. Click OK.

9. In the drop-down listbox, select Authors as the business object (see Figure 4-48). Click Next. You are essentially binding the ObjectDataSource control to the Authors class.

10. In the SELECT tab, select the "getAuthors(), returns DataSet" method (see Figure 4-49). Click Finish.

11. To test the application, press F5. You should now see the GridView control populated with records from the Authors table.

If you don't see the getAuthors() method, be sure to save your Authors.vb class file first.

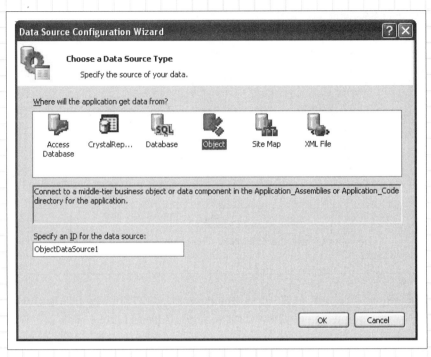

Figure 4-47. Select Object as the data source

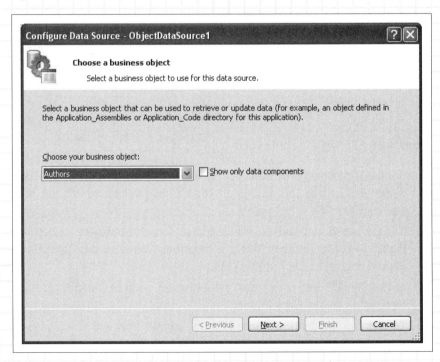

Figure 4-48. Selecting the object for the ObjectDataSource control

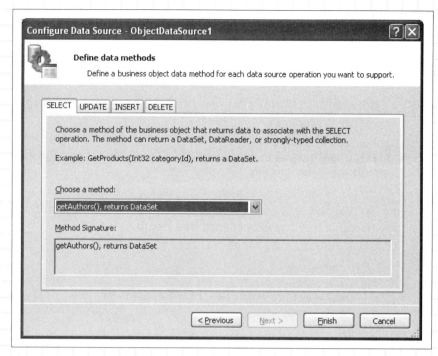

Figure 4-49. Selecting the method to bind to the SELECT tab

What about...

...editing the rows in the GridView control through the ObjectData-Source control?

You can also use the GridView control to update the rows through the ObjectDataSource control.

1. Add a new method, updateAuthors( ), to the Authors class, as shown in Example 4-10.

Example 4-10. updateAuthors( )

```
Public Sub updateAuthors(ByVal au_id As String, _
                         ByVal au_fname As String, _
                         ByVal au_lname As String)
    Dim conn As New SqlConnection( _
        ConfigurationManager.ConnectionStrings _
        ("pubsConnectionString").ConnectionString)

    Dim adapter As New SqlDataAdapter( _
        "SELECT au_id, au_fname, au_lname " & _
        "FROM Authors WHERE au_id=@au_id", conn)
```

Example 4-10. updateAuthors( ) (continued)

```
        Dim ds As New DataSet
        adapter.SelectCommand.Parameters.Add( _
            "@au_id", SqlDbType.NVarChar, 11).Value = au_id
        adapter.Fill(ds, "Authors")

        With ds.Tables(0).Rows(0)
            .Item("au_fname") = au_fname
            .Item("au_lname") = au_lname
        End With
        Dim cb As New SqlCommandBuilder(adapter)
        adapter.Update(ds, "Authors")
    End Sub
```

2. Click on the Configure Data Source... link in the ObjectDataSource Tasks menu of the GridView control (see Figure 4-50).

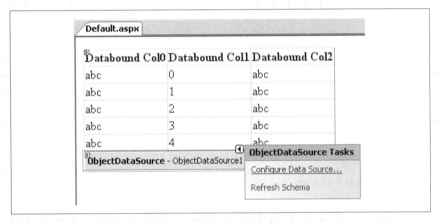

Figure 4-50. Configuring the ObjectDataSource control

3. Click Next, and in the UPDATE tab, select the updateAuthors( ) method (see Figure 4-51). The use of the updateAuthors( ) method is to update the changes made to the GridView back to the database. Click Finish.

TIP

Likewise for inserting and deleting records, you just need to add new methods to the Authors class and then select them in the INSERT and DELETE tabs.

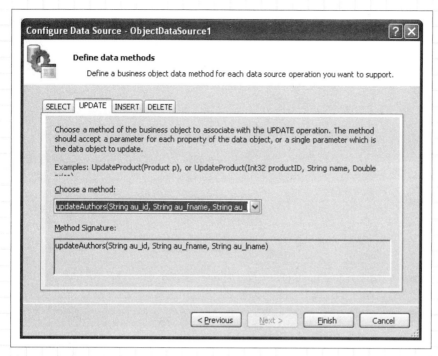

Figure 4-51. Selecting a method for the UPDATE tab

TIP

Note that the updateAuthors( ) method has parameters that are the same as the columns displayed in the GridView control.

---

4. On the GridView control, check the Enable Editing checkbox (see Figure 4-52) so that the GridView will display the Edit links in the leftmost column.

5. Press F5 to test the application. The GridView control is now editable with the changes passed to the updateAuthors( ) method for updating (see Figure 4-53).

...using a data component together with the ObjectDataSource control?

Instead of encapsulating the data access logic within a class, it would be easier if Visual Studio automatically generated all the required logic for standard data access tasks such as selecting, inserting, deleting, and updating. In fact, you can do so using a data component.

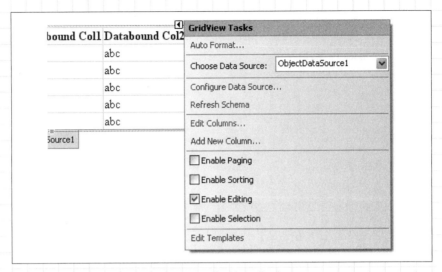

Figure 4-52. Enabling the GridView control to be edited

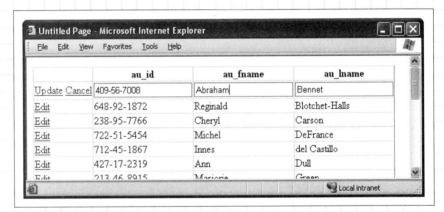

Figure 4-53. Updating a row in the GridView control via the ObjectDataSource control

1. Using the same project, right-click the project name in Solution Explorer and select Add New Item.... Select Web Form, and name the form *Default2.aspx*.

2. Right-click the project name in Solution Explorer and select Add New Item.... Select Dataset, and name the data set *Dataset.xsd*.

3. You will be prompted to save the data set in the special *App_Code* directory. Click Yes (see Figure 4-54).

4. The Data Component Configuration Wizard window will appear. Click Next.

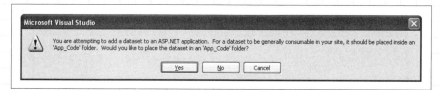

Figure 4-54. Saving the XSD file in the App_Code folder

5. Use the project's existing connection string (pubsConnectionString, saved in *Web.config*). Click Next (see Figure 4-55).

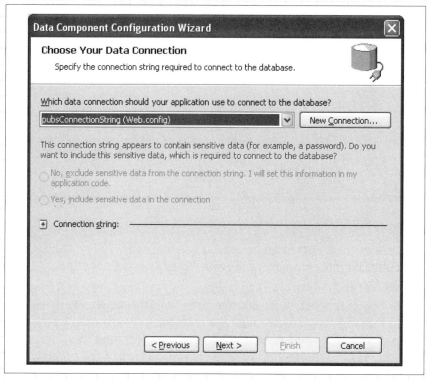

Figure 4-55. Choosing the connection string to use

6. In the next window, select the "Use SQL statements" option. Click Next (see Figure 4-56).

7. In the box "What data should the table load?", enter the following SQL statement:

```
SELECT au_id, au_fname, au_lname FROM Authors
```

8. Click the Advanced Options... button and check all three checkboxes (see Figure 4-57). Essentially, you want the Insert, Update, and

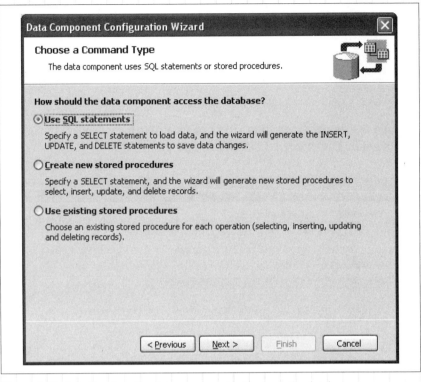

Figure 4-56. Selecting how the data component will access the database

Delete statements to be generated automatically. You would also use optimistic concurrency to prevent updating conflicts. Click OK and then Next.

9. In the next window, check the three checkboxes (see Figure 4-58). In this step, you are selecting the methods to be exposed by the data component. Use the default values and click Next and then Finish.

10. Save the project. Configure the GridView control to use a new data source (see Figure 4-59).

11. In the next window, select Object as the data source and use the default name of ObjectDataSource1 as the ID of the data source. Click OK.

12. Select the business object DataSetTableAdapter.authorsTableAdapter (see Figure 4-60). This table adapter is autocompiled based on the data set you added earlier (*Dataset.xsd*). Click Next.

13. The SELECT, UPDATE, INSERT, and DELETE tabs will all have a method assigned to them (see Figure 4-61). Click Finish.

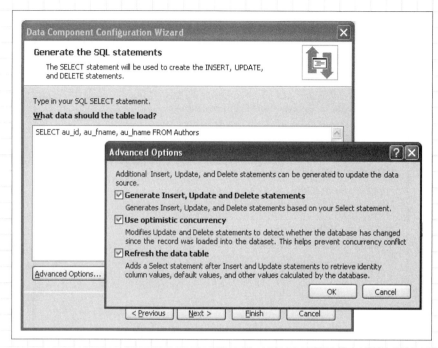

Figure 4-57. Generating all the required SQL statements

14. Finally, check the Enable Editing and Enable Deleting checkboxes in
the GridView Tasks menu (see Figure 4-62).

TIP

Due to a design decision made by Microsoft, you need to set the
ReadOnly attribute of the au_id field of the GridView control to
false, like this (in Source View):

```
<asp:BoundField
     ReadOnly="false" HeaderText="au_id"
     DataField="au_id" SortExpression="au_id">
</asp:BoundField>
```

This is because, by default, the GridView control assumes that primary keys are not updateable, whereas the data component allows
primary keys to be updated. Thus the GridView control will not pass
primary keys' values to the data component. So when you try to
update the GridView control, you will get an error stating that the
ObjectDataSource control could not find an Update method with the
correct parameters.

This behavior might change in the final release of Visual Studio 2005.

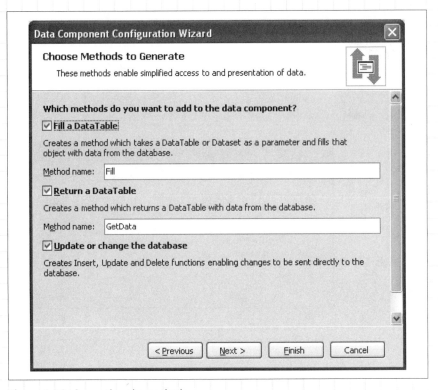

Figure 4-58. Generating the methods

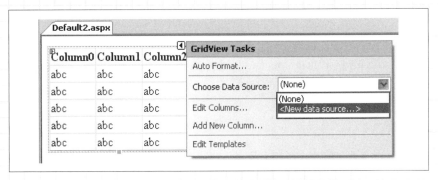

Figure 4-59. Configuring the GridView control to use a new data source

15. Press F5 to test the application. You will now be able to edit and delete records in the GridView control.

Where can I learn more?

To learn more about data access in .NET using ADO.NET, check out the following article: *http://msdn.microsoft.com/library/default.asp?url=/library/en-us/vbcon/html/vbconFundamentalDataConceptsInVisualStudioNET.asp.*

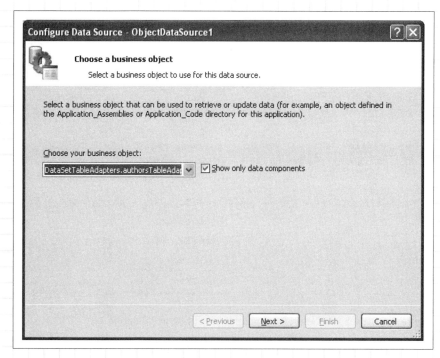

Figure 4-60. Choosing a business object

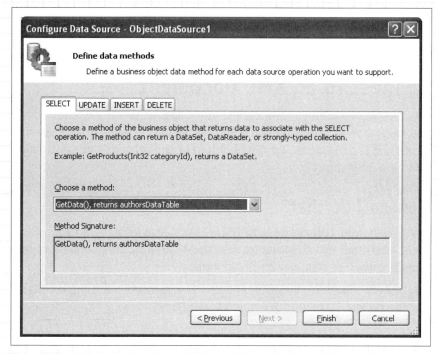

Figure 4-61. Choosing methods for the various operations

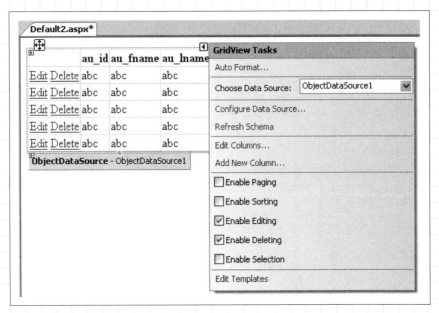

Figure 4-62. Enabling the GridView control for editing and deleting

To learn what is new in ADO.NET 2.0, check out the MSDN site at *http:// msdn.microsoft.com/data/DataAccess/Whidbey/default.aspx.*

If you are not familiar with data components, refer to this link for an introduction: *http://msdn.microsoft.com/library/default.asp?url=/library/ en-us/vbcon/html/vbconadonetdatasetcreationinvisualstudionet.asp.*

Connect to an XML Document

Use an XML document easily through the XmlDataSource control. No more lengthy code to write to manipulate XML documents.

Like the SqlDataSource control, the new XmlDataSource control allows you to deal with XML documents without having to write a large amount of code. It is most suited for data binding to controls such as the DataList and TreeView controls.

How do I do that?

In this lab, you will create an RSS reader that consumes an RSS document, and then use the DataList and the XmlDataSource controls to display the news in a human-readable form.

1. Launch Visual Studio 2005 and create a new web site project. Name the project *C:\ASPNET20\chap04-XMLDataSource.*

2. Right-click the project name in Solution Explorer and select Add New Item…. Select XML File and name it *RSS.xml*.

3. Populate the *RSS.xml* document as shown in Example 4-11.

Example 4-11. A sample RSS document

```
<?xml version="1.0"?>
<rss version="2.0">
    <channel>
        <title>Liftoff News</title>
        <link>http://liftoff.msfc.nasa.gov/</link>
        <description>Liftoff to Space Exploration.</description>
        <language>en-us</language>
        <pubDate>Tue, 10 Jun 2003 04:00:00 GMT</pubDate>
        <lastBuildDate>Tue, 10 Jun 2003 09:41:01 GMT</lastBuildDate>
        <docs>http://blogs.law.harvard.edu/tech/rss</docs>
        <generator>Weblog Editor 2.0</generator>
        <managingEditor>editor@example.com</managingEditor>
        <webMaster>webmaster@example.com</webMaster>
        <item>
            <title>Star City</title>
            <link>http://liftoff.msfc.nasa.gov/news/2003/news-starcity.asp</link>
            <description>How do Americans get ready to work with Russians aboard
the International Space Station? They take a crash course in culture, language
and protocol at Russia's &lt;a href="http://howe.iki.rssi.ru/GCTC/gctc_e.
htm"&gt;Star City&lt;/a&gt;.</description>
            <pubDate>Tue, 03 Jun 2003 09:39:21 GMT</pubDate>
            <guid>http://liftoff.msfc.nasa.gov/2003/06/03.html#item573</guid>
        </item>
        <item>
            <title>The Engine That Does More</title>
            <link>http://liftoff.msfc.nasa.gov/news/2003/news-VASIMR.asp</link>
            <description>Before man travels to Mars, NASA hopes to design new
engines that will let us fly through the Solar System more quickly.  The proposed
VASIMR engine would do that.</description>
            <pubDate>Tue, 27 May 2003 08:37:32 GMT</pubDate>
            <guid>http://liftoff.msfc.nasa.gov/2003/05/27.html#item571</guid>
        </item>
        <item>
            <title>Astronauts' Dirty Laundry</title>
            <link>http://liftoff.msfc.nasa.gov/news/2003/news-laundry.asp</link>
            <description>Compared to earlier spacecraft, the International Space
Station has many luxuries, but laundry facilities are not one of them.  Instead,
astronauts have other options.</description>
            <pubDate>Tue, 20 May 2003 08:56:02 GMT</pubDate>
            <guid>http://liftoff.msfc.nasa.gov/2003/05/20.html#item570</guid>
        </item>
    </channel>
</rss>
```

4. Drag and drop the DataList control (located in the Toolbox under the
   Data tab) onto the default form.

5. In the DataList Tasks menu of the DataList control, select <New data
   source...> (see Figure 4-63).

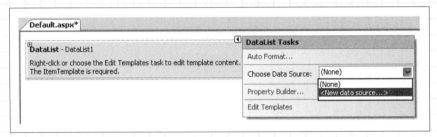

Figure 4-63. Creating a new data source for the DataList control

6. Select XML File (see Figure 4-64). Use the default `XmlDataSource1` as
   the ID for the XmlDataSource control. Click OK.

7. Enter `RSS.xml` for the datafile (see Figure 4-65) and `rss/channel/`
   `item` for the XPath Expression. Click OK.

8. Switch to Source View for the default Web Form and add in the following code (in bold) to configure the DataList control so that it will
   display the appropriate sections of the XML file:

```
<asp:DataList ID="DataList1" runat="server"
DataSourceID="XmlDataSource1">
    <itemtemplate>
        <b><%#XPath("title")%> </b><br />
        <i><%#XPath("description") %></i> <%#XPath("pubDate")%><br />
        <a href='<%#XPath("link") %>'>Link</a><br />
        <br />
    </itemtemplate>
</asp:DataList>
```

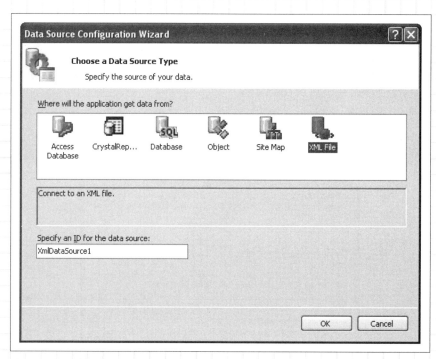

Figure 4-64. Choosing the XML File data source

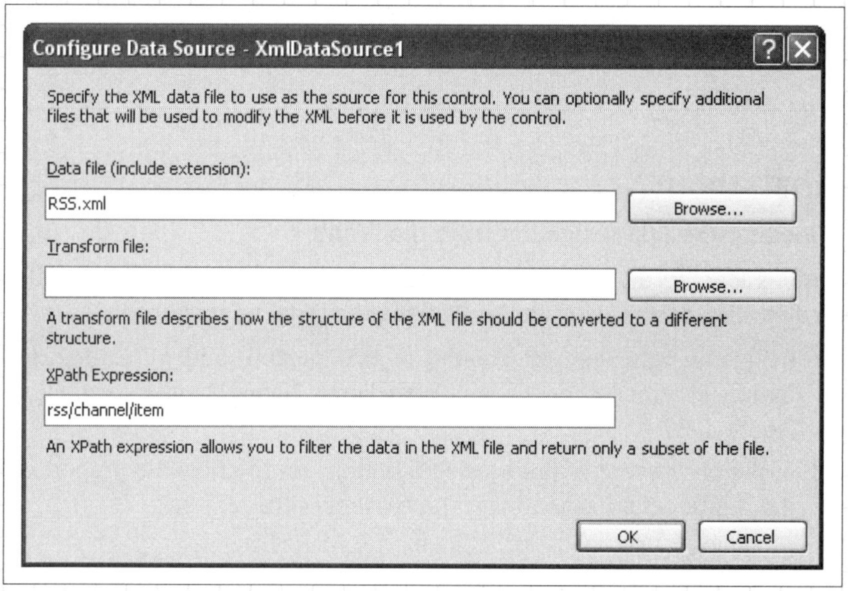

Figure 4-65. Loading the XmlDataSource control with an XML document

9. Apply the Sand & Sky theme to the DataList control using Auto Format... in the DataList Tasks menu.

10. To test the application, press F5, and you now see the XML document formatted as shown in Figure 4-66. Clicking on Link will bring you to the source of the news.

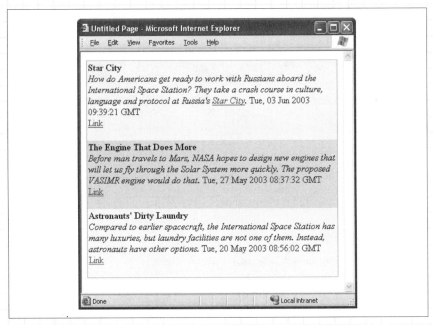

Figure 4-66. Displaying a weblog without writing code

What about...

...loading the RSS document from the Web?

Besides loading an XML document from your local storage, you can also load an XML document from the Web via the DataFile property.

1. Using the same project created in this section, add a TextBox and Button control to the default Web Form. Name them as shown in Figure 4-67.

2. In the click event of the Load RSS button, set the DataFile property of the XmlDataSource control to the content of the text box:

```
Protected Sub btnLoadRSS_Click(ByVal sender As Object, _
                               ByVal e As System.EventArgs) _
                               Handles btnLoadRSS.Click
    XmlDataSource1.DataFile = txtRssURL.Text
End Sub
```

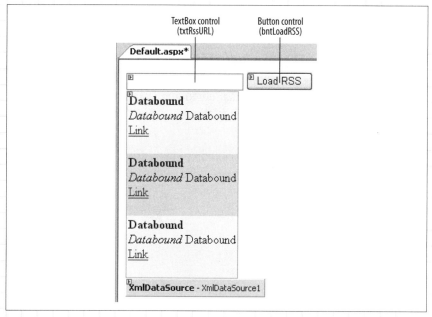

Figure 4-67. Adding the TextBox and Button controls to the form

3. To test the application, press F5, enter a URL pointing to an RSS feed, and click Load RSS. The RSS feed should be retrieved and displayed in the DataList control (see Figure 4-68).

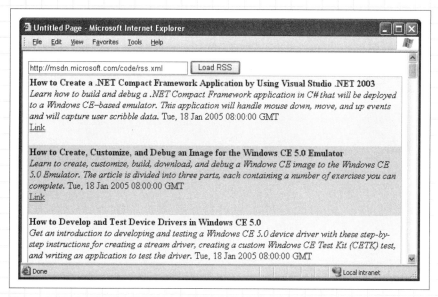

Figure 4-68. Feeding an XML document dynamically to the XmlDataSource control

Where can I learn more?

If you are new to the world of RSS and weblogs, check out my introductory article to weblogs at *http://www.oreillynet.com/pub/a/javascript/2002/12/30/weblog_intro.html*.

For more information on the XmlDataSource and DataList controls, check out the MSDN Help topics "XmlDataSource Members" and "DataList Members."

CHAPTER 5

Security

ASP.NET 2.0 comes with new security controls that aim to simplify the life of a developer. Using the new security controls, you can now perform user logins, registration, password changes, and more, with no more effort than dragging and dropping controls onto your Web Form.

Powering these new controls are the Membership APIs, which perform the mundane tasks of user management without your having to write your own code.

In this chapter, you will learn how the use the new security controls to secure your site. You will also learn about the Membership APIs and how they can be used to perform user administration.

Create a Login Page Using the New Security Controls

In ASP.NET 1.x, you can use form-based authentication to authenticate web users through a custom login page. While this is a useful and straightforward technique, it still requires you to write your own code to perform the authentication, most often through the use of a data store such as SQL Server. However, this mundane task has now been simplified by the introduction of new security controls in ASP.NET 2.0.

How do I do that?

In this lab, you will build a login page that employs the built-in security controls that ship with ASP.NET 2.0 to authenticate users. You will use the various new Login controls—in particular, Login, LoginView, LoginStatus, and LoginName—to help you accomplish tasks such as user authentication, display of login status and login name, and more. You

Using the various Login controls, you can now perform user authentication with ease!

will create two forms: one to display the login status of the user and another to allow the user to log into your application.

The Web Forms created in this lab will lay the groundwork for the next lab, "Add Users with WAT," which will add users to the site for you to test the security controls.

1. First, we'll create a new site to use as a test bed for the new security controls. Launch Visual Studio 2005 and create a new web site project. Name the project *C:\ASPNET20\chap-5-SecurityControls*.

2. You'll find the security controls you'll be using in this chapter in the Toolbox, under the Login tab, as shown in Figure 5-1.

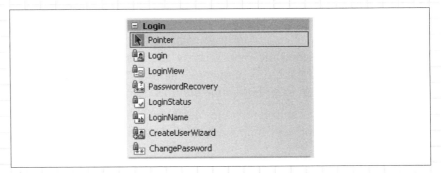

Figure 5-1. The security controls in ASP.NET 2.0

3. Populate the default Web Form with the control shown in Figure 5-2. The LoginView control is a container that displays different information depending on whether the user is logged in or not. This page will be used to display the status of the user (whether she is logged in or not). This *Default.aspx* form will be used to display the login status of a user.

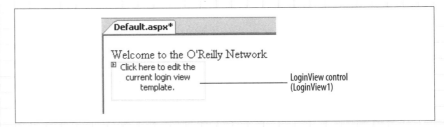

Figure 5-2. The LoginView control

4. Configure the LoginView control by clicking on it and selecting the AnonymousTemplate views in the LoginView Tasks menu (see Figure 5-3). Type the following text into the LoginView control:

"You must Login to the O'Reilly Network to post a talkback." The Anonymous view displays this content when a user is not yet authenticated.

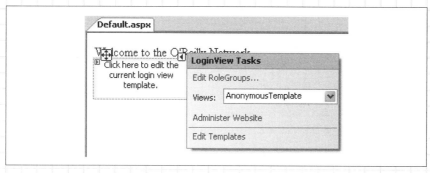

Figure 5-3. Configuring the LoginView control for Anonymous view

5. Drag and drop a LoginStatus control onto the LoginView control, as shown in Figure 5-4. The LoginStatus control displays a hyperlink that shows "Login" before the user is authenticated and "Logout" when the user is logged in. Using the LoginStatus control, you can let the user click on the link to either log into or log out of the site.

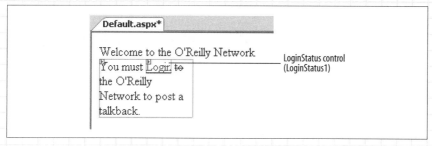

Figure 5-4. Using the LoginStatus control to display login status

6. Configure the LoginView control for Logged In View by selecting the LoggedInTemplate views in the LoginView Tasks menu (see Figure 5-3). Type the following text into the LoginView control: "You are logged in as." The LoggedIn view displays this content when a user is authenticated.

7. Drag and drop a LoginName control and an additional LoginStatus control onto the LoginView control in *Default.aspx*, as shown in Figure 5-5. When a user logs into the site, the LoginName control will display the user's name that was used to log into the application. The user will also be able to log out of the site by clicking on the LoginStatus control.

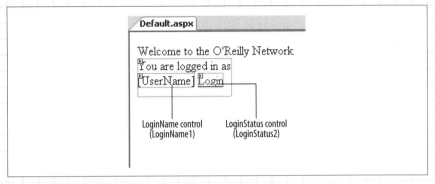

Figure 5-5. Using the LoginName control to display a username

8. Add a new Web Form to the project and name it *Login.aspx*. This form will be used to let users log into the site. Drag and drop a Login control (see Figure 5-6) onto the *Login.aspx* Web Form. The Login control provides user interface elements for logging into a web site.

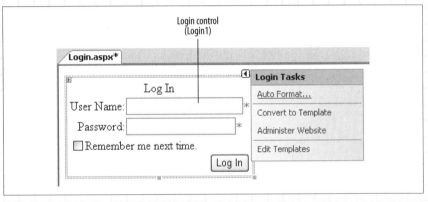

Figure 5-6. Add the Login control to the Web Form

Note that ASP.NET forms authentication does not perform any type of encryption on the credentials that are submitted via the login page, so any login page should be protected by SSL encryption so that credentials can't be stolen.

TIP

To learn how to configure SSL on IIS, check out *http://www.microsoft.com/resources/documentation/iis/6/all/proddocs/en-us/nntp_sec_securing_connections.mspx*.

Default Login Page in ASP.NET 2.0

Note that in ASP.NET 2.0, the default login page is named *Login.aspx* (this is the default "burned" into ASP.NET 2.0 and can be verified by looking at *machine.config.comments*).

However, if you do wish to use a different name for your login page, you can modify the *Web.config* file by adding the following lines (shown in bold). This will change the authentication mode from the default *Login.aspx* to *Authenticate.aspx*:

```
<system.web>
    <authentication mode="Forms">
        <forms name=".ASPXAUTH"
            loginUrl="Authenticate.aspx"
            protection="Validation"
            timeout="999999" />
    </authentication>
    ...
```

Here are the attributes of the <forms> element:

name
    Specifies the name of the HTTP cookie to use for authentication

loginUrl
    Specifies the name of the page to use for login

protection
    Specifies the type of encryption, if any, to use for cookies

timeout
    Specifies the amount of time, in integer minutes, after which the cookie expires

9. It's time to dress up the Login control. Apply the Elegant scheme to the control by clicking on the Auto Format... link in the Login Tasks menu. Your Login control should now look like the one shown in Figure 5-7.

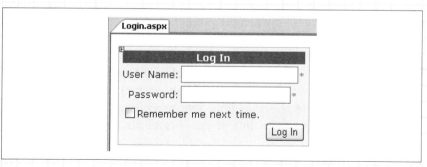

Figure 5-7. Applying autoformat to the Login control

10. Add a *Web.config* file to your project (right-click the project name in Solution Explorer and select Add New Item..., and then select Web Configuration File).

11. In *Web.config,* change the authentication mode from Windows to Forms by adding the following line of code. You use forms authentication so that you can add users to your web site without needing to create the user accounts in Windows:

```
<system.web>
    <authentication mode="Forms"/>
```

12. You are now ready to test your application. But before you do that, you have to add a user to your project. You will see how to do this in the next lab.

TIP

You should set the DestinationPageUrl property of the Login control to one of your sites pages so that if the *Login.aspx* page is loaded directly, it can direct the user to a default page once the user is authenticated. (The DestinationPageUrl property applies only when *Login.aspx* is loaded directly.)

How does it work?

ASP.NET 2.0 uses a new security model known as the Membership Provider Model. The Provider Model allows for maximum flexibility and extensibility by enabling developers to choose the way they add security features to their applications.

As an example of the extensibility of the Provider Model, consider the new set of Login controls, some of which you've put to work in this lab. The controls, APIs, and providers that make up this new model are shown in Figure 5-8.

At the top level are the various web server controls, such as the Login, LoginStatus, and LoginView controls. Underlying the controls are the APIs that perform the work required to implement their functionality. The Membership class takes care of tasks such as adding and deleting users, while the MembershipUser class is responsible for managing users' information, such as passwords, password questions, and so on. The Membership APIs use the Membership Providers to save—or *persist*, in today's jargon—user information in data stores. Visual Studio 2005 ships with

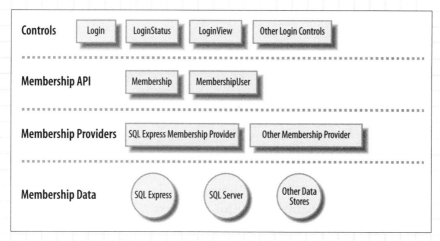

Figure 5-8. The Membership Provider Model

one default Membership Provider: the SQL Express 2005 Membership Provider. The role of the Membership Provider is to act as a bridge between the Membership APIs and the data stores, so that information can be persisted without requiring a developer to write the low-level code needed to access data.

If the provider supplied by Microsoft does not meet your needs, you can either extend them or simply write your own. For instance, if you want to save the membership information for your site in an XML document rather than a relational database (such as SQL Server), you can write your own provider to talk to the XML file.

What about...

...authenticating users without the use of cookies?

Forms authentication in ASP.NET 1.x uses an HTTP cookie to store the encrypted username. In ASP.NET 2.0, it now supports an additional mode of forms authentication: cookieless forms authentication. To use cookieless forms authentication, you just need to set the <cookieless> attribute within the *Web.config* file:

```
<authentication mode="Forms">
    <forms name=".ASPXAUTH"
           loginUrl="Login.aspx"
           protection="Validation"
           timeout="999999"
           cookieless="UseUri"/>
</authentication>
```

If you use cookie-less forms authentication, you will notice a long string of text embedded within your URL.

The cookieless attribute supports four modes:

AutoDetect
: Automatically detects whether the browser supports cookies and will automatically use cookies if the browser supports them

UseCookies
: Uses cookies for forms authentication (default behavior)

UseDeviceProfile
: Uses cookies (or not) based on device profile settings in *machine.config*

UseUri
: Uses cookieless forms authentication through the URL

...configuring the LoginView control in Source View?

If you do not like using the LoginView wizard, you can switch to Source View and manually add the attributes you need to configure the control. Here is the source view of the LoginView control that will achieve the same result as discussed earlier:

```
<asp:LoginView ID="LoginView1" runat="server">
    <LoggedInTemplate>
        You are logged in as
        <asp:LoginName ID="LoginName1" runat="server" />
        <asp:LoginStatus ID="LoginStatus2" runat="server" />
         
    </LoggedInTemplate>
    <AnonymousTemplate>
        You must <asp:LoginStatus ID="LoginStatus1"
        runat="server" /> to the O'Reilly Network to
        post a talkback.
    </AnonymousTemplate>
</asp:LoginView>
```

Where can I learn more?

For more information about the various parameters in the <forms> element in *Web.config*, check out the MSDN Help topic "<forms> Element."

For an overview of the Membership feature in ASP.NET 2.0, check out the MSDN Help topic "Introduction to Membership."

Add Users with WAT

Once you have set up your site to authenticate users, you need a way to add user accounts to your site. In ASP.NET 2.0, you can do this by using the ASP.NET Web Site Administration Tool (WAT). The user accounts you add will be stored in a SQL Server 2005 Express database by default (located under the *App_Data* folder in your project), as specified by the default Membership Provider. There is no longer any need for you to create your own custom databases for this purpose or to store the user account information in *Web.config* (which is insecure).

The ASP.NET Web Application Administration Tool (WAT) will help you create new users for your web site and then store the users' information in the database.

How do I do that?

In this lab, you will use the ASP.NET WAT to add new user accounts to your web application. The user accounts will be stored in the database specified by the Membership Provider (see the "How does it work?" section of "Create a Login Page Using the New Security Controls"). By default, the WAT adds new users to a SQL 2005 Express database.

1. Open the project created in the last lab (*C:\ASPNET20\chap-5-SecurityControls*).

2. To add a new user to your web site, you will use the ASP.NET Web Site Administration Tool (found in the Website → ASP.NET Configuration menu item; see Figure 5-9).

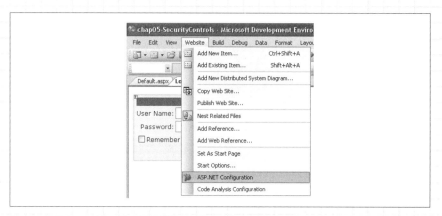

Figure 5-9. Launching the ASP.NET Configuration tool

Alternatively, you can invoke the ASP.NET WAT by clicking on the ASP.NET Configuration icon in Solution Explorer (see Figure 5-10).

3. To create a new user, click on the Security tab (see Figure 5-11).

4. Under the Users group, click on the "Create user" link to create a new user account (see Figure 5-12).

5. Enter the information needed to create a new user account (see Figure 5-13). Click the Create User button to complete the account creation.

Figure 5-10. Invoking the ASP.NET Configuration tool in Solution Explorer

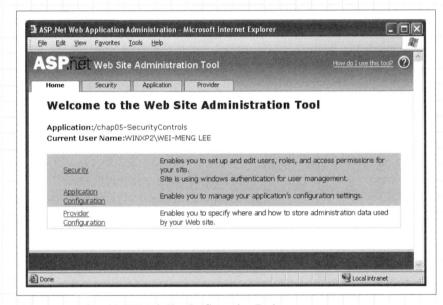

Figure 5-11. The ASP.NET Web Site Configuration Tool

6. Finally, you are now ready to test drive your application. In Solution Explorer, select *Default.aspx* and press F5. You should see the screen shown in Figure 5-14.

7. Click on the Login link to go to the *Login.aspx* page. Enter the account details of the account just created and click Log In (see Figure 5-15).

8. If the account is authenticated, you should see a screen like Figure 5-16.

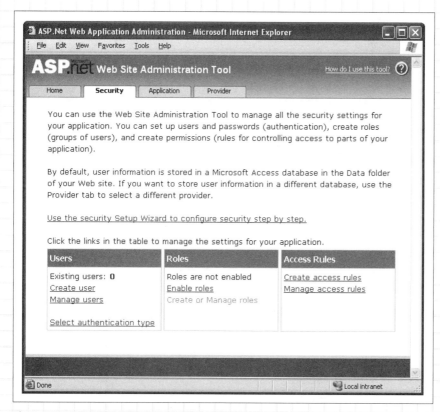

Figure 5-12. Creating a new user

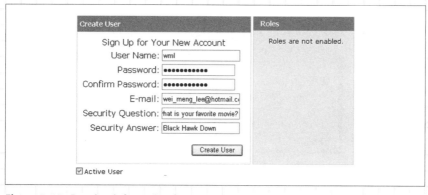

Figure 5-13. Entering information for a new user

Figure 5-14. The opening page: not logged in yet

Figure 5-15. Logging in

Figure 5-16. User authenticated

What just happened?

When you add a user to your application, the information is saved in two tables in SQL 2005 Express (located in the *App_Data* folder of the project):

- aspnet_Membership

- aspnet_Users

TIP

The aspnet_Membership table stores detailed information about a user (such as password, email, last login date, and more), whereas the aspnet_Users table stores information such as the name of the web application to which the user belongs.

Tables 5-1 and 5-2 show the values that are created in the two tables when I create an account for myself.

Table 5-1. Content of aspnet_Membership

Field	Value
ApplicationId	{B6677867-19E8-409B-B5CD-9D584B5F5647}
UserId	{03D7299A-2C80-4A3C-B6B7-818369526BEE}
Password	TyPAwmdjkASXx-ZAn+Kxy3U59qQO=
PasswordFormat	1
PasswordSalt	ZsmfGb76Jflh2+xmxcyXcA==
MobilePIN	
Email	wei_meng_lee@hotmail.com
LoweredEmail	wei_meng_lee@hotmail.com
PasswordQuestion	What is your favorite movie?
PasswordAnswer	Black Hawk Down
IsApproved	1
IsLockedOut	0
CreateDate	2/5/2005 6:58:05 PM
LastLoginDate	2/5/2005 6:58:05 PM
LastPasswordChangedDate	2/5/2005 6:58:05 PM
LastLockoutDate	1/1/1753
FailedPasswordAttemptCount	0
FailedPasswordAttemptWindowStart	1/1/1753
FailedPasswordAnswerAttemptCount	0
FailedPasswordAnswerAttemptWindowStart	1/1/1753
Comment	

Table 5-2. Content of aspnet_Users

Field	Value
ApplicationId	{B6677867-19E8-409B-B5CD-9D584B5F5647}
UserId	{03D7299A-2C80-4A3C-B6B7-818369526BEE}
UserName	wml
LoweredUserName	wml
MobileAlias	
IsAnonymous	0
LastActivityDate	2/5/2005 6:58:05 PM

Notice that the password has been *salt hashed* before it is stored in the Password field of the aspnet_Membership table (see the sidebar "Password Hashing").

What about...

...finding out whether a page is being viewed by an authenticated user?

You determine if a page is being viewed by an authenticated user by using the GetUser() method from the Membership class. Take the example of the *Default.aspx* page. You might want to display some customized welcome messages once a user has logged in successfully. You can do that by calling the GetUser() method in the Form_Load event-handling code. If the user viewing the page is not logged in, the GetUser() method will return null. The following code checks to see if an authenticated user is viewing the page, and if that's the case, it prints out the current time.

```
Protected Sub Page_Load(ByVal sender As Object, _
                    ByVal e As System.EventArgs) _
                    Handles Me.Load
    If Membership.GetUser IsNot Nothing Then
        Response.Write("Time is " & Now)
    End If
End Sub
```

...preventing a potential hacker from trying too many times to guess a user's password?

You can limit the number of unsuccessful attempts by setting the passwordAttemptThreshold and passwordAttemptWindow attributes of the Membership Provider in the *Web.config* file, as shown in Example 5-1.

Password Hashing

There are many ways to store a user's password in the database. The simplest (and most insecure) way is to store the user's password in clear text. However, doing so will expose all your users' passwords in the event that your database is compromised.

A better way would be to encrypt your password (using an encryption key or, better still, with keyless encryption). The best choice would be to apply a one-way function to the password so that no key is needed, reducing the chance that the key would be discovered by a potential hacker. Hashing is a cryptographic algorithm that takes in an input and produces a hash output. It does not require a key and, technically, there is little chance that two different inputs will produce the same hash value.

Therefore, the hashed values of passwords are often stored in the database. When a user logs in, the given password is hashed and its value is compared with that of the value stored in the database. If they are the same, the user is authenticated.

One pitfall of hashing is that a potential hacker may use a dictionary attack. He may generate a list of hash values of commonly used passwords and then compare them with the hash values stored in the database. Once a match is found, the attacker would know the password of a user.

To slow attackers down, a random string of values (known as a *salt*) is generated for each user and added to the password before it is hashed. The hashed value and the salt is then stored in the database. The advantage of this is that an attacker will now have to generate a separate list of hash values for each user (taking into consideration the random salt for each user), making it more difficult and time-consuming to get the exact password. Also, using a salted hash, two users having the same password will now have two different hash values, since a random salt is generated for each user.

Example 5-1. Limiting password attempts

```
...
<membership defaultProvider="SqlProvider"
          userIsOnlineTimeWindow="20">
   <providers>
      <add name="SqlProvider"
          type="System.Web.Security.SqlMembershipProvider"
          connectionStringName="LocalSqlServer"
          requiresQuestionAndAnswer="true"
          passwordAttemptThreshold="5"
          passwordAttemptWindow="30"
          applicationName="MyApplication" />
   </providers>
</membership>
```

The code in Example 5-1 limits a user to five password attempts within 30 minutes. If the user exceeds those numbers, her account will be locked.

Where can I learn more?

To learn more about how to use salted hashes in your own .NET applications, check out this MSDN article: *http://msdn.microsoft.com/msdnmag/issues/03/08/SecurityBriefs/*.

For more information on the passwordAttemptThreshold and passwordAttemptWindow attributes, check out the MSDN Help topics on "Membership.passwordAttemptThreshold property" and "Membership. passwordAttemptWindow property."

The Login controls are useful only if you restrict access to your pages in your site. Learn how to restrict user access to your ASP.NET application.

Restrict Unauthorized Access to Pages

So far, you have seen how to add a new login page to your web site and how you can add users to your application. In order to ensure that users provide a valid login credential before they are allowed access to a specific part of your site, you need to configure ASP.NET to require that *all* users be authenticated before they are given access.

How do I do that?

In the earlier lab "Create a Login Page Using the New Security Controls," you saw how to use the Login control to get a user's credentials. In this lab, you will learn how you can restrict access to certain pages based on the user's credentials. You will create a new folder in the existing project and then restrict access to this folder by modifying *Web.config*. When a page in the restricted folder is loaded, the login page will automatically be loaded to authenticate the user.

1. Using the project created in the previous lab (*C:\ASPNET20\chap-5-SecurityControls*), add a new folder named *Members* (right-click the project name in Solution Explorer and then select Add Folder → Regular Folder).

2. Add a Web Form to this folder (right-click the *Members* folder in Solution Explorer and then select Add New Item…; select Web Form) and name it *MemberDefault.aspx*.

3. Add a *Web.config* file to this folder (right-click the project name in Solution Explorer and then select Add New Item…; select Web Configuration File) and insert the following lines:

```
<!-- Remove this line
    <authentication mode="Windows" />
-->
<authorization>
    <deny users="?" />
</authorization>
```

4. The <deny> element specifies which users to deny access to the current folder (*Members*, in this case). You can also use the <allow> element to specifically state which users have access to the current folder. The question mark (?) specifies that anonymous users, or non-authenticated users, have access, while an asterisk (*) specifies that all users have access.

5. Your Solution Explorer should now resemble the one shown in Figure 5-17.

Figure 5-17. The Solution Explorer

6. Select *MemberDefault.aspx* in Solution Explorer and press F5. You will be redirected to the *Login.aspx* page, as this page is accessible only to an authenticated user. Log in with the user account created in the last lab. If the authentication is successful, the *MemberDefault.aspx* page will be loaded.

What about...

...using a single *Web.config* file to specify the access permission of the entire web application?

Besides adding a separate *Web.config* file to each folder in your web application to specify the access permission for each folder, you can also use the <location> element in the *Web.config* file in the root folder. The following entry in the *Web.config* file in the root of the web application is equivalent to Step 3:

```
...
</system.web>

<location path="Members">
    <system.web>
        <authorization>
            <deny users="?" />
        </authorization>
    </system.web>
</location>
</configuration>
```

Using this method will eradicate the need to have multiple *Web.config* files in your project. You can use multiple <location> elements to specify the permission for each folder.

Where can I learn more?

Check out the MSDN Help topic on the <location> element to learn more about the use of this element in *Web.config* files.

Recover Passwords for Users

Let users recover their lost passwords automatically through email.

Users sometimes (in reality, a lot of times!) forget their passwords, and you need to have a mechanism to help them recover their passwords easily. One of the most common ways is for the site to ask for your email address so that it can send you the password. In ASP.NET 2.0, this functionality is accomplished by the PasswordRecovery control.

The PasswordRecovery control allows users to retrieve their forgotten passwords via email and makes it a snap to implement this functionality for your site.

How do I do that?

In this lab, you will use the PasswordRecovery control to allow users to recover their forgotten passwords. You will extend the *Default.aspx* page

Password Recovery

Password recovery makes sense only if you store the password as plain text and not its hashed value. However, by default, the settings in the *machine.config* file specify that all passwords be hashed before they are stored in the member database. *machine.config* also disables password retrieval by default.

To store the user's password in plain text, add the following to *Web.config*:

```
...
<system.web>
    <membership
        defaultProvider="SqlProvider"
        userIsOnlineTimeWindow="15">
        <providers>
            <clear />
            <add
                name="SqlProvider"
                type="System.Web.Security.
                    SqlMembershipProvider"
                connectionStringName="LocalSqlServer"
                applicationName="chap05-SecurityControls"
                enablePasswordRetrieval="true"
                enablePasswordReset="true"
                requiresQuestionAndAnswer="true"
                requiresUniqueEmail="true"
                passwordFormat="Clear" />
        </providers>
    </membership>
...
```

Specifically, you are clearing all the Membership Providers and then adding a new SqlMembershipProvider. Note that you need to set the enablePasswordRetrieval and passwordFormat attributes (to true and Clear, respectively) in order to allow passwords to be retrieved.

If you set the passwordFormat as Hashed, then the enablePasswordReset must be set to false.

created in the earlier lab with the PasswordRecovery control so that users who have forgotten their passwords can retrieve them through email.

1. Using the project created in the last lab (*C:\ASPNET20\chap-5-SecurityControls*), drag and drop the PasswordRecovery control onto *Default.aspx* (see Figure 5-18).

2. Set the From and Subject properties from the MailDefinition node in the Properties window of the PasswordRecovery control (see Figure 5-19).

3. Apply the Elegant scheme to the PasswordRecovery control (through the Auto Format… link in the PasswordRecovery Tasks menu).

Figure 5-18. Adding the PasswordRecovery control to the Default.aspx form

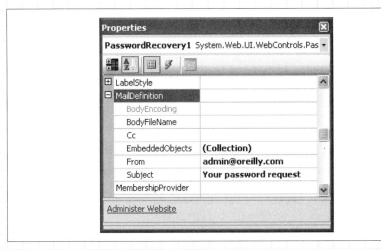

Figure 5-19. Configuring the PasswordRecovery control

4. Press F5 to test the application. You will first be prompted to enter your username, followed by the question that you set when you first registered. If your answer matches the one stored in the database, an email is sent to you; otherwise, you have to try again. The dialog is shown in Figure 5-20.

TIP

You need to have SMTP service configured on your machine for the PasswordRecovery control to send an email.

You can configure SMTP service on your machine by using the ASP.NET Web Application Administration → Application → Configure SMTP email settings.

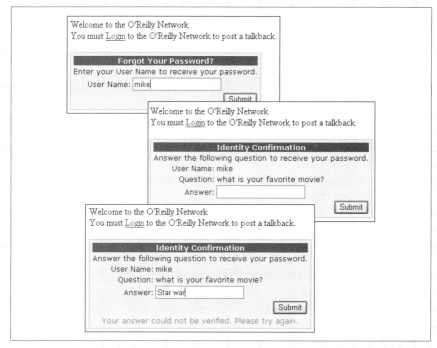

Figure 5-20. Recovering lost passwords

For security reasons, it is not a good idea to send a user's password through email. Hence, you need to carefully consider this option before you decide to use it.

What about...

...resetting a password?

You will learn how to reset a user password in the lab "Manage User Settings," later in this chapter.

Where can I learn more?

To see the various methods and properties supported by the Password-Recovery control, check out the MSDN Help topic "PasswordRecovery Members."

For more information on SMTP, check out the following SMTP chapter from the book *Exchange Server 2003 Transport and Routing Guide*:

> *http://www.microsoft.com/technet/prodtechnol/exchange/guides/*
> *E2k3TransnRouting/1bee564f-a307-4b65-83f4-61c1b5dcc744.mspx*

Let Users Change Passwords

Changing passwords is another common task performed by users of a web site. ASP.NET 2.0 has replaced the mundane task of writing low-level code to change passwords with a brand new ChangePassword control.

How do I do that?

In this lab, you will create a page that allows users to change their passwords. You will use the ChangePassword control to do the work. You will create a new Web Form in the restricted *Members* folder so that authenticated users can change their passwords.

1. Using the project created in the previous lab (*C:\ASPNET20\chap-5-SecurityControls*), drag and drop the ChangePassword control onto the *MemberDefault.aspx* Web Form located in the *Members* folder.

2. Apply the Elegant scheme to the ChangePassword control (through the Auto Format... link in the ChangePassword Tasks menu). The Change-Password control will now look like that shown in Figure 5-21.

Figure 5-21. The ChangePassword control

The ChangePassword control must be used on a form that is located within an authenticated directory so that it is accessible only after a user has logged in.

3. Press F5 to test the application. You will need to be authenticated first, so log in using the account created in the lab "Add Users with WAT." After authentication, the *MemberDefault.aspx* page will be displayed. Enter the current password and the new password. Click the Change Password button to change the password.

4. If the password is changed successfully, you will see the notification shown in Figure 5-22.

Figure 5-22. Changing password using the ChangePassword control

---

TIP

You need to set the ContinueDestinationPageUrl property of the ChangePassword control so that when the Continue button is clicked, the user can be redirected to another page. It's a good idea to set the property to point to the home page of your site.

---

5. If the new passwords do not match, an error message will be displayed (see Figure 5-23).

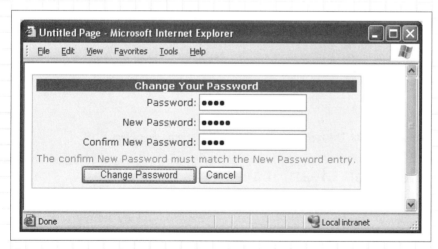

Figure 5-23. Error in changing the password

What about...

...adding regular expressions to ensure that the user's new password is of a certain length and complexity?

You can do this by adding a NewPasswordRegularExpression attribute to the <asp:changepassword> element (in Source View):

```
<asp:changepassword id="ChangePassword2" runat="server"
        PasswordHintText = "Password must be 8 characters long
                            and includes two numbers and two
                            special character."
        NewPasswordRegularExpression =
           '@\"(?=.{8,})(?=(.*\d){2,})(?=(.*\W){2,})'
        NewPasswordRegularExpressionErrorMessage=
           "Error: Your password must be 8 characters long
            and includes two numbers and two special character." >
</asp:changepassword>
```

If you apply the Elegant scheme to the ChangePassword control, it will appear like Figure 5-24 during runtime (shown displaying the different error messages).

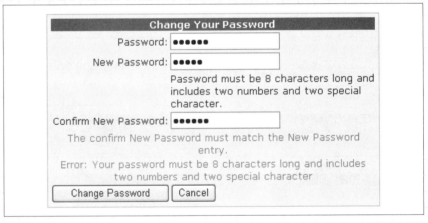

Figure 5-24. The ChangePassword control with the error messages

Where can I learn more?

For more information on using regular expressions for pattern matching, check out the book *Mastering Regular Expressions* by Jeffrey E. F. Friedl (O'Reilly).

Create Accounts with CreateUserWizard

Simplify user account creation with the new CreateUserWizard control.

Because creating user accounts is such as common task for most web sites, Microsoft has provided a new CreateUserWizard control in ASP.NET 2.0. The CreateUserWizard control takes the drudgery out of creating user accounts by providing a highly customizable control that accepts users' information. It performs such tasks as verifying users' passwords and authenticating email addresses. It then automatically adds the user account using the specified Membership Provider.

How do I do that?

In this lab, you will create a page to let users create an account on your web site. You will use the CreateUserWizard control to perform this task.

1. Using the same project created in the last lab (*C:\ASPNET20\chap-5-SecurityControls*), add a new Web Form to the project (right-click the project name in Solution Explorer and then select Add New Item...; select Web Form). Name the Web Form *NewUser.aspx*.

2. Drag and drop the CreateUserWizard control onto the form.

3. Apply the Elegant scheme to the CreateUserWizard control (through the Auto Format... link in the CreateUserWizard Tasks menu).Your page should now look like the one shown in Figure 5-25.

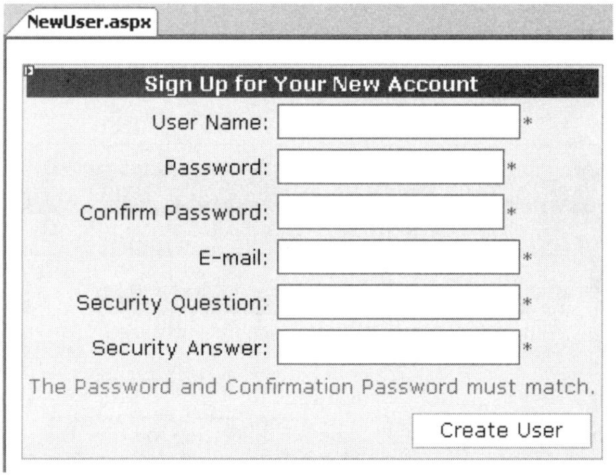

Figure 5-25. Using the CreateUserWizard control

You can customize the look and feel of the CreateUserWizard control by using the CreateUserWizard Tasks menu. You can apply formatting templates, add a sidebar to it (via the DisplaySideBar property), or set the CreateUserWizard control to display the Cancel button (via the DisplayCancelButton property).

4. Press F5 to test the application. Enter the information shown in Figure 5-26 and then click the Create User button.

Figure 5-26. Creating a new user account

5. If the account is created is successfully, you should see a notification like the one shown in Figure 5-27.

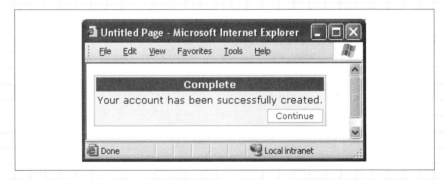

Figure 5-27. Successful creation of a new user account

You can verify the correct format of the email address by specifying a
regular expression for the CreateUserWizard control. This is set via the
EmailRegularExpression property of the CreateUserWizard control.

What about...

...adding a user to your site programmatically?

Besides using the ASP.NET Web Site Administration Tool or CreateUser-
Wizard control to add users to your web site, you can use the Membership class to add users programmatically to your web site. The
Membership class allows you to perform common tasks involved in
user management, such as user addition, deletion, and changing of
passwords.

1. Using the same project created in this lab (*C:\ASPNET20\chap-5-
   SecurityControls*), add a new Web Form to the project (right-click the
   project name in Solution Explorer and then select Add New Item...;
   select Web Form). Name the Web Form *AddUser.aspx*.

2. Add a 2×6 table to the Web Form (Layout → Insert Table) and populate it with the controls shown in Figure 5-28.

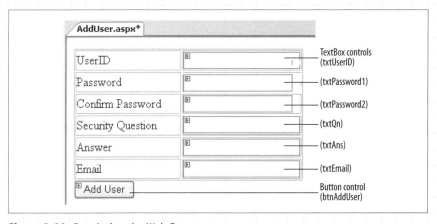

Figure 5-28. Populating the Web Form

3. Set the TextMode property of both the txtPassword1 and txt-Password2 controls to Password so that the password entered will not be displayed as plain text on the form.

4. Double-click the Add User button to switch to code-behind, and type in the following code:

```
Imports System.Web.Security
Partial Class AddUser_aspx
    Inherits System.Web.UI.Page

    Protected Sub btnAddUser_Click(ByVal sender As Object, _
                                    ByVal e As System.EventArgs) _
                                    Handles btnAddUser.Click
        Dim IsCreated As MembershipCreateStatus
        If (txtPassword1.Text = txtPassword2.Text) Then
            Membership.CreateUser(txtUserID.Text, txtPassword1.Text, _
                txtEmail.Text, txtQn.Text, txtAns.Text, True, IsCreated)
            Response.Write("Add user: " & IsCreated.ToString)
        Else
            Response.Write("Passwords do not match")
        End If
    End Sub
End Class
```

5. The MembershipCreateStatus enumeration returns the status of the user creation process. To test the application, press F5 and add a new user. The user information is saved in the aspnet_Users and aspMembership tables on the database specified by the Membership provider (by default, it is the SQL 2005 Express database).

You can verify that the new user has been added by loading the *Login.aspx* form and logging in with the new user credential.

...deleting a user?

You can delete a user by using the DeleteUser( ) method in the Membership class:

```
Dim username as String
Dim deleted as Boolean= _
    Membership.DeleteUser(username)
```

The DeleteUser( ) method returns a Boolean result indicating whether the specified user is deleted successfully.

Where can I learn more?

To learn more about the various methods in the Membership class, check out the MSDN Help topic on "Membership Methods."

Group Users into Roles

Simplify user management by using roles to group users by function.

Besides restricting access to individual users, it is sometimes much easier to restrict access based on the groups, or roles, to which users belong. You can use the ASP.NET Web Site Administration Tool (WAT) to classify users into roles and determine their access rights based on the function of each role. For example, users who administer the site might be grouped under an Admin role that you define. This role—and, by implication, the users assigned to it—can then be given permission via the *Web.config* file to access certain parts of the web site that are off-limits to others.

How do I do that?

In this lab, you will learn how to create roles for your web site through the use of the ASP.NET WAT. You will create a new role called Admin and then assign a newly created user, Administrator, to this role. After that, you will see how you can limit access to folders in your application based on the role of the user.

1. Open the project used in the last lab (*C:\ASPNET20\chap-5-SecurityControls*).

2. Invoke the ASP.NET WAT in Visual Studio 2005 (Website → ASP.NET Configuration).

3. Click on the Security tab, where you'll find the tools you need to set up roles for your site (see Figure 5-29).

4. Let's start by creating a special account for administrators of your site. Click the Create User link to add a new user account. Name the new user account Administrator.

5. Under the Roles section, click "Enable roles" to enable you to add roles in your web site. This step enables the "Create or Manage roles" link.

6. Click on the "Create or Manage roles" link to create a new role.

7. Enter a name for the new role you are creating: Admin. Click Add Role (see Figure 5-30). The role will now be created and displayed in the same page.

8. To add/remove users from a role, click on the Manage link (see Figure 5-31).

9. You will be able to search for users to be added into this role. Click on the All link to view all the users. Select the "User Is In Role" checkbox for the Administrator account. This will assign the Admin role to the Administrator account (see Figure 5-32).

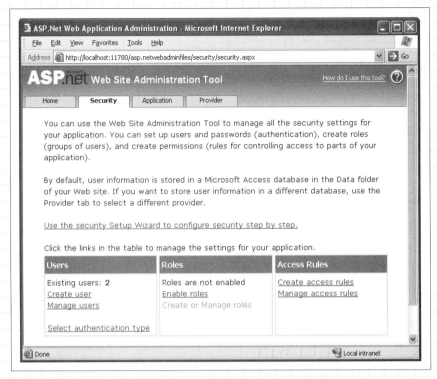

Figure 5-29. The Security tab in the ASP.NET Web Site Administration Tool

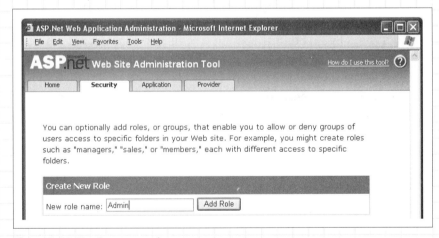

Figure 5-30. Naming a new role

10. Now Administrator is a member of the Admin role. Add the following lines to the *Web.config* file located within the */Members* folder:

```
<authorization>
    <allow roles="Admin" />
```

Figure 5-31. Managing a role

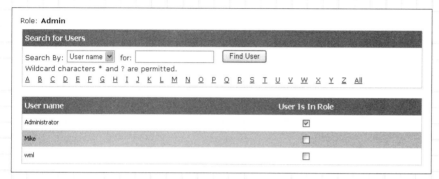

Figure 5-32. Assigning users to a role

```
        <deny users="*" />
    </authorization>
```

Only users belonging to the Admin role can now access the pages in the */Members* folder (others are denied access).

11. To test the new Admin role, select the *MemberDefault.aspx* page in Solution Explorer and then press F5.

You will be redirected to the login page, as pages in this folder can be viewed only by users in the Admin role. Log in using the wml account created in the lab "Add Users with WAT." You will notice that you will be prompted to log in again. This is because wml does not belong to the Admin role. Try the Administrator account. This time, the *MembersDefault.aspx* page will be loaded.

What about...

...programmatically creating roles and assigning users to roles?

Besides using the ASP.NET Web Site Administration Tool (WAT) to create roles and then assigning users to a role, you can programmatically create and manipulate role information via the Roles class. Let's see how this is done.

1. To illustrate how to use the Roles class, add a new Web Form to the *Members* folder (right-click the *Members* folder in Solution Explorer and then select Add New Item...; select Web Form). Name the Web Form *Roles.aspx*.

2. Populate the *Roles.aspx* Web Form with the controls shown in Figure 5-33. It will list the various roles defined in the web application as well as the users assigned to a particular role.

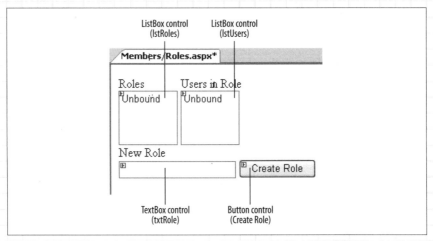

Figure 5-33. The various controls to display roles and users

3. In the ListBox Tasks menu of the lstRoles control, check the Enable AutoPostBack checkbox (see Figure 5-34). This will cause a postback to occur whenever a role is selected in the listbox, so that all users in that selected role can be retrieved and displayed in the second listbox.

Figure 5-34. Setting the AutoPostBack property of the lstRoles control

4. Double-click the Web Form to switch to the code-behind. Code the following in the Form_Load event. You use the GetAllRoles() method

from the Roles class to retrieve all the roles defined in the web application when the page is loaded for the first time. When a role is selected, you retrieve all the users in that role using the GetUsersInRole() method.

```
Protected Sub Page_Load(ByVal sender As Object, _
                        ByVal e As System.EventArgs) _
                        Handles Me.Load
    '---display roles when the page is first loaded
    If Not IsPostBack Then
        Dim allRoles() As String
        allRoles = Roles.GetAllRoles()
        lstRoles.Items.Clear()
        For i As Integer = 0 To allRoles.Length - 1
            lstRoles.Items.Add(allRoles(i).ToString)
        Next
    End If
    '---displays users in selected role
    lstUsers.Items.Clear()
    If lstRoles.SelectedItem IsNot Nothing Then
        Dim allUsersInRole() As String = _
            Roles.GetUsersInRole(lstRoles.SelectedItem.ToString)
        For i As Integer = 0 To allUsersInRole.Length - 1
            lstUsers.Items.Add(allUsersInRole(i).ToString)
        Next
    End If
End Sub
```

5. To create a new role, use the CreateRole() method. Code the Create Role Button control as follows:

```
Protected Sub btnCreateRole_Click(ByVal sender As Object, _
                        ByVal e As System.EventArgs) _
                        Handles btnCreateRole.Click
    Roles.CreateRole(txtRole.Text)
    lstRoles.Items.Add(txtRole.Text)
End Sub
```

6. Press F5 to test the application. When the page is loaded, you will be prompted to log in (use the Administrator account created in the previous lab). Once authenticated, you should be able to see the Admin role. Click on the Admin role, and the user(s) in the role will be displayed (see Figure 5-35).

7. You can also enter the name of a new role and then click on the Create Role button to create a new role.

The Roles class also supports other methods, including:

- Roles.GetRolesForUser
- Roles.GetUsersInRole
- Roles.GetUsersInRole

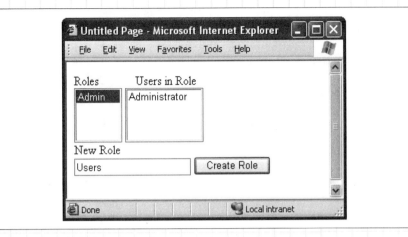

Figure 5-35. Displaying roles and users

- Roles.IsUserInRole
- Roles.RemoveUserFromRole
- Roles.RemoveUserFromRoles
- Roles.RemoveUsersFromRole
- Roles.RemoveUsersFromRoles
- Roles.RoleExists
- Roles.FindUsersInRole
- Roles.AddUsersToRole
- Roles.AddUsersToRoles
- Roles.AddUserToRole
- Roles.AddUserToRoles

Where can I learn more?

To understand how ASP.NET 2.0 stores role information through the role provider, check out the MSDN Help topic "ASP.NET Role Management Providers."

The MSDN Help topic "Implementing a Role Provider" also discusses how you can implement your own role provider.

To learn more about the various methods in the Roles class, check out the MSDN Help topic on "Roles Methods."

Manage User Settings

Learn how to programmatically modify user's account information using the Membership class.

So far, you have seen how to modify users' information using the built-in controls that ship with ASP.NET 2.0. A much more versatile approach would be to modify user data programmatically. The Membership class makes this possible and is, in fact, the source of many of the APIs driving all the new Login controls in ASP.NET 2.0.

How do I do that?

In this lab, you will learn how to programmatically modify and access a user's settings. You will create a Web Form and populate it with text boxes and Button controls to let users perform tasks such as changing their passwords and identity validation questions, as well as updating their email addresses. All these tasks will be performed using the Membership and MembershipUser classes.

1. Using the same project created in the last lab (*C:\ASPNET20\chap-5-SecurityControls*), add a new Web Form to the project (right-click the *Members* folder in Solution Explorer and then select Add New Item...; select Web Form). Name the Web Form *UserInfo.aspx*.

2. Add a 3×6 table to the Web Form (Layout → Insert Table) and populate it with the controls shown in Figure 5-36.

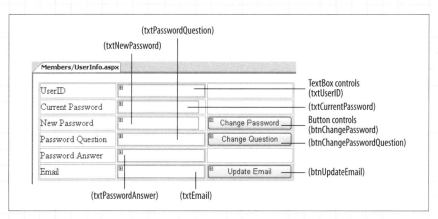

Figure 5-36. The various controls on the UserInfo.aspx page

3. When the form is first loaded, retrieve the user's information using the GetUser() method from the Membership class. It returns a

MembershipUser object. To code the Form_Load event, double-click on the Web Form to switch to the code-behind:

```
Protected Sub Page_Load(ByVal sender As Object, _
                        ByVal e As System.EventArgs) _
                        Handles Me.Load
    Dim user As MembershipUser
    '---get info about current user
    user = Membership.GetUser
    Response.Write("Your last login was on: " & _
                   user.LastLoginDate & "<br/>")
    Response.Write("Your account was created on: " & _
                   user.CreationDate & "<br/>")
    Response.Write("Your password was last changed on: " & _
                   user.LastPasswordChangedDate & "<br/>")
    If Not IsPostBack Then
        txtUserID.Text = user.UserName.ToString
        txtPasswordQuestion.Text = user.PasswordQuestion
        txtEmail.Text = user.Email
    End If
End Sub
```

Note that the MembershipUser class contains several pieces of information about the user, such as last login date, user creation date, and password last changed date. You can also retrieve the password question (but not the answer to the question).

TIP

If the user is not authenticated, the Membership.GetUser method returns a null reference.

---

4. Add the following displayMessage() subroutine to format and display a message on the page:

```
Private Sub displayMessage(ByVal str As String)
    Response.Write("<br/><b>" & str & "</b>")
End Sub
```

5. When the Change Password button is clicked, you can change the user's password via the ChangePassword() method in the MembershipUser class. This method returns a Boolean value indicating whether the change is successful:

```
Protected Sub btnChangePassword_Click(ByVal sender As Object, _
                                      ByVal e As System.EventArgs) _
                                      Handles btnChangePassword.Click
    Dim user As MembershipUser = Membership.GetUser
    '==change password===
    If txtCurrentPassword.Text <> "" And _
       (txtNewPassword.Text <> txtCurrentPassword.Text) And _
```

```
        txtNewPassword.Text <> "" Then
          '---means the user wants to change password
          If user.ChangePassword(txtCurrentPassword.Text, _
                              txtNewPassword.Text) Then
              displayMessage("Password Changed.")
          Else
              displayMessage("Password Changed Failed.")
          End If
      Else
          displayMessage("Required fields missing")
      End If
  End Sub
```

6. You can change the password question and answer using the ChangePasswordQuestionAndAnswer() method. It, too, returns a value indicating whether the change is successful:

```
Protected Sub btnChangePasswordQuestion_Click( _
          ByVal sender As Object, _
          ByVal e As System.EventArgs) _
          Handles btnChangePasswordQuestion.Click
  Dim user As MembershipUser = Membership.GetUser
  If txtCurrentPassword.Text <> "" And _
     txtPasswordQuestion.Text <> "" And _
     txtPasswordAnswer.Text <> "" Then
      If user.ChangePasswordQuestionAndAnswer( _
          txtCurrentPassword.Text, _
          txtPasswordQuestion.Text, _
          txtPasswordAnswer.Text) Then
          displayMessage("Password Question Changed.")
      Else
          displayMessage("Password Question Failed.")
      End If
  Else
      displayMessage("Required fields missing")
  End If
  End Sub
```

7. When the user clicks on the Update Email button, the email is updated via the UpdateUser() method in the Membership class:

```
Protected Sub btnUpdateEmail_Click(ByVal sender As Object, _
                            ByVal e As System.EventArgs) _
                            Handles btnUpdateEmail.Click
  Dim user As MembershipUser = Membership.GetUser
  user.Email = txtEmail.Text
  Membership.UpdateUser(user)
  displayMessage("Email Updated.")
  End Sub
```

8. Press F5 to test the page. When the page is loaded, you will be prompted to log in (use the Administrator account created in the previous lab). Figure 5-37 shows the page in action. To change the password, type in the current and new passwords and then click on

Change Password. To change the password question and answer, fill in the new question and answer and then click Change Question. To change the email address, fill in the new email address and click Update Email.

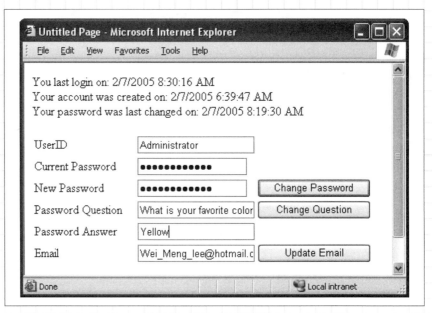

Figure 5-37. Modifying a user's information

Take note that this *UserInfo.aspx* page should be appropriately protected (using SSL, for example), since passwords are transmitted in the clear.

What about ...

...retrieving all users' information?

You can retrieve all the users' information in your application using the GetAllUsers() method in the MembershipUser class:

```
Dim users As MembershipUserCollection
users = Membership.GetAllUsers
```

The users' information is returned as a MembershipUserCollection. You can then bind it to, say, a GridView control:

```
GridView1.DataSource = users
GridView1.DataBind( )
```

If you need to reset a user's password, you can use the ResetPassword()
method in the MembershipUser class. You just need to supply a password answer (if your user account requires one):

```
Dim newPassword As String = user.ResetPassword(txtPasswordAnswer.Text)
```

The ResetPassword() method returns the new randomly generated
password.

Where can I learn more?

Check out the MSDN Help topics "Membership Members" and
"MembershipUser Members" for all the properties and methods in the
two classes.

For more comprehensive coverage of the GridView control, refer to
Chapter 4.

To learn how to configure SSL on IIS, check out:

*http://www.microsoft.com/resources/documentation/iis/6/all/
proddocs/en-us/nntp_sec_securing_connections.mspx*

Performance

ASP.NET 2.0 includes new features that enhance the performance of your web applications. For example, in ASP.NET 1.x, pages are dynamically compiled and cached the first time a user loads a page. As a result, an ASP.NET 1.x web application is typically slower the first time it is loaded. In ASP.NET 2.0, you can now precompile your site so that it's already compiled when the first user pays a visit.

ASP.NET 2.0 also supports fragment caching for the first time, which means you can now cache parts of your page rather than the entire page. An example of the usefulness of this feature is when you need to display the current time on a page while caching data retrieved from a database. In this case, the page output could be cached while on every request the current time could be inserted into the page.

Consuming web services is also now made easier with the automatic generation of a web proxy class based on a WSDL document. Simply drop a WSDL document into the *App_Code* folder and the web proxy class would be generated automatically.

Finally, ASP.NET 2.0 now includes the Client Callback Manager, which allows you to update your page with information from the server without performing a postback.

Configure Your App to Recompile on the Fly Whenever You Make a Change

In ASP.NET 1.x, all code-behinds are compiled into an assembly and stored in the /bin directory of the application, while the web pages (.*aspx*) are

In this chapter:
- *Configure Your App to Recompile on the Fly Whenever You Make a Change*
- *Dynamically Generate Web Service Proxy Classes*
- *Precompile Your Site*
- *Cache Fragments of a Page*
- *Lower the Cost of Server Callbacks*

You can now make changes to your ASP.NET 2.0 web application and it will recompile on the fly.

compiled on demand. And so any changes made to the *.aspx* page will automatically be updated, whereas changes to the code-behind of the page will not be recompiled until you explicitly request it.

In ASP.NET 2.0, you can use dynamic runtime compilation so that any changes made to either the *.aspx* or *.vb* (or *.cs*) files will automatically trigger a recompilation of the page.

How do I do that?

To verify that ASP.NET 2.0 will dynamically recompile your *.aspx* and code-behind files, you will create a web application that uses a class stored in a special directory called *App_Code*. When the class stored in the *App_Code* folder is modified, ASP.NET 2.0 will automatically recompile it when the page is requested.

1. Launch Visual Studio 2005 and create a new web site project. Name the project *C:\ASPNET20\chap06-DynamicRecompilation*.

2. To use dynamic runtime compilation for your ASP.NET 2.0 application, you need to add a special folder called *App_Code* to your project. Right-click the project name in Solution Explorer and select Add New Folder → Application Code Folder. You should now see the *App_Code* folder (see Figure 6-1).

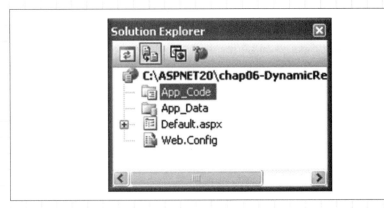

Figure 6-1. The App_Code folder in Solution Explorer

3. Right-click the *App_Code* folder and select Add New Item. Select Class and name it *TimeClass.vb*.

If you right-click the project name and try to add a class file to your project, you will be prompted to add the class within the *App_Code* folder. If the folder does not exist, one will be created automatically.

Special Folders in ASP.NET 2.0

In ASP.NET 2.0, there are several of directories under your project that have special significance. They are:

App_Code
> The *App_Code* folder is a container for class files and WSDL and XSD documents. All files contained within this folder are automatically compiled during runtime.

App_Data
> The *App_Data* folder is used to contain database files as well as XML and schema files.

App_LocalResources
> The *App_LocalResources* folder stores the resource files generated by Visual Studio to be used for implicit localization. See Chapter 8 for more information.

App_GlobalResources
> The *App_GlobalResources* folder is used to store resource files required for globalizations. Note that the resource files (*.resx*) placed in this folder are automatically exposed via the Resources class, providing IntelliSense statement completion for the resources contained within. See Chapter 8 for more information.

App_Themes
> The *App_Themes* folder stores themes and skin files.

App_Browsers
> The *App_Browsers* folder is used to store browser files for supporting different types of clients.

App_WebReferences
> The *App_WebReferences* folder stores *.wsdl* and *.discomap* files of web services.

The */Bin* directory is still supported for backward compatibility with ASP.NET 1.x applications.

4. Code *TimeClass.vb* as follows:

```
Imports Microsoft.VisualBasic

Public Class TimeClass
    Public Function getCurrentTime() As String
        Return "The current time is " & Now
    End Function
End Class
```

5. Switch to the code-behind of the default Web Form and in the Form_ Load event, code the following:

```
Protected Sub Page_Load(ByVal sender As Object, _
                        ByVal e As System.EventArgs) _
                        Handles Me.Load
    Dim time As New TimeClass
    Response.Write(time.getCurrentTime())
End Sub
```

6. Press F5 to test the application. You should see something like Figure 6-2.

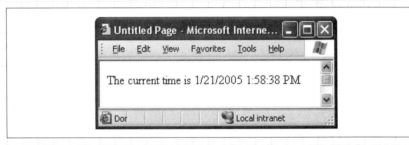

Figure 6-2. Testing the application

7. Without closing IE, make some modifications to the *TimeClass.vb* file. Use Notepad and load *TimeClass.vb* from *C:\ASPNET20\chap06-DynamicRecompilation\App_Code*. Change the code shown in bold in the following snippet:

```
Imports Microsoft.VisualBasic

Public Class TimeClass
    Public Function getCurrentTime() As String
        Return "Server time is now" & Now
    End Function
End Class
```

8. Refresh the IE web browser. You will notice that it takes a while to reload. This is because ASP.NET has detected that the *TimeClass.vb* file has changed and hence is recompiling it. Once compilation is complete, you should see the updated output from the TimeClass class shown in Figure 6-3.

What about...

...using multiple languages in the same project?

As you have seen, you can place your class files into the *App_Code* folder so that ASP.NET can dynamically compile them. However,

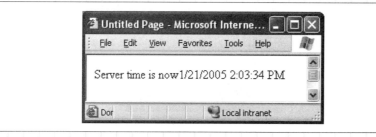

Figure 6-3. Displaying the updated page

because all these files will be compiled into a single assembly, you cannot have files of different languages (such as VB2005 and C#) all contained within this folder.

If you want to keep multi-language files within the *App_Code* folder, you need to separate them into different subfolders within the *App_Code* folder.

ASP.NET will automatically use the correct language compiler to compile the files contained in the App_Code folder.

TIP

As mentioned in Chapter 1, while support for multiple languages is a useful feature, developers should weigh the pros and cons of mixing languages in a project. The pro is that you can have different programmers (with different language preferences) working together on a project. However, this also may increase the effort required in maintaining the project in the future.

---

1. To create subfolders within the *App_Code* folder, add the <codeSub-Directories> element to the *Web.config* file:

```
<compilation debug="true">
   <codeSubDirectories>
      <add directoryName="VB" />
      <add directoryName="CS" />
   </codeSubDirectories>
</compilation>
```

TIP

The names of the subfolders under *App_Code* are purely arbitrary and will not influence the type of language files you can store. ASP.NET will examine the file types within the subfolders and use the appropriate compiler to compile the source code in each folder. The important point is this: files of the same language must be in the same folder.

---

2. Right-click the *App_Code* folder, and then select Add Folder → Regular Folder. Name the folder *VB*. Repeat this step one more time and name the folder *CS*. Your *App_Code* folder tree should now look like the one shown in Figure 6-4.

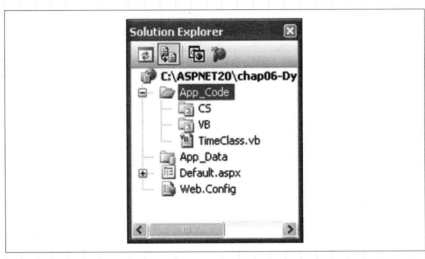

Figure 6-4. The subfolders within the App_Code folder

3. You can now drag and drop the *TimeClass.vb* file into the *VB* folder. You can also add a new class file (say, *Employee.cs*, written in C#) to the *CS* folder (see Figure 6-5).

Figure 6-5. Adding source files to the respective folders

Where can I learn more?

The choice of which language to use has always been a hotly debated topic. If you are also pondering whether to use VB.NET or C#, check out some of the discussions on the Web and decide for yourself:

- *http://blogs.msdn.com/csharpfaq/archive/2004/03/11/87816.aspx*
- *http://dotnetjunkies.com/WebLog/sahilmalik/archive/2004/05/07/13071.aspx*
- *http://www.developerdotstar.com/community/node/61*

Dynamically Generate Web Service Proxy Classes

Now you can simply drop a WSDL file into the App_Code folder and the web proxy class is dynamically generated. Cool!

In Visual Studio .NET 2003, you must manually add a web reference to a web service using Add Web Reference or the *WSDL.exe* tool so that the appropriate web proxy class is generated. In Visual Studio 2005, this step is no longer required. Instead, you simply add a WSDL document that describes the service into the *App_Code* folder and the web proxy class needed to access the service is generated automatically. This allows you to handle situations where you are only provided a WSDL file by a web service provider and not a browsable URL endpoint containing the WSDL document.

How do I do that?

In this lab, you will see how easy it is to consume a web service, given its WSDL document. You will enable an application to consume a language translation web service by simply saving the WSDL document in the *App_Code* folder. IntelliSense will then show the web proxy class generated, based on the WSDL document.

1. Launch Visual Studio 2005 and create a new web site project. Name the project *C:\ASPNET20\chap06-DynamicWebProxy*.

2. Right-click the project name in Solution Explorer and select Add Folder → App_Code Folder.

3. Use IE to load the WSDL document located at *http://www.webservicex.com/TranslateService.asmx?WSDL*. Save the file as *TranslateService.wsdl* in *C:\ASPNET20\chap06-DynamicWebProxy\App_Code*.

4. To see the WSDL document in Solution Explorer, right-click the *App_Code* folder and select Refresh Folder (see Figure 6-6).

What Is a Web Service?

I have always liked to describe a web service as a web application without a user interface. Technically, a web service is a business object residing on a server that you can programmatically access through the network. For example, a stock exchange could deploy a web service that allows its customers to check for the latest stock prices. Rather than using a web browser to check for current stock prices, customers can write their own custom applications and programmatically access price data through the web service and then integrate the results back into their application.

To ensure interoperability between web services and its users (known as *web service consumers*), most web services use standards such as XML, HTTP, and WSDL:

- XML is used as the language for exchanging messages between a web service and its consumer.
- HTTP is used as the transport protocol to carry web services messages.
- WSDL is used to write the contract that defines what the web service has to offer.

In Visual Studio (2003 and 2005), you need to obtain the WSDL file of a web service so that you know how to communicate with it. The advantage of using Visual Studio for web services is that it will automatically generate a proxy class for you (based on the WSDL document) so that you can simply invoke the web service just like a normal object.

Figure 6-6. Saving a WSDL file within the App_Code folder

5. A web proxy class would then be dynamically generated.

6. To test the web proxy class, populate the default Web Form for the project with the controls shown in Figure 6-7.

Chapter 6: Performance

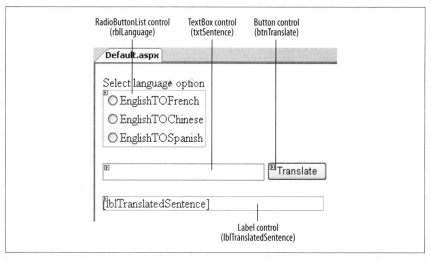

Figure 6-7. Populating the default Web Form

7. Double-click the Translate button to reveal the code-behind of the Web Form. Code the Click event of the Translate button as follows:

```
Protected Sub btnTranslate_Click(ByVal sender As Object, _
                                 ByVal e As System.EventArgs) _
                                 Handles btnTranslate.Click
    Dim ws As New TranslateService
    Dim targetLanguage As String
    Select Case rblLanguage.SelectedIndex
        Case 0 : targetLanguage = _
                 ws.Translate(Language.EnglishTOFrench, _
                 txtSentence.Text)
        Case 1 : targetLanguage = _
                 ws.Translate(Language.EnglishTOChinese, _
                 txtSentence.Text)
        Case 2 : targetLanguage = _
                 ws.Translate(Language.EnglishTOSpanish, _
                 txtSentence.Text)
    End Select
    lblTranslatedSentence.Text = targetLanguage
End Sub
```

IntelliSense will automatically display the web proxy class that was dynamically generated (TranslateService) as one of its choices.

8. Press F5 to test the application. Enter a sentence, select a language option, and then click the Translate button (see Figure 6-8).

TIP

Your browser must be installed with the language pack for you to display some languages correctly. To do so, in IE select View → Encoding → More and select the desired language (Chinese, for example). You will then be prompted to install the language pack (you need the Windows installation disk).

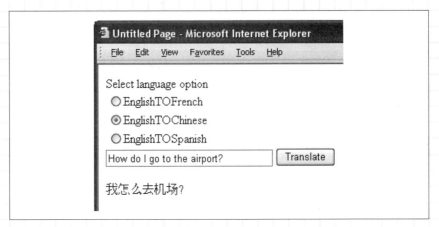

Figure 6-8. Testing the application

What about...

...the old way of generating a web service proxy class using Add Web Reference?

In ASP.NET 2.0, you can still use Add Web Reference to add a reference to a web service. Simply right-click the project name in Solution Explorer and select Add Web Reference... (see Figure 6-9).

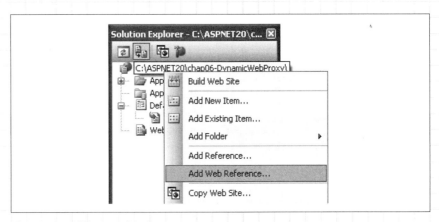

Figure 6-9. Adding a web reference

You will be prompted to enter the URL of the web service. If you enter *http://www.webservicex.com/TranslateService.asmx?WSDL*, the web reference will then be added to the project under the *App_WebReferences* folder (see Figure 6-10).

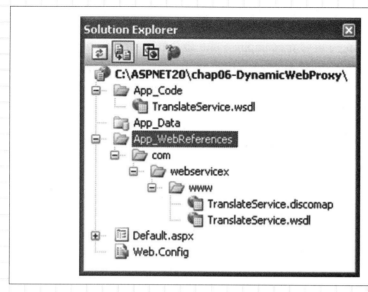

Figure 6-10. The web reference added to the project

To invoke the web service, add the following statement to your code:

```
Dim ws As New com.webservicex.www.TranslateService
```

Where can I learn more?

If you want to learn how to develop web services using Visual Studio, check out the following tutorials: *http://www.programmingtutorials.com/webservices.aspx*.

For a whitepaper on web services architecture and its specifications, read the following article from MSDN: *http://msdn.microsoft.com/webservices/default.aspx?pull=/library/en-us/dnwebsrv/html/introwsa.asp*. Note that this paper contains a lot of information, and you may find it overwhelming, especially if you are a newcomer to web services. However, I do recommend that you read it once you have mastered the fundamentals of the topic.

Precompile Your Site

In ASP.NET 1.x, you deploy files with *.aspx* extensions to the web server that hosts the application. To safeguard your business logic, ASP.NET does not require you to deploy the code-behinds of your Web Forms. However, the user interface of your web application is still encapsulated within the *.aspx* file, and these files must be deployed to the web server, opening

You can now precompile and deploy your ASP.NET web application without exposing the source, thereby improving first user response time and protecting your IP.

the possibility that someone at the web server end (especially for web hosting scenarios) may read your UI code. ASP.NET 2.0 has gone a step further, allowing you to precompile a site so that when you deploy it:

- There is no code (neither *.aspx* nor code-behind sources) on the server side.
- The site is precompiled, which shortens first-use response time.

TIP

If your web application uses client-side scripts, they would still be visible on the user's web browser side, since they have to be sent to the web browser for processing.

How do I do that?

ASP.NET 2.0 supports two precompilation options:

- Precompile for site deployment
- Precompile In–Place

Precompile for site deployment allows to you to deploy the compiled binaries of your web site to the hosting machine without the need to deploy your source code. This is a great boost to protecting your source, especially when you are deploying to a remote hosting machine and do not want others to see the source code behind your web site. It also precompiles the site and so reduces the first-use response time of the application.

Let's see how you can precompile a site for deployment.

1. Launch Visual Studio 2005 and create a new web site project. Name the project *C:\ASPNET20\chap06-Precompile*.

2. To precompile the web site, use the *aspnet_compiler* utility available in the *C:\WINDOWS\Microsoft.NET\Framework\<version>* folder.

3. In the command-line window, type the following:

```
C:\Windows\Microsoft.NET\Framework\version>aspnet_compiler -v /
Precompile -p C:\ASPNET20\chap06-Precompile c:\Precompile_Target
```

4. Your compiled web site can now be found in *C:\Precompile_Target* (see Figure 6–11).

5. If you view the content of the placeholder *Default.aspx* file, you will see that it contains the following single sentence (all the logic is compiled into files located in the *bin* folder):

```
This is a marker file generated by the precompilation tool, and should
not be deleted!
```

The aspnet_compiler Utility

The syntax of the *aspnet_compiler* utility is:

```
aspnet_compiler [-?] [-m metabasePath | -v virtualPath [-p
physicalDir]] [[-u] targetDir]
```

-m

> The full IIS metabase path of the application. This switch cannot be combined with the -v or -p switches.

-v

> The virtual path of the application to be compiled (e.g., "/MyApp"). If -p is specified, the physical path is used to locate the application. Otherwise, the IIS metabase is used, and the application is assumed to be in the default site (under "/LM/W3SVC/1/Root"). This switch cannot be combined with the -m switch.

-p

> The physical path of the application to be compiled. If -p is missing, the IIS metabase is used to locate the app. This switch must be combined with -v.

-u

> If specified, the precompiled application is updatable.

-f

> Overwrites the target directory if it already exists. Existing contents are lost.

-nologo

> Suppresses the compiler copyright message.

targetDir

> The physical path to which the application is compiled. If not specified, the application is precompiled in-place.

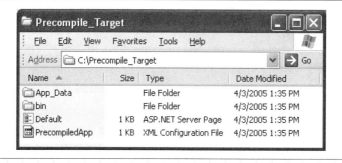

Figure 6-11. The folder containing the compiled page

6. To deploy the application to the target web server, you can now create a virtual directory in IIS and point it to the *C:\Precompile_Target* directory. To access the web site, simply use the following URL format: *http://webserver/virtualdir/default.aspx*.

What about...

Precompile In-Place is useful for web sites that change often.

...precompiling in-place?

That's certainly possible. Precompile In-Place allows you to precompile a web site before the user loads the page. Traditional ASP.NET pages are dynamically compiled and cached the first time a user loads the page, so the load time is always higher the first time the site is accessed. With precompilation, the web site is compiled and cached before a user loads a page for the first time, eliminating the long wait for the page to be compiled. Another benefit to this approach is the ability to check for bugs before the user discovers them.

To precompile your site before the first user loads it, you simply invoke the special handler *precompile.axd* located in the virtual root of your web application, like this:

http://localhost/chap06-Precompile/precompile.axd

After precompilation, you will notice that there are no delays when the application is first accessed.

TIP

Precompiling works by compiling the entire site (including subdirectories).

...hackers launching a denial-of-service attack at my site by forcing it to constantly precompile?

ASP.NET 2.0 will turn off remote precompiling in-place. You can only perform a precompile in-place locally.

...updating an application once I have precompiled it?

Once you have precompiled an application, you can only deploy the directory that has been generated. To update an application, you would need to modify the original application files and perform the precompilation steps again.

Where can I learn more?

To learn how you can precompile ASP.NET 1.x applications, check out the article at *http://www.codeproject.com/aspnet/PreCompileAspx.asp*.

Cache Fragments of a Page

In ASP.NET 1.x, you can either cache an entire page or cache fragments of the page using user controls. In ASP.NET 2.0, you can cache the output of a page while designating a portion of the page to be updated on every request.

You can now cache portions of a page, instead of the entire page, and thereby speed up page updates.

How do I do that?

In this lab, you will create a page that uses fragment caching. The main page will use output caching, while a part of the page will be updated on every request.

1. Launch Visual Studio and create a new web site project. Name the project *C:\ASPNET20\chap06-CacheFragments*.

2. In the default Web Form, switch to Source View and add the @OutputCache directive. You will cache the output of this page for five seconds:

   ```
   <%@ Page Language="VB" AutoEventWireup="false" CodeFile="Default.aspx.
   vb" Inherits="Default_aspx" %>
   <%@ OutputCache Duration="5" VaryByParam = "none" %>
   ```

3. Switch to the code-behind of default Web Form. In the Page_Load event, type the following code:

   ```
   Protected Sub Page_Load(ByVal sender As Object, _
                           ByVal e As System.EventArgs) _
                           Handles Me.Load
       Response.Write("Current (cached) Time is :" & Now)
   End Sub
   ```

4. The output of the Write statement will be cached for five seconds, meaning the time will be updated every five seconds. Now, add a shared function in the default Web Form that also displays the current time:

   ```
   Public Shared Function getServerTime( _
        ByVal context As System.Web.HttpContext) _
        As String
        Return "Current Time is :" & Now.ToString
   End Function
   ```

Note the parameter of the shared function. This is required for the HttpResponseSubstitutionCallback class, as you will see later.

5. Instead of using the Response.Write() method to display the time returned by this function, use the new Response.WriteSubstitution() method. Add the lines shown in bold to the Page_Load event:

```
Protected Sub Page_Load(ByVal sender As Object, _
                        ByVal e As System.EventArgs) _
                        Handles Me.Load
    Response.Write("Current (cached) Time is :" & Now)
    Response.Write("<br/>")
    Response.WriteSubstitution(New _
        HttpResponseSubstitutionCallback(AddressOf _
        getServerTime))
End Sub
```

6. The Response.WriteSubstitution() method basically calls the getServerTime() method on every request, and the output is then inserted into the cached response.

7. Press F5 to test the application. Refresh the page regularly and you will see that the time shown on the first line is refreshed every five seconds, while the second line is refreshed on every request (see Figure 6–12).

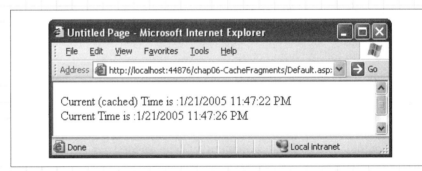

Figure 6-12. The time displays are different: one is cached while the other is fresh

What about...

...saving output caching on disk?

By default, ASP.NET 2.0 saves the output caching on disk. This has the advantages of caching more information than what your memory allows you, as well as the ability to retrieved cached data when the web server undergoes a restart.

You can, however, turn off disk caching by modifying the DiskCacheable attribute in the OutputCache directive:

```
<%@ OutputCache Duration="120" VaryByParam="name"
    DiskCacheable="false" %>
```

To affect all the pages in an application, insert the <outputCache> element into *Web.config*. You can also specify the size of the disk to cache for the application.

```
<?xml version="1.0"?>
<configuration>
    <system.web>
        <caching>
            <outputCache>
                <diskCache enabled="true" maxSizePerApp="5" />
            </outputCache>
        </caching>
    </system.web>
</configuration>
```

Is there a better way to manage cache profiles for the entire application? If you have many pages that you need to manage, it is always better to control the caching profile of all pages centrally. Instead of modifying the cache duration of each page individually, a much more efficient way would be to specify sets of caching profiles in the *Web.config* file.

The following entries in *Web.config* specify several caching profiles:

```
<system.web>
    <caching>
        <outputCacheSettings>
            <outputCacheProfiles>
                <add name="Cache30sec" duration="30" />
                <add name="Cache5min" duration="300" />
                <add name="Cache1hr" duration="3600" />
                <add name="ShortTerm" duration="1800" />
                <add name="LongTerm" duration="7200" />
            </outputCacheProfiles>
        </outputCacheSettings>
    </caching>
</system.web>
```

To use the policies defined in *Web.config*, simply set the profiles via the CacheProfile attribute:

```
<%@ OutputCache CacheProfile="ShortTerm" VaryByParam="name" %>
```

One advantage of the cache profile is that you can change the cache duration via the *Web.config* file without modifying the source of the page. In the previous example, if you think that the short term caching should be more than half an hour (1800 seconds), you can just change it to a larger value.

Where can I learn more?

To learn more about the various ways you can improve your web application by using caching, check out my article at *http://www.devx.com/asp/Article/21751*.

Send data back to the server without a postback by using the Client Callback Manager.

Lower the Cost of Server Callbacks

One of the inherent limitations of web applications is the costly delay that occurs when a web page posts data to the server that requires the page to be reloaded. Instead of updating only the portion of the page affected by the postback, the entire page has to be refreshed when some elements of the page need to be changed. For example, if a user selects "US" as the country in a registration web page, a drop-down list should display all the states in the U.S. If the user selects a country other than the U.S., the drop-down list should change to display the states of the selected country. Current implementation refreshes the entire page, which is often slow and frustrating. (Another technique is to send all of the states to the client and use JavaScript to display the related states when the user chooses a country, but this method largely inflates the size of the page and increases loading time.)

One technique that current ASP.NET 1.x developers use to overcome this postback problem is employing the Microsoft XMLHTTP ActiveX object to send requests to server-side methods from client-side JavaScript. In ASP.NET 2.0, this process has been simplified and encapsulated within the function known as the *Client Callback Manager*.

XMLHTTP

The ASP.NET Client Callback Manager uses XMLHTTP behind the scenes to encapsulate the complexities in sending data to and from the servers and clients. And so, in order for the Callback Manager to work, you need a web browser that supports XMLHTTP. Internet Explorer is, obviously, one of them. To use the Client Callback Manager, you need IE 5.0 or higher.

How do I do that?

To see how the Callback Manager in ASP.NET 2.0 works, let's build the simple web application shown in Figure 6-13.

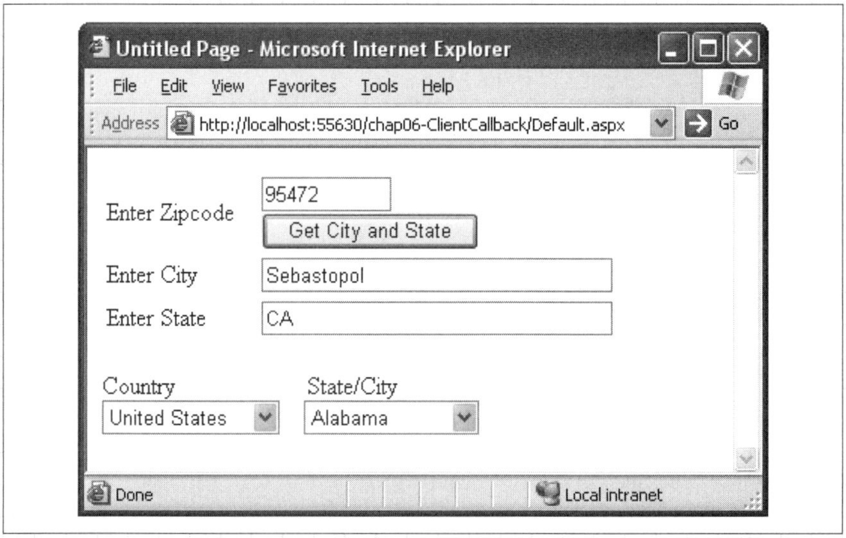

Figure 6-13. Developing the sample application for client callback

The example will allow a user to enter a Zip Code into a text box and retrieve the city and state information without posting back to the server. A TextBox control is used for entering a Zip Code, while a Button control is used to invoke the code (to get the city and state based on the Zip Code) on the server. The result is then displayed in the city and state text boxes.

The application also has two DropDownList controls on the form. When a user selects a particular country, the states (or cities) belonging to the selected country are retrieved from the server and displayed in the second DropDownList control.

1. Launch Visual Studio 2005 and create a new web site project. Name the project *C:\ASPNET20\chap06-ClientCallback*.

2. Populate the default Web Form with the controls shown in Figure 6-14.

3. Add three items to the ddlCountry DropDownList control. You can add them by switching the default Web Form to Source View and entering the following bold lines:

```
<asp:DropDownList ID="ddlCountry" Runat="Server" >
  <asp:ListItem>Select Country</asp:ListItem>
  <asp:ListItem Value="US">United States</asp:ListItem>
  <asp:ListItem Value="Sing">Singapore</asp:ListItem>
  <asp:ListItem Value="UK">United Kingdom</asp:ListItem>
</asp:DropDownList>
```

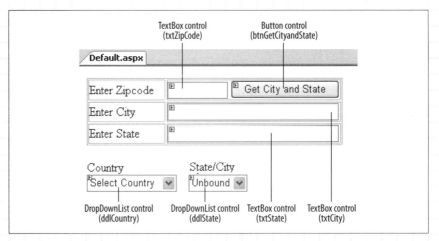

Figure 6-14. Populating the form with controls

4. Switch to the code-behind of the default Web Form. The Web Form that is going to receive the postback needs to implement the ICall-backEventHandler interface. You also need to declare a public String (its use will be evident later on):

```
Partial Class Default_aspx
    Inherits System.Web.UI.Page
    Implements ICallbackEventHandler
    Public callbackStr As String
```

The ICallbackEventHandler interface has only one method to implement: RaiseCallbackEvent( ). This method is invoked when the client sends a postback to the server. In this case, this is the place to check the city and state information of a Zip Code, as well as retrieve the states and cities of a country.

5. Ideally, all of this information should be retrieved from a web service, but for simplicity you will hardcode the result to be returned for a limited number of queries. Code the RaiseCallbackEvent( ) method as shown in Example 6-1.

Example 6-1. ClientCallBack Server-side RaiseCallbackEvent( )

```
Public Function RaiseCallbackEvent(ByVal eventArgument As String) As _
  String Implements _
  System.Web.UI.ICallbackEventHandler.RaiseCallbackEvent

  If eventArgument.StartsWith("1:") Then
    '---strips away the command
    eventArgument = eventArgument.Substring(2)
```

Example 6-1. ClientCallBack Server-side RaiseCallbackEvent( ) (continued)

```
     '---get city and state based on Zipcode
     Select Case eventArgument
        Case "95472" : Return "Sebastopol,CA"
        Case "02140" : Return "Cambridge,MA"
        Case Else
           Throw (New Exception("ZipCode not valid!"))
     End Select
  ElseIf eventArgument.StartsWith("2:") Then
     '---strips away the command
     eventArgument = eventArgument.Substring(2)
     '---get states and cities related to country
     Select Case eventArgument
        Case "Sing" : Return "Singapore,"
        Case "US" : Return _
  "Alabama,California,Maryland,Massachusetts,New York,Oklahoma,Wisconsin,"
        Case "UK" : Return _
  "Birmingham,Cambridge,Christchurch,Leeds,Sheffield,"
        Case Else
           Return ""
     End Select
  Else
        Return "Command not recognized"
  End If
End Function
```

Notice that the RaiseCallbackEvent( ) function takes in and returns a result of String data type. Therefore, if you have complex data types to transfer from the client to the server (and vice versa), you need to serialize the complex object into a string and then back.

The eventArgument parameter is passed from the client. To retrieve the state and city based on Zip Code, the eventArgument parameter would look like this:

```
1:02140
```

where 1: is the command and 02140 is the Zip Code.

To retrieve all states and cities based on country, the eventArgument parameter would look like this:

```
2:US
```

where 2: is the command and US is the country code.

TIP

Note that for the first command, the returning result (city and state) is separated by a comma—for example, Sebastopol,CA. For the second command, the returning result (states or cities) is also separated by commas—for example, Alabama,California, Maryland,Massachusetts,New York,Oklahoma,Wisconsin,.

---

6. In the Page_Load event, you need to wire up the "Get City and State" button and the Country drop-down list. You also need to generate the code that performs the callback by using the GetCallbackEventReference() method from the ClientScriptManager class:

The ClientScriptManager class is the one that handles tasks such as client-side scripts registration. You can get an instance of the ClientScriptManager class through the Page's ClientScript property.

```
Sub Page_Load(ByVal sender As Object, ByVal e As System.EventArgs) _
    Handles Me.Load

    '---prevent the Get City & State button from postback
    btnGetCityandState.Attributes.Add("onClick", "return false")

    ddlCountry.Attributes.Add("onChange", "GetStatesFromServer()")
    callbackStr = Page.ClientScript.GetCallbackEventReference(_
                    Me, "Command", "CallBackHandler", _
                    "context", "onError", False)
End Sub
```

The parameters for the GetCallbackEventReference() method are:

control *(control)*
    A reference to the caller itself

argument *(string)*
    The string to be passed to the server side for processing

clientCallback *(string)*
    The reference to the callback handler on the server side

context *(string)*
    A token used to identify who actually initiated the callback

errorCallback *(string)*
    The reference to the callback handler when an error occurs

async *(Boolean)*
    Specifies if the callback script should be called asynchronously

The callbackStr variable will store the following string when the form is loaded:

```
WebForm_DoCallback('__Page',Command,
                    CallBackHandler,context,onError,false)
```

What is important here is that Command refers to the string that is going to be passed to the server, while CallBackHandler is the function that is invoked (on the client) when the server returns a result to the client.

7. Let's now define the functions required on the client side. Switch to Source View for the default Web Form and add in the script block shown in Example 6-2.

Example 6-2. Script for ClientCallback client-side functions

```
...
<head runat="server">
    <title>Untitled Page</title>
<script>
function GetStateFromZip(){
  var Command = "1:" + document.forms[0].elements['txtZipCode'].value;
  var context = new Object();
  context.CommandName = "GetStateFromZip";
  <%=callbackStr%>
}

function GetStatesFromServer() {
  var Command = "2:" + document.forms[0].elements['ddlCountry'].value;
  var context = new Object();
  context.CommandName = "GetStatesFromCountry";
  <%=callbackStr%>
}

function CallBackHandler(result, context) {
  if (context.CommandName == "GetStateFromZip" ) {
    var indexofComma = result.indexOf(",");
    var City = result.substring(0,indexofComma);
    var State = result.substring(indexofComma+1,result.length);
    document.forms[0].elements['txtState'].value = State;
    document.forms[0].elements['txtCity'].value = City;
  } else
  if (context.CommandName == "GetStatesFromCountry")
  {
    document.forms[0].elements['ddlState'].options.length=0;
    while (result.length>0) {
      var indexofComma = result.indexOf(",");
      var State = result.substring(0,indexofComma);
      result = result.substring(indexofComma+1);

      opt = new Option(State,State);
      document.forms[0].elements['ddlState'].add(opt);
    }
  }
}

function onError(message, context) {
  alert("Exception :\n" + message);
}

</script>
</head>
...
```

The GetStateFromZip() and GetStatesFromServer() methods basically formulate the request to be sent to the server side; in this case, it takes the value of the TextBox control (and DropDownList control) and puts it into the callbackStr variable. The <%=callbackStr%> statement will insert the generated string into the function, so that at runtime it becomes:

```
function GetStateFromZip(){
  var Command = "1:" + document.forms[0].elements['txtZipCode'].value;
  var context = new Object();
  context.CommandName = "GetStateFromZip";
  WebForm_DoCallback('__Page',Command,CallBackHandler,context,onError,
  false)
}

function GetStatesFromServer(){
  var Command = "2:" + document.forms[0].elements['ddlCountry'].value;
  var context = new Object();
  context.CommandName = "GetStatesFromCountry";
  WebForm_DoCallback('__Page',Command,CallBackHandler,context,onError,
  false)
}
```

Notice that both functions return the call to the CallBackHandler() method; the CallBackHandler() method will be invoked when the server returns the result to the client. Hence, there is a need to differentiate who the return caller is. You use the context variable to set the command name for each type of call (GetStateFromZip or GetStatesFromCountry).

The result will be returned as the variable result. The result is then parsed and displayed accordingly in the controls on the page.

8. To complete this example, remember to wire the GetStateFromZip() function to the Button control.

JavaScript is case sensitive, so be sure to use the correct case for control names.

```
<asp:Button ID="btnGetCityandState"
    OnClientClick="GetStateFromZip()"
    runat="server" Text="Get City and State"
    Width="144px" />
```

9. As for the Country DropDownList control, recall that earlier in the Page_Load event we have this statement:

```
ddlCountry.Attributes.Add("onChange", "GetStatesFromServer()")
```

Essentially, this means that when the item in the DropDownList control changes, the GetStatesFromServer() function will be called.

10. Press F5 to test the application. You can now access the server without a postback (see Figure 6-15).

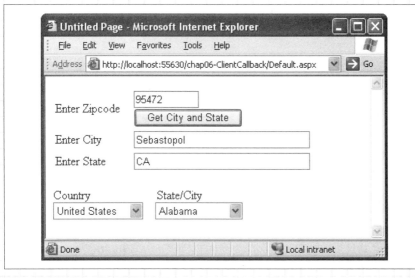

Figure 6-15. Using the Callback Manager to avoid a postback

11. If you click the "Get City and State" button without supplying a Zip Code, a JavaScript pop-up window will display the error message (see Figure 6-16). This is handled by the onError() function on the client side.

Figure 6-16. Displaying the error pop-up window when an error occurs

What about...

...detecting web browsers that do not support Client Callback?

As I mentioned, you need IE 5.0 or higher to use the Client Callback manager. So how do you detect if the user's browser could support Client Callback? Use the SupportsCallback property, like this:

```
Protected Sub Page_Load(ByVal sender As Object, _
                ByVal e As System.EventArgs) _
                Handles Me.Load
```

```
If Request.Browser.SupportsCallback Then
    '---prevent the Get City & State button from postback
    btnGetCityandState.Attributes.Add("onClick", "return false")

    ddlCountry.Attributes.Add("onChange", "GetStatesFromServer()")
    callbackStr = Page.ClientScript.GetCallbackEventReference(Me,
                  "Command", _"CallBackHandler", "context",
                  "onError", True)
Else
    Response.Write("Your browser does not support Client Callback.")
End If

End Sub
```

Where can I learn more?

For a discussion of the implications of script callbacks in ASP.NET 2.0, check out this article: *http://msdn.microsoft.com/msdnmag/issues/04/12/CuttingEdge/*.

For a basic understanding of how the XMLHTTP ActiveX object works, check out *http://www.devx.com/getHelpOn/10MinuteSolution/20358*.

CHAPTER 7

Profiles

Personalizing your web site is a way to enhance the experiences of your users. Personalization allows information about visitors to be preserved so that the information can be reused when they come to your site again. For example, Amazon.com uses personalized information to remember the books and DVDs that you have purchased and to make suitable recommendations based on your interests (see Figure 7-1).

In this chapter:
- *Personalize Your Application*
- *Authenticate Users with Forms Authentication*
- *Save Anonymous User Profiles*
- *Transfer an Anonymous Profile to an Authenticated Profile*

Figure 7-1. Amazon.com's personalized recommendation

In ASP.NET 2.0, the new Profile service gives you a way to store information about your users.

Personalize Your Application

Chapter 5 introduces the new ASP.NET Membership Provider and shows you how to use it to manage users easily. Using the new Membership Provider makes managing user logins straightforward. However, the membership feature does not store information about the users it lists, such as their preferences for themes, their shipping addresses, or lists of previous purchases.

To remember a user's preferences, you can use the new Profile service (exposed via the Profile object) in ASP.NET 2.0. Think of the Profile service as a mechanism to persistently store a user's information, similar to the Session object. Unlike a Profile object, however, a Session object is valid only for the duration of a session; after the session has expired, the Session object is deleted. The Profile service, however, retains its information until you explicitly remove it from the data store.

Moreover, the Profile object has several advantages over the Session object, such as:

Nonvolatility
Profile object data is persisted in data stores, whereas Session variables are saved in memory.

Strong typing
Profile object properties are strongly typed, unlike Session variables, which are stored as Objects and typecast during runtime.

Efficient implementation
Profile properties are loaded only when they're needed, unlike Session variables, which are all loaded whenever any one of them is accessed.

In ASP.NET 2.0, the new Profile object allows user's data to be persisted in a much more efficient manner.

How do I do that?

If you want to use the Profile object to store personalized information about your users, you need a way to identify users so their usernames can act as keys to the information stored in the data store. In this lab, you will build an application that prompts the user to save her name when she first visits your site. Subsequently, when she visits the page again, you will be able to retrieve her name from the Profile object.

1. Launch Visual Studio 2005 and create a new web site project. Name the project *C:\ASPNET20\chap07-Profile*.

2. Drag and drop a Panel control onto the default Web Form and add a 2×3 table (Layout → Insert Table) into the Panel control. Populate the form with the controls shown in Figure 7-2.

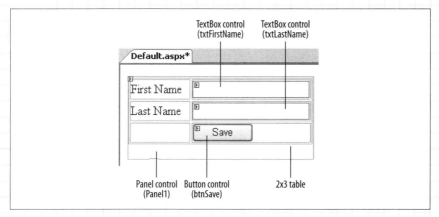

Figure 7-2. Populating the default page with all the controls

3. The default Web Form will prompt the user to enter her name when she first visits the page. The next time the user visits the page, the application will be able to remember her name. You will use the Profile object to save the user's name. To use the Profile object, you first need to add a web configuration file to your project. Right-click on the project name in Solution Explorer, select Add New Item..., and select Web Configuration File from the Template pane of the Add New Item dialog.

4. Add the <profile> element to the *Web.config* file as follows:

```
<system.web>
  <profile>
  <properties>
      <add name="FirstName" type="System.String"/>
      <add name="LastName" type="System.String"/>
  </properties>
  </profile>
  ...
```

5. You have defined two Profile properties, FirstName and LastName, which will be used to store a user's first and last name, respectively. You have also specified the data types to be used for the properties. You can use any type that is available in the framework (so long as they are serializable). To use either of the two

Profile properties, simply prefix the property name with the keyword Profile. That is, Profile.FirstName and Profile.LastName.

Attributes in the Profile Property

Besides the name and the type attribute (any .NET data type; the default is string), you can also specify the following attributes:

readOnly
> Indicates whether the property is read-only.

serializeAs
> Represents how the property value should be stored in the database. Possible values are String (default), Xml, Binary, and ProviderSpecific.

provider
> The name of the profile provider to use.

defaultValue
> The default value of the property.

allowAnonymous
> Whether the property can store values by anonymous users.

---

6. Double-click the default Web Form to switch to its code-behind page. In the Page_Load event, first check to see if the FirstName property is nonempty. If it is nonempty, you will retrieve the first and last name of the user from the Profile properties. If it is empty, you can assume this is the first time the user is visiting the page, and you can show the Panel control to allow the user to enter her first and last name.

```
Protected Sub Page_Load(ByVal sender As Object, _
                        ByVal e As System.EventArgs) _
                        Handles Me.Load
    If Profile.FirstName <> "" Then
        Panel1.Visible = False
        Response.Write("Welcome back, " & _
                        Profile.FirstName & ", " & _
                        Profile.LastName)
    Else
        Panel1.Visible = True
    End If
End Sub
```

7. When the user clicks the Save button, you save the first and last names by simply assigning them to the Profile properties. Code the Save button as:

```
Protected Sub btnSave_Click(ByVal sender As Object, _
                        ByVal e As System.EventArgs) _
                        Handles btnSave.Click
```

```
' save the profile
Profile.FirstName = txtFirstName.Text
Profile.LastName = txtLastName.Text
Response.Write("Thank you, " & _
    txtFirstName.Text & ", " & txtLastName.Text)
End Sub
```

8. To test the application, press F5. Figure 7-3 shows what happens when the user loads the Web Form for the first time. The user can then enter her name and click Save to save her name in the Profile object. When the user comes back to visit the page again, she will be greeted with a welcome message, instead of having to reenter her name (see Figure 7-4).

Figure 7-3. Loading the page for the first time

Figure 7-4. Subsequent visit by the user

What just happened?

When you run the application, the user's first and last names are saved in the Profile properties. So where are these values stored?

ASP.NET 2.0 uses a Profile Provider to store the data saved in the Profile object. By default, the SQL Server 2005 Express Provider is used.

1. To examine the values stored by the Profile object, double-click the *ASPNETDB.MDF* file located under the *App_Data* folder in your project.

2. You should now see the *ASPNETDB.MDF* database under the Data Connections item in Server Explorer (see Figure 7-5). Expand the Tables node to view the list of tables within this database.

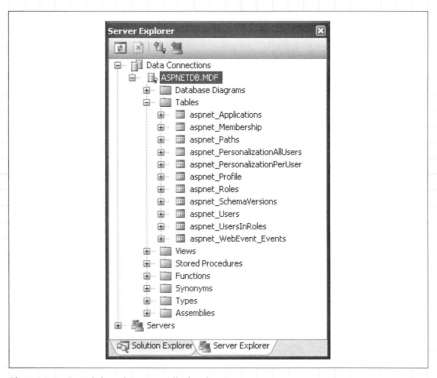

Figure 7-5. Examining the aspnetdb database

3. Right-click on the aspnet_Profile table and select Show Table Data. You should now be able to see the values stored in the table (see Figure 7-6).

Figure 7-6. Examining the aspnet_Profile table

4. Note the UserID field of the aspnet_Profile table. It is used to uniquely identify the Profile object associated with a particular user for this application. If you further examine the aspnet_Users table (see Figure 7-7), the UserID field has a corresponding ApplicationID field

(that identifies the application) and a UserName field (that identifies the user).

Figure 7-7. Examining the aspnet_Users table

5. Notice that the UserName is "WINXP2\Wei-Meng Lee." For this application, you are using the default Windows authentication for your ASP.NET application. Therefore, you should see your own Windows login name.

What about...

...grouping related Profile properties?

Suppose you want to save the address of a user. Instead of using the following structure:

```
Profile.Line1 = ""
Profile.Line2 = ""
Profile.State = ""
Profile.Zip = ""
```

it would be more logical to organize all related information into a group, like this:

```
Profile.Address.Line1 = ""
Profile.Address.Line2 = ""
Profile.Address.State = ""
Profile.Address.Zip = ""
```

To do so, simply use the <group> element in *Web.config*:

```
<configuration xmlns="http://schemas.microsoft.com/.NetConfiguration/v2.0">
    <system.web>
        <profile>
            <properties>
                <add name="FirstName" type="System.String" />
                <add name="LastName" type="System.String" />
                <add name="LastLoginTime" type="System.DateTime" />
                <group name="Address">
                    <add name="Line1" type="System.String" />
                    <add name="Line2" type="System.String" />
                    <add name="State" type="System.String" />
                    <add name="Zip" type="System.String" />
                </group>
            </properties>
        </profile>
    </system.web>
</configuration>
```

Where can I learn more?

You can write your own Profile Provider if you do not want to use the one provided by Microsoft. For example, you may wish to persist the Profile properties in an XML file instead of a SQL Server database. For more information on the ASP.NET 2.0 Provider Model, check out these two articles by Rob Howard:

- *http://msdn.microsoft.com/library/default.asp?url=/library/en-us/dnaspnet/html/asp02182004.asp*

- *http://msdn.microsoft.com/library/default.asp?url=/library/en-us/dnaspnet/html/asp04212004.asp*

Forms authentication, the preferred authentication mode for web applications, works just fine with the Profile service.

Authenticate Users with Forms Authentication

The lab "Personalize Your Application" shows how you can use Windows authentication for your ASP.NET web application. While this is useful for Intranet applications, a better way to authenticate external users is to use forms authentication. In this section, you will use the Profile object together with forms authentication.

Forms Versus Windows Authentication

In forms authentication, unauthenticated requests are redirected to a Web Form using HTTP client-side redirection. The user provides a username and password and then submits the form. If the application authenticates the request, the system issues a cookie containing the credentials or a key for reacquiring the identity. Subsequent requests are issued with the cookie in the request headers. They are then authenticated and authorized by an ASP.NET event handler using whatever validation method the application developer specifies.

In Windows authentication, ASP.NET works in conjunction with Microsoft Internet Information Services (IIS) authentication. Authentication is performed by IIS in one of three ways: basic, digest, or Integrated Windows Authentication. When IIS authentication is complete, ASP.NET uses the authenticated identity to authorize access.

It is not feasible for you to create separate Windows accounts for users accessing your application through the Internet. So, forms authentication should be used for Internet applications.

How do I do that?

In this lab, you will see how you can authenticate your users via forms authentication. You will add users to a web site using the ASP.NET Web Site Administration Tool. You will then use the Profile object to save the user's preferences based on the username provided at login.

1. Using the same project created in the last section (*C:\ASPNET20\ chap07-Profile*), add a new folder to your project by right-clicking the project name in Solution Explorer, selecting New Folder → Regular Folder, and naming the new folder *Members*.

2. Move the *Default.aspx* page into the *Members* folder.

3. Add a new Web Configuration File (*Web.config*) to the *Members* folder.

4. Finally, add a new Web Form to your project and name it *Login.aspx* (see Figure 7-8). Populate the form with the Login control.

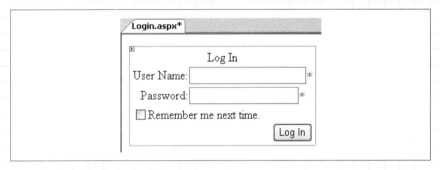

Figure 7-8. The login page with the Login control

5. Your project should now look like the one shown in the Solution Explorer in Figure 7-9.

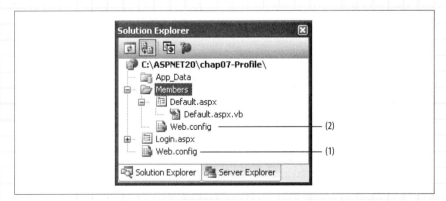

Figure 7-9. The project with two Web.config files

---

6. In the application *Web.config*, marked (1) in Figure 7-9, change the authentication mode from Windows to Forms:

```
<authentication mode="Forms"/>
```

Default Values in machine.config

In ASP.NET 1.x, you need to explicitly specify the name of the login page when you use forms authentication. Your code looks something like this:

```
<authentication mode="Forms">
    <forms name=".ASPXAUTH"
        loginUrl="login.aspx"
        protection="Validation"
        timeout="999999" />
</authentication>
```

And so, if an anonymous user tries to load a page that is protected, he will be redirected to the *Login.aspx* page for authentication.

In ASP.NET 2.0, there is no need to perform this step. Rather, the above settings (plus many others) are "burned" into ASP.NET as defaults. Each application now includes three different *machine.config* files, all located in *C:\ WINDOWS\Microsoft.NET\Framework\<version>\CONFIG*:

- *machine.config*
- *machine.config.default*
- *machine.config.comments*

The *machine.config.default* file contains all the default system-wide configuration settings. To see the default settings defined in *machine.config.default*, check the *machine.config.comments* file for details. For example, the default settings for forms authentication found in *machine.config.comments* are:

```
<forms
    name=".ASPXAUTH"
    loginUrl="login.aspx"
    protection="All"
    timeout="30"
    path="/"
    requireSSL="false"
    slidingExpiration="true"
    defaultUrl="default.aspx"
    cookieless="UseCookies"
    enableCrossAppRedirects="false" >
```

If you want to override the default settings, you should modify *machine.config* (for machine-wide configuration) or *Web.config* (for application-wide configuration). The rationale for splitting the original *machine.config* file into three different files is to reduce the size of *machine.config* and hence improve the performance.

7. In the *Members* folder *Web.config*, marked (2) in Figure 7-9, add the <authorization> element so that all anonymous users are denied access to the *Members* folder. Also, remove the <authentication> element:

```
<system.web>
  <authorization>
    <deny users="?" />
  </authorization>
  ...
  <!--
  <authentication mode="Windows"/>
  -->
```

8. Using the ASP.NET Web Site Administration Tool (Website → ASP.NET Configuration, and then click on the Security tab), add a new user to your application (see Figure 7-10).

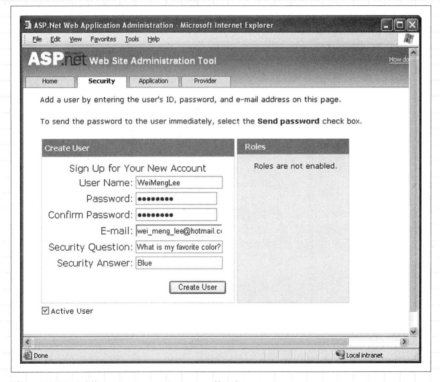

Figure 7-10. Adding a new user to my application

TIP

See Chapter 5 for more information on how to add a new user to your web application.

---

9. To test the application, press F5. Load the *Default.aspx* page located in the *Members* folder using a web browser. Since all unauthenticated users are denied access, you will be redirected to the *Login.aspx* page.

10. Log in using the username that you added in Step 8, and you will see the *Default.aspx* page. As usual, enter your first and last names and click on the Save button.

11. Examine the aspnet_Profile and aspnet_Users tables again. This time, you will see a second user in the table. In my case, not surprisingly, the name is "WeiMengLee," which is the username I used to log in. Contrast this to the Windows username ("WINXP2\Wei-Meng Lee") used in the previous lab, which used Windows authentication.

What about...

...sites that store the Default.aspx file outside of the Members folder, thereby allowing users to access the site without logging in?

Figure 7-11 shows the location of *Default.aspx* at such a site, namely the one we're working with in this chapter.

Figure 7-11. Moving Default.aspx out of the Members folder

If the *Default.aspx* file is accessed directly when the user has not yet been authenticated, trying to set the Profile properties will result in a runtime error. This is because ASP.NET requires a key to uniquely identify the user. Using the Profile object for a user that has not yet been authenticated is known as *anonymous profiling*. The next lab, "Save Anonymous User Profiles," discusses this in more detail.

Where can I learn more?

To learn more about how to secure your ASP.NET web applications, check out the following article, which provides a checklist for securing your ASP.NET application:

> *http://msdn.microsoft.com/library/default.asp?url=/library/en-us/ secmod/html/secmod98.asp.*

Save Anonymous User Profiles

While ASP.NET 2.0 employs a unique user ID to associate a user with a profile, it is often desirable to associate an anonymous user with a profile as well. For example, at a typical e-commerce web site, users who have not yet been authenticated are typically encouraged to add items to their shopping carts while they browse the merchandise. Only when a user is ready to check out is she then required to log into the system and supply other information, such as credit card numbers and a shipping address.

In ASP.NET 2.0, you can keep track of anonymous users through the use of the Globally Unique Identifier (GUID).

You can use the Profile service to store information about anonymous users, instead of an authenticated user ID.

How do I do that?

In this lab, you will see how you can implement anonymous personalization in ASP.NET 2.0. You will also learn how you can store complex data types into the profile property.

1. Using the same project created in the last lab (*C:\ASPNET20\chap07-Profile*), create a new *Images* folder in your project and add the images as shown in Figure 7-12 (you can download these images from the O'Reilly support site at *http://www.oreilly.com/catalog/aspnetadn/*). We'll use these images to represent items that can be ordered on our test page.

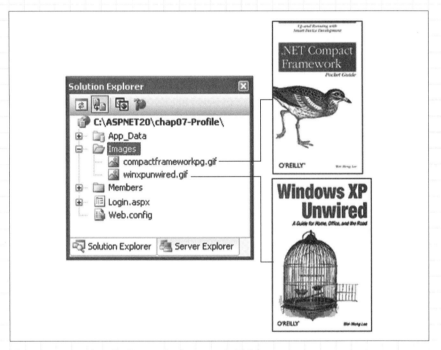

Figure 7-12. Saving the images in the Images folder

2. Now we need to create a test page. Add a new Web Form to the root of the project and name it *Products.aspx*.

3. Populate the *Products.aspx* page with the images you added to your project in Step 1, as shown in Figure 7-13.

4. Now add two "Add to cart" buttons to the page so users can drop the two items into a shopping cart, regardless of whether they've been authenticated. The best place to save shopping cart items is the Profile object.

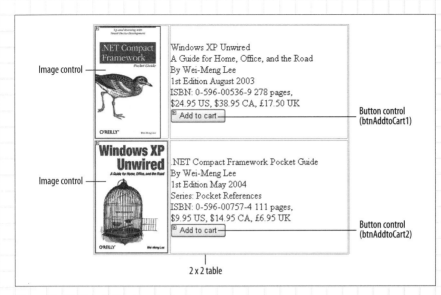

Figure 7-13. Populating the Products.aspx page

5. Add a new class to the project and name it *ShoppingCart.vb*. You will be prompted to save the file in the *App_Code* folder. Click Yes. This new class will implement the shopping cart used in this application.

6. Code the *ShoppingCart.vb* class as shown in Example 7-1. The Cart class allows items to be added to an ArrayList object.

Example 7-1. ShoppingCart.vb

```
Imports Microsoft.VisualBasic
Imports System.Xml.Serialization

Namespace OReilly

    Public Structure itemType
        Dim isbn As String
        Dim qty As Integer
    End Structure

    <XmlInclude(GetType(itemType))> _
    Public Class Cart
        '---use public for Xml serialization---
        Public items As New ArrayList
        Public Sub AddItem(ByVal isbn As String, ByVal qty As Integer)
            Dim cartItem As New itemType
            cartItem.isbn = isbn
            cartItem.qty = qty
            items.Add(cartItem)
        End Sub
    End Class
End Namespace
```

7. To allow anonymous identification, add the following code to the *Web.config* file for your application (shown in Figure 7-14). In particular, you need to specify the <anonymousIdentification> element:

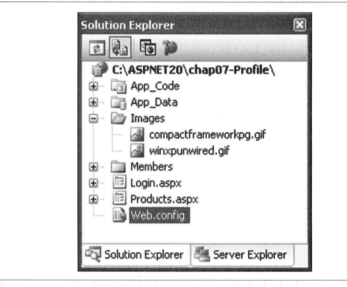

Figure 7-14. Modifying the Web.config file in the root of the application

```
<system.web>
    <anonymousIdentification enabled="true"/>
    <profile>
        <properties>
            <add name="FirstName" type="System.String"/>
            <add name="LastName" type="System.String"/>
            <add name="shoppingcart" allowAnonymous="true"
                type="OReilly.Cart" serializeAs="Xml"/>
        </properties>
    </profile>
    ...
```

8. You define the type for the shoppingcart profile property as OReilly. Cart. This type refers to the Cart class that you have defined in *ShoppingCart.vb*. The profile property shoppingcart will be serialized as an XML string so that it can be stored in a database.

9. Switch to the code-behind of *Products.aspx* and add the code for the btnAddToCart_Click() method shown in this step. This method will retrieve the shopping cart associated with the current user (authenticated or anonymous) and then add the item selected. The new shopping cart is then saved back into the Profile object:

```
Protected Sub btnAddToCart_Click(ByVal sender As Object, _
                                 ByVal e As System.EventArgs) _
```

```
                                        Handles btnAddtoCart1.Click, _
                                        btnAddtoCart2.Click
        Dim myCart As OReilly.Cart
        '---retrieve the existing cart
        myCart = Profile.shoppingcart
        If myCart Is Nothing Then
            myCart = New OReilly.Cart
        End If

        Dim isbn As String
        Select Case CType(sender, Button).ID
            Case "btnAddtoCart1" : isbn = "0-596-00536-9"
            Case "btnAddtoCart2" : isbn = "0-596-00757-4"
        End Select
        myCart.AddItem(isbn, 1)
        '---save the cart back into the profile
        Profile.shoppingcart = myCart
    End Sub
```

10. Code the Page_Load event so that when the page is loaded, you can use the Membership class to check whether the user is authenticated and print out the related information about the user:

```
    Protected Sub Page_Load(ByVal sender As Object, _
                            ByVal e As System.EventArgs) _
                            Handles Me.Load
        Dim user As MembershipUser = Membership.GetUser
        If user Is Nothing Then
            Response.Write("You have not logged in yet.")
        End If
    End Sub
```

11. To test the application, press F5. In *Products.aspx,* you should see the message "You have not logged in yet" (see Figure 7-15).

12. Click on the two "Add to cart" buttons, and the two items are added to the Profile object. To view the information saved by the Profile object, use Server Explorer to view the content of the aspnet_Profile table in the *ASPNETDB.MDF* file. Notice that the shoppingcart profile property is saved as an XML string PropertyValuesString field:

```
    <?xml version="1.0" encoding="utf-16"?>
    <Cart xmlns:xsi="http://www.w3.org/2001/XMLSchema-instance" xmlns:
    xsd="http://www.w3.org/2001/XMLSchema">
      <items>
        <anyType xsi:type="itemType">
          <isbn>0-596-00536-9</isbn>
          <qty>1</qty>
        </anyType>
        <anyType xsi:type="itemType">
          <isbn>0-596-00757-4</isbn>
          <qty>1</qty>
        </anyType>
      </items>
    </Cart>
```

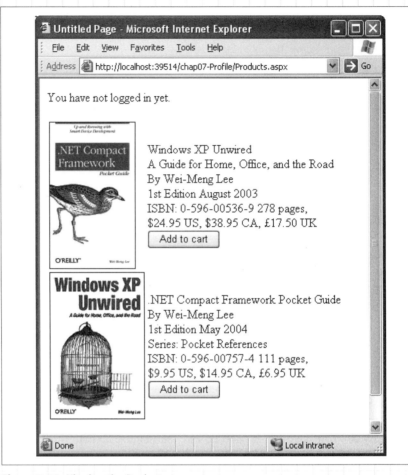

Figure 7-15. Viewing the Products.aspx page

13. Also, if you examine the aspnet_Users table, you will notice that a new user has been created. This user account is created to identify the anonymous user.

Anonymous ID and GUID

If anonymous identification is enabled, when an unauthenticated user tries to save information into the Profile object, an anonymous user ID is generated for the user. This ID is a GUID (Globally Unique Identifier) that is guaranteed to be unique for each user.

You can programmatically retrieve the anonymous ID for the user via `Request.AnonymousId`.

What about...

...binary serialization?

To use binary serialization instead of XML serialization, you need to explicitly mark your object to be persisted as serializable by using the Serializable( ) attribute:

```
Imports Microsoft.VisualBasic
Imports System.Xml.Serialization
<Serializable( )> _
Public Structure itemType
    Dim isbn As String
    Dim qty As Integer
End Structure

Namespace OReilly
    <Serializable( ), _
     XmlInclude(GetType(itemType))> _
    Public Class Cart
        '---use public for Xml serialization---
        Public items As New ArrayList
        Public Sub AddItem(ByVal isbn As String, ByVal qty As Integer)
            Dim cartItem As New itemType
            cartItem.isbn = isbn
            cartItem.qty = qty
            items.Add(cartItem)
        End Sub
    End Class
End Namespace
```

The object that is persisted will then be saved in the PropertyValuesBinary field instead of the PropertValuesString field in the aspnet_Profile table.

Where can I learn more?

Notice that in the Cart class, I have used the Public access modifier for the items array. This is because only member variables that are defined as public can be persisted in XML serialization. If you choose to use binary serialization instead, you can define items as private. For more information on Binary and XML Serialization, refer to my two articles at ONDotNet.com:

- *http://www.ondotnet.com/pub/a/dotnet/2003/10/13/serializationpt1.html*
- *http://www.ondotnet.com/pub/a/dotnet/2003/11/03/serializationpt2.html*

When an
anonymous user is
authenticated,
you need to
manually migrate
his profile
properties.

Transfer an Anonymous Profile
to an Authenticated Profile

Although ASP.NET 2.0 lets you maintain information for both authenticated and anonymous users, you need to take special steps to preserve data when you authenticate an anonymous user. For example, an anonymous user may already have items in her shopping cart when she logs in. In this situation, profile data that was saved while she was an anonymous user would normally be lost when the user switches from using a GUID to using a user ID for identification. To migrate the profile of the user, you need to transfer whatever information has been saved as an anonymous profile to the user profile.

How do I do that?

In this lab, you will build on the previous lab, "Save Anonymous User Profiles," and learn how you can migrate an anonymous profile to an authenticated profile once a user has been authenticated.

1. Using the project created in the last lab (*C:\ASPNET20\chap07-Profile*), add a new Web Form to the *Members* folder. Name the Web Form *Checkout.aspx*.

2. Add a *Global.asax* file to the project (right-click the project name in Solution Explorer and then select Add New Item...; select Global Application Class).

3. The Solution Explorer should now look like Figure 7-16.

4. Add the following method to *Global.asax*. The MigrateAnonymous event is raised whenever a user changes his status from anonymous to authenticated.

   You can get the anonymous ID from the AnonymousId property and then use the GetProfile() method to retrieve the anonymous profile. The retrieved profile can then be assigned to the authenticated user profile.

   ```
   Sub Profile_MigrateAnonymous(ByVal sender As Object, _
                         ByVal e As ProfileMigrateEventArgs)
       Dim anonymousProfile As ProfileCommon = _
           Profile.GetProfile(e.AnonymousId)
       If anonymousProfile.shoppingcart IsNot Nothing Then
           Profile.shoppingcart = anonymousProfile.shoppingcart
       End If

       '---delete the items associated with the anonymous user
       ProfileManager.DeleteProfile(e.AnonymousID)
   ```

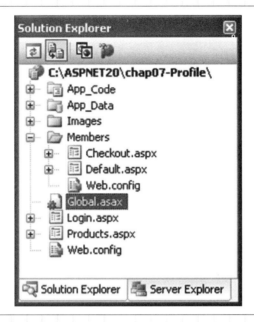

Figure 7-16. Adding the Global.asax file to the project

```
'---clear the anonymous identifier from the request
' so that this event will not fire for an authenticated user
AnonymousIdentificationModule.ClearAnonymousIdentifier()

End Sub
```

5. In the code-behind of *Checkout.aspx*, code the following in the Form_Load event. The *Checkout.aspx* page will print out all the items in the cart:

```
Protected Sub Page_Load(ByVal sender As Object, _
                        ByVal e As System.EventArgs) _
                        Handles Me.Load
    Dim myCart As OReilly.Cart
    myCart = Profile.shoppingcart
    Dim item As OReilly.itemType
    Response.Write("Your cart contains:<br/>")
    For Each item In myCart.items
        Response.Write(item.isbn & " - " & item.qty & "<br/>")
    Next
End Sub
```

6. Add a Button control to *Products.aspx* and set its Text property to Check Out (see Figure 7-17) so that the user can proceed to *Checkout.aspx* after he is done adding the item. Set the PostBackUrl property of the Button control to *Members/Checkout.aspx*.

7. To test the application, you should first load the *Products.aspx* page anonymously and then add a few items to your shopping cart. Once

Figure 7-17. Adding the Check Out button

this is done, click the Check Out button to proceed to the checkout page. You will be prompted to log in. When you are authenticated, the MigrateAnonymous event fires and the profile properties are transferred. The *Checkout.aspx* page will list all the items in the shopping cart.

TIP

Check the aspnet_profile table to verify that the profiles have been migrated successfully.

What about...

...the old entries in the aspnet_Profile table that were saved by the anonymous user? Will they be deleted when the user's profile is moved?

The answer is no. You need to manually clear away the entries. Fortunately, ASP.NET 2.0 comes with the ProfileManager class (which contains the DeleteProfile() method) to help you manage profile properties.

Where can I learn more?

Check out the Visual Studio 2005 documentation to see how you can use the ProfileManager class to manage profiles and generate reports on profiles. Also, check out the following article for more information on the Profile service:

http://msdn.microsoft.com/library/default.asp?url=/library/en-us/dnvs05/html/userprofiles.asp

Themes, Skins, and Localization

Designing a consistent and friendly user interface for a web application is an integral part of every developer's job. Yet, this seemingly easy job requires a lot of planning and architecting to ensure a clean separation of UI from business logic.

In this chapter, we will learn about the new themes and skins feature in ASP.NET 2.0 and how you can use them to maintain a consistent user interface for your application. In addition, localization in ASP.NET 2.0 has gotten easier with the new auto-culture handling mechanism. You will learn how to create applications that support multiple cultures.

In this chapter:
- *Create Themes and Skins*
- *Apply Themes at Runtime*
- *Store Themes in User Profiles*
- *Localize Your Application*

Create Themes and Skins

Most web designers use Cascading Style Sheets (CSS) to give their web sites a consistent look and feel. In ASP.NET 2.0, you can now create themes and skins that extend a consistent look and feel to your server controls. In this lab, you will learn how to create skins for your web controls and how to group them into themes.

How do I do that?

In this lab, you'll create some skin files and group them into a theme. Then, you'll apply this theme to a page to change its look and feel and observe the result.

1. Launch Visual Studio 2005 and create a new web site project. Name the project *C:\ASPNET20\chap08-Themes*.

2. Populate the default Web Form (*Default.aspx*) with the Label, Calendar, and Button controls shown in Figure 8-1.

Learn how to maintain a consistent look and feel for your web site by creating themes and skins for your web server controls.

Themes Versus CSS Stylesheets

While both themes and CSS stylesheets let you apply common sets of attributes to web pages, they do have their differences:

- Themes can define properties of controls, such as the images to be used for an ImageMap control. CSS stylesheets, on the other hand, can define only certain sets of style properties.
- Theme property values always override local property values, while stylesheets can cascade.

Note that you can use themes and CSS together.

Themes and skins allow you to cleanly separate your UI into layers, separating form from function. This greatly increases the manageability of your project.

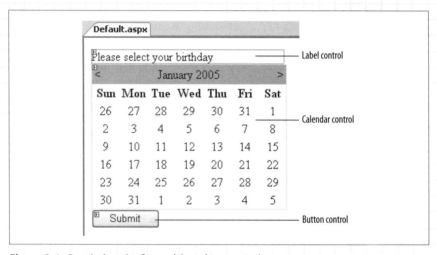

Figure 8-1. Populating the form with various controls

3. Create a new folder in your project by right-clicking the project name in Solution Explorer and then selecting Add Folder → Themes Folder. The folder will be used to hold various themes folders for your application.

The names of the folders under the App_Themes folder are also the theme names.

4. Note that a new folder named *Theme1* will be created under *App_Themes*. Change the name of this folder to *Classic*. You'll use this folder to store the skin files for the Classic theme (the name of the folder is also the theme name).

5. Add three *.skin* files to the *Classic* folder by right-clicking the *Classic* folder and selecting Add New Item…. Select Skin File and name the new files *Button.skin*, *Calendar.skin*, and *Label.skin*, respectively. A

skin file contains formatting information used to change the look and feel of a control. The Solution Explorer should now look like Figure 8-2.

Figure 8-2. Adding skin files to a theme

6. Populate the *Button.skin* file with the following line of code:

```
<asp:Button runat="server" Width="90px" Font-Bold="True" />
```

7. Populate the *Calendar.skin* file as follows:

```
<asp:Calendar runat="server" Width="400px"
    Font-Names="Times New Roman" Font-Size="10pt"
    Height="220px" BorderColor="Black" ForeColor="Black"
    BackColor="White" NextPrevFormat="FullMonth"
    TitleFormat="Month" DayNameFormat="FirstLetter">
  <SelectedDayStyle ForeColor="White" BackColor="#CC3333" />
  <SelectorStyle ForeColor="#333333" Font-Names="Verdana"
            Font-Size="8pt" Font-Bold="True"
            Width="1%" BackColor="#CCCCCC" />
  <OtherMonthDayStyle ForeColor="#999999" />
  <TodayDayStyle BackColor="#CCCC99" />
  <DayStyle Width="14%" />
  <NextPrevStyle ForeColor="White" Font-Size="8pt" />
  <DayHeaderStyle ForeColor="#333333" Height="10pt"
            Font-Size="7pt" Font-Bold="True"
            BackColor="#CCCCCC" />
  <TitleStyle ForeColor="White" Height="14pt"
            Font-Size="13pt" Font-Bold="True"
            BackColor="Black" />
</asp:Calendar>
```

8. Populate the *Label.skin* file as follows:

```
<asp:Label runat="server" Width="256px"
    Font-Bold="True" Font-Names="Arial Narrow"
    Font-Size="Medium" />
```

Tips for Creating Skin Files

Since skin files are nothing more than just the Source View of controls (with the exception of attributes such as id), it is very easy to create skin files. One good way to do so is to give your controls the look and feel you want them to have on a normal Web Form in Design View. Then switch to Source View, copy the control element from the source code created for the control, and paste it into the skin file. Finally, remove the id attribute and add a skinid attribute in its place.

9. For the default Web Form, switch to Source View and add in the following Theme attribute:

```
<%@ Page Language="VB"  AutoEventWireup="false"
        CodeFile="Default.aspx.vb" Inherits="Default_aspx"
        Theme="Classic" %>
```

10. To test your application, press F5. You will notice that the controls on the page look different from their original design (see Figure 8-3). This is because the settings in the .skin files have been applied to the controls on the page.

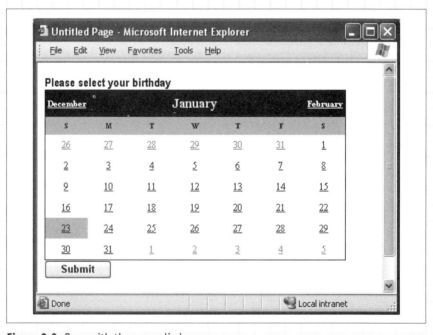

Figure 8-3. Page with theme applied

What just happened?

You have just created three skin files and grouped them together as a single theme. Each skin file is used to define the look and feel of a particular control.

A theme contains one or more skins. A skin file defines the look and feel of a control.

For example, the *Button.skin* file under the Classic theme defines the style of a Button control:

```
<asp:Button runat="server" Width="90px" Font-Bold="True" />
```

While the *Button.skin* file used in this lab contains only one Button definition, you can, if you wish, include multiple Button definitions in the same file, as shown in the following code snippet:

```
<asp:Button runat="server" Width="90px" Font-Bold="True" />

<asp:Button skinid="Italic" runat="server" Width="90px"
    Font-Bold="True" Font-Italic="True" />

<asp:Button skinid="Underline" runat="server" Width="90px"
    Font-Bold="True" Font-Italic="True" Font-Underline="True" />
```

Remember, a skin definition cannot contain the id attribute. Including it will trigger a compile-time error.

You identify each skin in a *.skin* file by the value of its skinid attribute. The first button style defined in a *.skin* file typically does not contain a skinid attribute and is regarded as the *default* skin for the Button control.

If you examine the Button control's properties by displaying its Properties window, you will find a SkinID property. By default, the SkinID property is not set, but if a skin file that is part of a selected theme contains multiple definitions, you can select a particular definition from the list of skins that it displays (see Figure 8-4). If the SkinID property of a control is not set, the default skin will be applied during runtime.

By specifying a theme to use for the page, the default skins in all the skin files will apply to all the relevant controls on the page, unless a particular skin is specified in the skinid attribute of each control.

TIP

While you need not necessarily create multiple skin files for your project (in fact, a single skin file can contain all the style definitions for all controls), the recommended practice is that you hold the styles for each control in a separate skin file. A good practice is to name each skin file after the control that it defines.

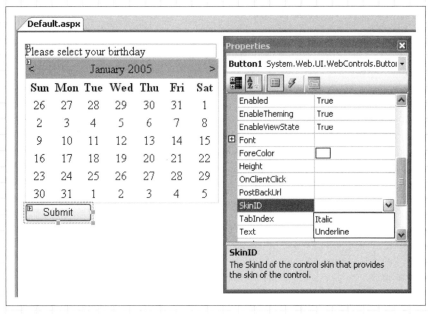

Figure 8-4. Specifying a SkinID for a control

Disabling Skinning for Controls

When a theme is applied to a page, all controls will be affected if there are styles defined in the various skin files. To prevent a control from being applied a theme, set the EnableTheming property of the control to False, like this:

```
<asp:Button ID="btnGetTitle"
      Runat="server"
      Text="Get Title"
      EnableTheming="False" />
```

What about...

...applying a theme programmatically?

To programmatically change the theme of a page, you use the Theme property exposed by the Page class. However, you need to set the theme before the page is loaded (before the Page_Load event is fired). In fact, you have to set it in the PreInit event, which is fired before all the controls are loaded and initialized:

```
Protected Sub Page_PreInit(ByVal sender As Object, _
                    ByVal e As System.EventArgs) _
```

Chapter 8: Themes, Skins, and Localization

```
                        Handles Me.PreInit
        Page.Theme = "Classic"
    End Sub
```

Where can I learn more?

Microsoft has a good quick-start guide to themes and skins at *http://beta.asp.net/quickstart/aspnet/*.

Apply Themes at Runtime

The previous lab, "Create Themes and Skins," shows how to apply themes to a web site at design time. A better way to use themes is to let users to select their preferred themes at runtime, when they visit site. In this section, you will see how themes can be applied during runtime.

Allow your users to customize your web site by letting them select the theme they want.

How do I do that?

Instead of setting the theme of a page at design time, in this lab you are going to let the users choose a theme they like. In addition to the Classic theme, you will create a theme called Colorful.

1. Using the same project created in the previous lab (*C:\ASPNET20\chap08-Themes*), add a new folder under the *App_Themes* folder. Name the folder *Colorful*.

2. Add three skin files to the *Colorful* folder (see Figure 8-5). The three skin files under the *Colorful* folder will define the look and feel of the various controls on the page.

3. Code the *Button.skin* file as follows:

```
<asp:Button runat="server" Width="90px" Font-Bold="True"
    BackColor="#C0C0FF" />
```

4. Code the *Calendar.skin* file as follows:

```
<asp:Calendar runat="server" Width="220px"
    Font-Names="Verdana" Font-Size="8pt"
    Height="200px" BorderColor="#FFCC66"
    ForeColor="#663399" BackColor="#FFFFCC"
    DayNameFormat="FirstLetter" BorderWidth="1px"
    ShowGridLines="True">
    <SelectedDayStyle BackColor="#CCCCFF" Font-Bold="True" />
    <SelectorStyle BackColor="#FFCC66" />
    <OtherMonthDayStyle ForeColor="#CC9966" />
    <TodayDayStyle BackColor="#FFCC66" ForeColor="White" />
    <NextPrevStyle ForeColor="#FFFFCC" Font-Size="9pt" />
    <DayHeaderStyle Height="1px" Font-Bold="True"
            BackColor="#FFCC66" />
```

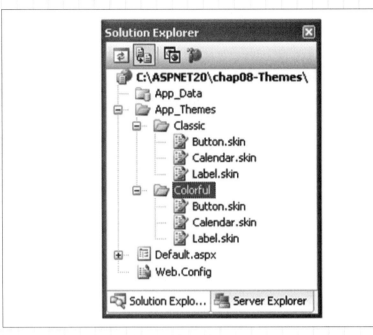

Figure 8-5. Adding a new theme to the project

```
<TitleStyle ForeColor="#FFFFCC" Font-Size="9pt"
            Font-Bold="True" BackColor="#990000" />
</asp:Calendar>
```

5. Code the *Label.skin* file as follows:

```
<asp:Label runat="server" Width="256px"
     Font-Bold="True" Font-Names="Arial Narrow"
     Font-Size="Medium" BackColor="#FFFFC0" />
```

6. To the default Web Form, add the DropDownList and Button controls as shown in Figure 8-6.

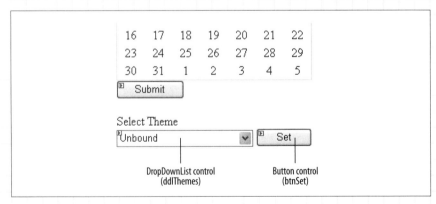

Figure 8-6. Adding new controls to the page

7. To get a list of available themes, check the list of folders under the *App_Themes* folder. Then iteratively add the list of themes to the DropDownList control. In the Page_Load event for the default Web Form, code the following.

```
Protected Sub Page_Load(ByVal sender As Object, _
                        ByVal e As System.EventArgs) _
                        Handles Me.Load
    If Not IsPostBack Then
        '---get all folders under the App_Themes folder
        Dim themes As String() = _
            Directory.GetDirectories( _
            Request.PhysicalApplicationPath & "App_Themes")
        '---add the themes into the DropDownList
        ddlThemes.Items.Clear()
        For Each theme As String In themes
            '---add only the theme name and not full path
            ddlThemes.Items.Add( _
                theme.Substring(theme.LastIndexOf("\") + 1))
        Next
    End If
End Sub
```

8. In the Page_PreInit event, get the value of the DropDownList control using the Request object and set the theme of the page using the Theme property:

```
Protected Sub Page_PreInit(ByVal sender As Object, _
                           ByVal e As System.EventArgs) _
                           Handles Me.PreInit
    Dim Theme As String = Request("ddlThemes")
    Page.Theme = Theme
End Sub
```

TIP

You cannot directly access the DropDownList control's properties to get the theme selected, because the PreInit event is executed before the postback is processed. Hence, when the Set button is clicked and results in a postback, the theme selected would not have been available yet in the PreInit event.

---

9. Press F5 to test the application. You can now select a theme to apply to the page from the Select Theme drop-down list. Try it (see Figure 8-7).

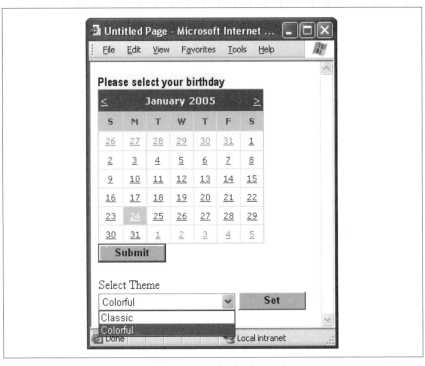

Figure 8-7. Dynamically applying a theme to a page

What about...

...mixing themes with CSS?

CSS styles apply at the client side. Hence, in this example, you define the style to be applied to the <input> element, which is the HTML code generated by the Button control.

Apart from applying themes to your web pages, you can also mix themes with CSS stylesheets.

1. Using the project created in this section, add a stylesheet to the *Classic* folder by right-clicking the *Classic* folder and selecting Add New Item.... Select Style Sheet, and name the CSS stylesheet *Button.css*. Likewise, add another stylesheet to the *Colorful* folder.

2. The content of the two *Button.css* stylesheets are as shown in Figure 8-8.

3. Press F5 to test the application. You will notice that when the Classic theme is applied, the font used for the Button controls is Courier New. Likewise, if you change the theme to Colorful, the font is now Arial Narrow and the text is now in red (see Figure 8-9).

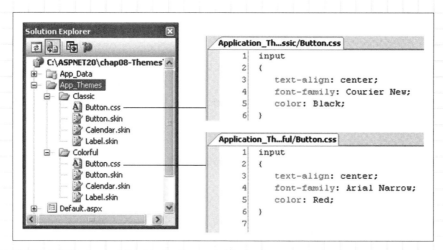

Figure 8-8. Content of the two Button.css stylesheets

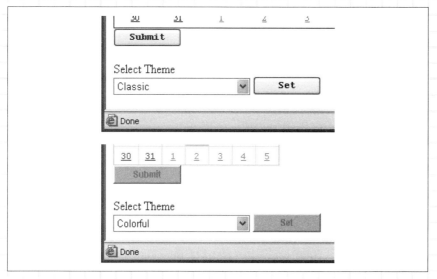

Figure 8-9. The effects of applying CSS stylesheets to a page

Where can I learn more?

If you want to learn more about CSS, I strongly suggest you take a look at this tutorial: *http://www.w3schools.com/css/default.asp*. There is also a good discussion of the use of themes in web applications at *http://mgemmons.com/blog/archive/0001/01/01/156.aspx*.

Allowing users to select a theme is one thing, but you need to be able to remember their preferences so that when they return, their choice remains the one they selected.

Store Themes in User Profiles

In the previous lab, "Apply Themes at Runtime," you saw how to make it possible for your users to change the theme of a page dynamically. The technique is fine as far as it goes, but the next time the user visits your site, she will have to select the theme again. Instead of asking a user to select a theme every time she visits your site, it is better for you to store the user's preferred theme in the Profile object.

How do I do that?

In this lab, you will use the Profile object to store the theme selected by the user. When the user visits the page again, the theme is then retrieved from the Profile object and reapplied to the page.

1. Using the project created in the previous lab, add a *Web.config* file to the project.

2. Add the <profile> element to the *Web.config* file and add a Theme profile property. The Theme property will be used to save the theme selected by a user:

```
<system.web>
    <profile>
        <properties>
            <add name="Theme" type="System.String" />
        </properties>
    </profile>
    . . .
```

If you want to allow anonymous users to save their profiles, remember to add the <anonymousIdentification> element and the allowAnonymous attribute for each profile property.

The Profile object is used to personalize a site or a user. Use the Profile object to remember a user's preferences.

3. To save the theme into the Profile object, switch to the code-behind of the default form and code the Set button. The theme selected in the drop-down listbox is saved into the theme property:

```
Protected Sub btnSet_Click(ByVal sender As Object, _
                           ByVal e As System.EventArgs) _
                           Handles btnSet.Click
    Profile.Theme = ddlThemes.SelectedValue
End Sub
```

4. In the Page_PreInit event, first check to see if there is any item selected in the drop-down list control. If it is empty, proceed to retrieve the profile saved in the Profile property. Otherwise, load the theme set in the drop-down list control:

```
Protected Sub Page_PreInit(ByVal sender As Object, _
                           ByVal e As System.EventArgs) _
```

```
                    Handles Me.PreInit
        Dim Theme As String = Request("ddlThemes")
        '---theme is not set in the DropDownList...
        If Theme = "" Then
            '---get it from profile
            Page.Theme = Profile.Theme
        Else
            '---get it from DropDownList
            Page.Theme = Theme
        End If
    End Sub
```

5. Press F5 to test the application. Select the Colorful theme. Stop debugging in Visual Studio 2005 and then press F5 again. You will notice that the Colorful theme is selected. This proves that your page can now remember the user's selected theme the next time she visits.

What about...

...applying themes at the application level?

You can apply a theme to an entire application by adding the <pages> element in *Web.config*:

```
<configuration xmlns="http://schemas.microsoft.com/.NetConfiguration/v2.0">
    <system.web>
        <pages theme="Colorful" />
    </system.web>
</configuration>
```

In the previous example, pages that do not have the Theme attribute in the Page directive will use the Colorful theme. If a page has the Theme attribute set, it will override the settings in *Web.config*.

Where can I learn more?

To learn more about the Profile service, refer to Chapter 7, where I discuss in more detail how to use the Profile service for authenticated and anonymous users.

Localize Your Application

As global competition heats up, companies are increasingly developing their applications to serve a worldwide audience. One of the challenges in developing a truly global site is in understanding the language and culture of the local audience. An application written for the American market may not be usable in the Asian market. For your application to reach all its potential users, you need to *localize* it for each audience you plan to serve.

ASP.NET 2.0 makes globalizing and localizing your web application easy with its new auto-culture handling feature.

Auto-Culture Handling in ASP.NET 2.0

ASP.NET 2.0 comes with the new auto-culture handling feature. Auto-culture handling can be enabled for each page by including the Culture="auto" and UICulture="auto" attributes in the Page directive of each page.

Once enabled, ASP.NET will automatically map Accept-Language headers to CultureInfo objects and attach them to the current thread (unlike ASP.NET 1.x, where you need to do this manually). As a developer, you simply need to prepare the resources for the different cultures you want to support. ASP.NET will then do the work of loading the appropriate resources for each culture as they are needed.

As a developer, you need to be concerned with the following:

Globalization
> When designing your application, you plan for all the necessary resources you'll need to enable your application to be modified with ease to suit different cultures.

Localization
> You perform the actual transformation to ensure that the user sees the application using the culture he has selected.

Localizing an application for a particular audience involves tasks such as the following:

Properly formatting dates
> People in the United States represent dates in a different format than someone in, say, the United Kingdom. Does "2/7/2004" represent 2 July 2004, or does it represent February 7, 2004? The answer depends on where you are located.

Translating content from one language to another
> For example, the text in your application must change to Chinese if you are targeting the Chinese market.

Setting text direction
> Does text read from left to right or from right to left?

In this lab, you will learn to use the localization feature in ASP.NET 2.0 and see how it simplifies the tasks you need to perform to create international applications.

How do I do that?

In this lab, you are going to create an application that supports two languages: English and Chinese. You will learn how to prepare the language

Localization Basics

If you are not familiar with the concept of localization, let's go through some terminologies first:

- A *culture* is a way to identify a particular setting pertinent to a location or country. You use a culture code to represent a culture.

- A *neutral* culture is a culture that is associated with a language but is not specific to a particular location. For example, "en" is a neutral culture, because it represents the English language but does not provide a specific instance of where it is used.

- A *specific* culture is a culture that is specific to a region or country. For example, "en-GB" is a specific culture.

- Finally, the *invariant* culture is neither a neutral nor a specific culture. It is English, but is not associated with any location. The invariant culture is used to represent data that is not shown to the user. For example, you use the invariant culture to persist date information to a file. This ensures that the date information would not be misrepresented if is it going to be interpreted in another specific culture.

resources needed so that when the user selects a language preference in IE, the application will display in the language selected by the user.

ASP.NET 2.0 supports *implicit localization*, where the values of controls are checked at runtime against a particular resource file based on the specified culture.

In implicit localization, the values of controls are checked at runtime against a particular resource file based on the specified culture.

1. To see how to use implicit localization in ASP.NET 2.0, launch Visual Studio 2005 and create a new web site project. Name the project *C:\ASPNET20\chap08-Localization*.

2. Populate the default Web Form with the controls shown in Figure 8-10. Apply the "Colorful 1" scheme to the Calendar control (through the Auto Format... link in the Calendar Tasks menu).

3. When a date is selected in the Calendar control, display the date in the Label control (lblDate). To do so, double-click the Calendar control and add the following code:

```
Protected Sub Calendar1_SelectionChanged(ByVal sender As Object, _
                            ByVal e As System.EventArgs)
    lblDate.Text = Calendar1.SelectedDate.ToShortDateString
End Sub
```

4. Once the form is populated, go to Tools → Generate Local Resource and Visual Studio 2005 will generate a resource file containing all the text resources used by your controls (see Figure 8-11).

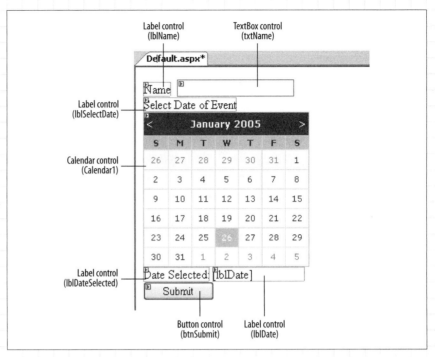

Figure 8-10. Populating the Default.aspx page

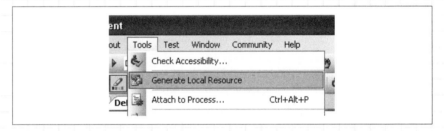

Figure 8-11. Generating the local resource in Visual Studio 2005

5. Step 4 causes a new folder named *App_LocalResources* to be automatically created, and within this folder you will find the resource file generated by Visual Studio 2005. The name of the resource file follows that of the Web Form and ends with a *.resx* extension (see Figure 8-12).

6. To view the resource file, double-click *App_LocalResources* to invoke the Resource Editor (see Figure 8-13).

7. If you now switch the default Web Form to Source View, you will see that each control now has an additional attribute called `meta:resourcekey`. Its value corresponds to each field in the resource file:

Figure 8-12. The App_LocalResources folder in Solution Explorer

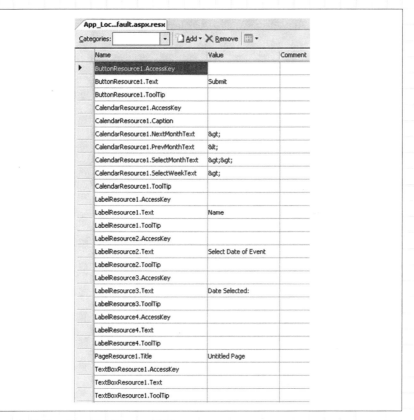

Figure 8-13. Invoking the Resource Editor

```
...
<asp:Label ID="lblName" runat="server"
    Text="Name"
    meta:resourcekey="LabelResource1">
</asp:Label>
```

```
...
<asp:TextBox ID="txtName" runat="server"
    meta:resourcekey="TextBoxResource1">
</asp:TextBox>
...
```

8. Suppose we want to be able to display this application in both the Chinese and the default English languages. To do so, you'll need to go to Solution Explorer and make a copy of the *Default.aspx.resx* file (right-click *Default.aspx.resx* and select Copy, then right-click *App_Resources* and select Paste). Rename the copy *Default.aspx.zh-CN.resx* (see Figure 8-14). The culture code must be used as part of the name of the resource file. In general, the resource files are named in the following format: *<filename>.aspx.<culturecode>.resx*.

Figure 8-14. Duplicating the resource file

9. Open the new resource file and add in the values as shown in Figure 8-15 using the Resource Editor.

ButtonResource1.Text	提交表格
LabelResource1.Text	姓名
LabelResource2.Text	请选择日期
LabelResource3.Text	日期:

Figure 8-15. The content of the resource file for Chinese culture

---

TIP

You can input Chinese characters using Windows, but first you need to install the language pack from the Windows CD. Refer to the section "Where can I learn more?" at the end of this lab to learn how to configure your computer for Chinese Input. Alternatively, you can use any third-party software that allows you to enter Chinese characters.

---

10. To use the auto-culture handling feature of ASP.NET 2.0, add the following two attributes into the Page directive (see Figure 8-16):

- Culture="auto"
- UICulture="auto"

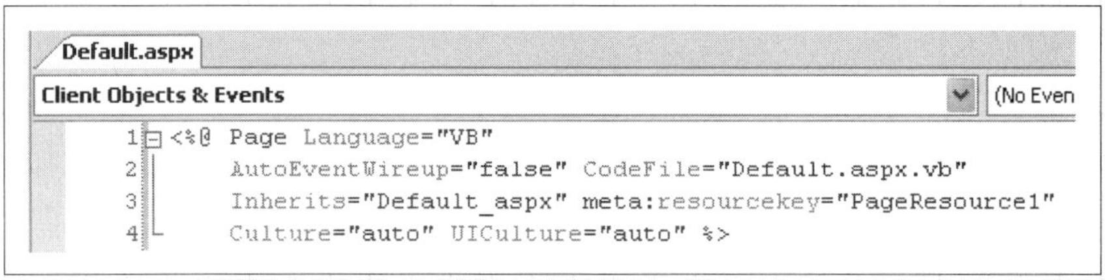

Figure 8-16. The Culture and UICulture attributes

TIP

To apply auto-culture handling at the application level, add the <globalization> element to *Web.config*:

```
<system.web>
    <globalization culture="auto" uiCulture="auto" />
```

The Culture and UICulture attributes automatically map information received in the Accept-language headers to the CurrentCulture and CurrentUICulture properties of the current thread, thus allowing controls on the page that are culture-aware to localize.

11. To test the application, press F5. You should see the Web Form displayed in English. To display the web application in Chinese, go to Tools → Internet Options... (in Internet Explorer) and click the Languages... button. In the Language Preference window (see Figure 8-17), click the Add... button to add a new language—in this case, you should select "Chinese (China) [zh-cn]". Move the desired language to the top of the list and then click OK.

12. To see the page in Chinese, refresh Internet Explorer. Figure 8-18 shows the page displayed in both English and Chinese.

What just happened?

At runtime, ASP.NET will automatically detect the culture settings of the requester. Using the culture setting, it then looks for the relevant resource file. If one is found, the values defined in the resource file are used. The *Default.aspx.resx* resource file is the resource for the default culture. It will also be used if the requester specifies a culture that is not defined in the *App_LocalResources* folder.

Figure 8-17. Changing the language preference in Internet Explorer

Figure 8-18. Displaying the page in English and Chinese

It is worth noting that some controls, like the Calendar control, already support localization. In this case, you do not need to do any work on the Calendar control, since it is already able to display the date in Chinese. Also note that the format of the date displayed is different in the English culture and the Chinese culture.

What about...

...explicit Localization?

In implicit localization, each Web Form has a separate set of resource files. This method is useful for cases where you need to localize the output of controls. However, it is not feasible when you need to localize large amounts of text or need to constantly reuse them (such as welcome or error messages). In this case, explicit localization is more useful. Explicit localization allows you to define a set of resources that can be used by all the pages in your project.

Explicit localization allows you to define a set of resources that can be used by all the pages in your project.

Using the same project created earlier (*C:\ASPNET20\chap08-Localization*), you will now use explicit localization to store a message written in both English and Chinese. Using the Resources class, the application can then display the message in the appropriate language (based on the preference set in IE).

1. To see how explicit localization works, use the same project (*C:\ASPNET20\chap08-Localization*) and add a new folder named *App_GlobalResources* (right-click the project name and select Add Folder → App_GlobalResources) in Solution Explorer.

2. Add a new resource file to the project by right-clicking on the *App_GlobalResources* folder and selecting Add New Item.... Select Assembly Resource File (see Figure 8-19). Name the resource file *Resource.resx*. Make a copy of the resource file and name it *Resource.zh-CN.resx*.

3. The Solution Explorer should now look like Figure 8-20.

4. In the *Resource.resx* file, enter a new key/value pair as shown in Figure 8-21. Likewise, do the same for *Resource.zh-CN.resx*, but this time the string is in Chinese.

5. Add the following Click event handler to the Submit button in *Default.aspx.vb*:

```
Protected Sub btnSubmit_Click(ByVal sender As Object, _
                        ByVal e As System.EventArgs) _
                        Handles btnSubmit.Click
    Dim message As String = _
        Resources.Resource.ThankYouMessage.ToString()
    Dim script As String = "alert('" & _
        message & "');"
```

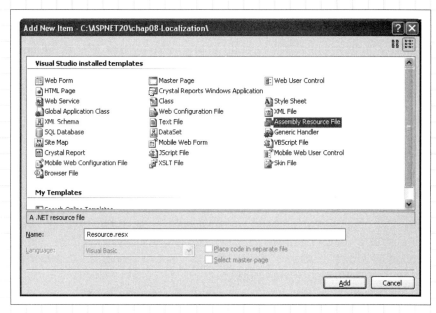

Figure 8-19. Adding a resource file to the project

Figure 8-20. The new App_GlobalResources folder

```
      Page.ClientScript.RegisterClientScriptBlock(Me.GetType, _
        "MyKey", script, True)
    End Sub
```

6. The Resources class provides a programmatic way to dynamically access the resources located in the resource file. IntelliSense will automatically display the keys defined in the resource file.

7. Press F5 to test the application. Set the language preference in IE to Chinese (see Figure 8-17). When you click on the Submit button (at

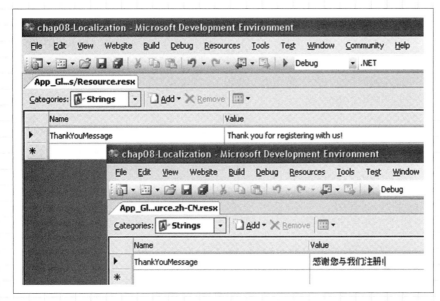

Figure 8-21. Creating resource strings

the bottom of the form), the thank you message is retrieved and then displayed on the client side as a pop-up window (see Figure 8-22), using the egisterClientScriptBlock( ) method.

Figure 8-22. Displaying a localized string

Where can I learn more?

If you want to learn more about configuring Windows XP for foreign language input, check out my article on O'Reilly Network:

http://www.ondotnet.com/pub/a/dotnet/2003/09/29/globalization_pt2.html?page=3

Retrieving Values from Resource Files

Besides programmatically retrieving values from resource files, you can also do it declaratively. For example, you can bind a Label control's Text property to the resource file by using the Expressions field in the Properties window (see Figure 8-23).

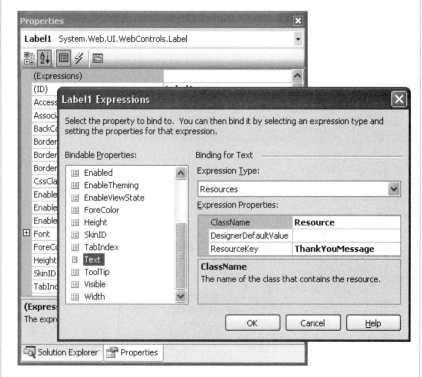

Figure 8-23. Binding a control to the Resource file

Alternatively, you can do this declaratively via the Source View window:

```
<asp:Label ID="Label1"
    Runat="server"
    Text="<%$ Resources:Resource,
          ThankYouMessage %>">
</asp:Label>
```

Index

We'd like to hear your suggestions for improving our indexes. Send email to *index@oreilly.com*.

C

C++, 13
CacheDuration attribute, SqlDataSource
     control, 173
caching
    levels in SQL Server, 179
    page fragments, update speed
       and, 261
    page output caching, 180
    sliding cache policy, 174
    SQL Cache Dependency, 174–181
    SqlDataSource control
       and, 172–174
Calendar control, 132
Callback Manager, 264
CatalogPart controls, 121
CatalogZone control, Web Part listing
      for users, 121
ChangePassword control, 228
ChangePasswordQuestionAndAnswer( )
      method, 243
CircleHotSpot, 39
classes, partial classes, 9
Client Callback, browsers
      supporting, 271
Client Callback Manager, 247
ClientScript property, 20
client-side script, inserting, 20
code modification, 8
Code-Behind View, switching
      between, 7
CollapseAll( ) method, 87
configuration
    DropDownList control, 153
    LoginView control, 214
connection strings, encryption,
      Web.config and, 182–187
ConnectionConsumer attribute, 135
ConnectionProvider attribute, 134
<connectionStrings> element, 153
ConnectionZone control
    Web Parts, 137
Content controls, 53
Content pages
    adding, 52
    <asp:Content>, 56
    convert from web page, 56
    nested Master pages, 55
    templates, Master pages as, 51
ContentLength property, 38

controls, 1
    AppearanceEditorPart, 127
    BehaviorEditorPart, 127
    Calendar, 132
    CatalogPart, 121
    CatalogZone, 121
    ChangePassword, 228
    ConnectionZone, 137
    Content controls, 53
    CreateUserWizard, 231
    DataGrid, GridView control
      and, 141
    DataList, 200
    DeclarativeCatalogPart, 121
    DetailsView, 165–172
    EditorPart controls, 127
    EditorZone controls, 128
    FileUpload, 35
    FindControl( ) method, 62
    focus, setting, 13
    GridView, 141
      tables, 141–155
    groups, display selectively, 29
    ImageMap, 38
    ImportCatalogPart, 121
    LayoutEditorPart, 127
    LoginName, 209
    LoginStatus, 209
    LoginView, 208, 209
    Menu, 89
    MultiView, 29
    ObjectDataSource, 187–198
    PageCatalogPart, 121
    PasswordRecovery, 224
    PropertyGridEditorPart, 127
      display, 130
    security controls, 207
    skins, disabling, 300
    SqlDataSource, 163
    validation
      group, 17
      SetFocusOnError property, 19
    View, MultiView control and, 29
    WebPartManager, 97
    WebPartMenuManager, 98
    WebPartZone, 97
    Wizard, screen dividing, 32
    XmlDataSource, 200–206
converting web page to Content
      page, 56
cookies, authentication without, 213

About the Author

Wei-Meng Lee is a technologist and founder of Developer Learning Solutions (*http://www.developerlearningsolutions.com*), a technology company specializing in hands-on training on the latest Microsoft technologies.

Wei-Meng speaks regularly at international conferences and has authored and coauthored numerous books on .NET, XML, and wireless technologies, including *Windows XP Unwired* and the *.NET Compact Framework Pocket Guide* (both from O'Reilly). He writes extensively for the O'Reilly Network on topics ranging from .NET to Mac OS X.

Wei-Meng is currently a Microsoft Regional Director for Singapore.

Colophon

Our look is the result of reader comments, our own experimentation, and feedback from distribution channels. Distinctive covers complement our distinctive approach to technical topics, breathing personality and life into potentially dry subjects.

The *Developer's Notebook* series is modeled on the tradition of laboratory notebooks. Laboratory notebooks are an invaluable tool for researchers and their successors.

The purpose of a laboratory notebook is to facilitate the recording of data and conclusions as the work is being conducted, creating a faithful and immediate history. The notebook begins with a title page that includes the owner's name and the subject of research. The pages of the notebook should be numbered and prefaced with a table of contents. Entries must be clear, easy to read, and accurately dated; they should use simple, direct language to indicate the name of the experiment and the steps taken. Calculations are written out carefully and relevant thoughts and ideas recorded. Each experiment is introduced and summarized as it is added to the notebook. The goal is to produce comprehensive, clearly organized notes that can be used as a reference. Careful documentation creates a valuable record and provides a practical guide for future developers.

Genevieve d'Entremont was the proofreader and production editor for *ASP.NET 2.0: A Developer's Notebook*. Linley Dolby was the copyeditor. Matt Hutchinson and Colleen Gorman provided quality control. Abigail Fox provided production assistance. Johnna VanHoose Dinse wrote the index.

Edie Freedman designed the cover of this book. Karen Montgomery produced the cover layout with InDesign CS using the Officina Sans and JuniorHandwriting fonts.

David Futato designed the interior layout. This book was converted by Keith Fahlgren to FrameMaker 5.5.6 with a format conversion tool created by Erik Ray, Jason McIntosh, Neil Walls, and Mike Sierra that uses Perl and XML technologies. The text font is Adobe Boton; the heading font is ITC Officina Sans; the code font is LucasFont's TheSans Mono Condensed; and the handwriting font is a modified version of JuniorHandwriting made by Tepid Monkey Foundry, and modified by O'Reilly. The illustrations that appear in the book were produced by Robert Romano, Jessamyn Read, and Lesley Borash using Macromedia FreeHand 9 and Adobe Photoshop 6. This colophon was written by Colleen Gorman.

Related Titles Available from O'Reilly

O'REILLY®

Our books are available at most retail and online bookstores.
To order direct: 1-800-998-9938 • *order@oreilly.com* • *www.oreilly.com*
Online editions of most O'Reilly titles are available by subscription at *safari.oreilly.com*

Keep in touch with O'Reilly

1. Download examples from our books

To find example files for a book, go to:

www.oreilly.com/catalog

select the book, and follow the "Examples" link.

2. Register your O'Reilly books

Register your book at *register.oreilly.com*

Why register your books?
Once you've registered your O'Reilly books you can:

- Win O'Reilly books, T-shirts or discount coupons in our monthly drawing.
- Get special offers available only to registered O'Reilly customers.
- Get catalogs announcing new books (US and UK only).
- Get email notification of new editions of the O'Reilly books you own.

3. Join our email lists

Sign up to get topic-specific email announcements of new books and conferences, special offers, and O'Reilly Network technology newsletters at:

elists.oreilly.com

It's easy to customize your free elists subscription so you'll get exactly the O'Reilly news you want.

4. Get the latest news, tips, and tools

www.oreilly.com

- "Top 100 Sites on the Web"—PC Magazine
- CIO Magazine's Web Business 50 Awards

Our web site contains a library of comprehensive product information (including book excerpts and tables of contents), downloadable software, background articles, interviews with technology leaders, links to relevant sites, book cover art, and more.

5. Work for O'Reilly

Check out our web site for current employment opportunities:

jobs.oreilly.com

6. Contact us

O'Reilly & Associates
1005 Gravenstein Hwy North
Sebastopol, CA 95472 USA

TEL: 707-827-7000 or 800-998-9938
      (6am to 5pm PST)

FAX: 707-829-0104

order@oreilly.com
For answers to problems regarding your order or our products. To place a book order online, visit:

www.oreilly.com/order_new

catalog@oreilly.com
To request a copy of our latest catalog.

booktech@oreilly.com
For book content technical questions or corrections.

corporate@oreilly.com
For educational, library, government, and corporate sales.

proposals@oreilly.com
To submit new book proposals to our editors and product managers.

international@oreilly.com
For information about our international distributors or translation queries. For a list of our distributors outside of North America check out:

international.oreilly.com/distributors.html

adoption@oreilly.com
For information about academic use of O'Reilly books, visit:

academic.oreilly.com

O'REILLY®

Our books are available at most retail and online bookstores.
To order direct: 1-800-998-9938 • *order@oreilly.com* • *www.oreilly.com*
Online editions of most O'Reilly titles are available by subscription at *safari.oreilly.com*